GAPS IN NATURE

SUNY Series, The Margins of Literature
Mihai I. Spariosu, Editor

Gaps in Nature

Literary Interpretation and the Modular Mind

Ellen Spolsky

State University of New York Press

Published by
State University of New York Press, Albany

Printed in the United States of America

For information, address State University of New York
Press, State University Plaza, Albany, NY 12246

Production by Bernadine Dawes
Marketing by Fran Keneston

Library of Congress Cataloging-in-Publication Data

Spolsky, Ellen, 1943–
Gaps in nature : literary interpretation and the modular mind /
Ellen Spolsky.
p. cm. — (SUNY series, the margins of literature)
Includes bibliographical references and index.
ISBN 0-7914-1387-X (alk. paper) : $49.50. — ISBN 0-7914-1388-8
(pbk. : alk. paper) : $16.95
1. Literature — History and criticism — Theory, etc. 2. Criticism.
3. Human information processing in literature. 4. Cognition in
literature I. Title. II. Series.
PN441.S63 1993
801'.95—dc20 92-13360
CIP

10 9 8 7 6 5 4 3 2 1

To my husband,

אִישׁ אֲשֶׁר-רוּחַ בּוֹ

Contents

Acknowledgments

I am grateful to the following for permission to reprint the material indicated below:

Lee Patterson, for excerpts from "'No man his reson herde': Peasant Consciousness, Chaucer's Miller, and the Structure of the Canterbury Tales," *South Atlantic Quarterly,* 86:4 copyright 1987, Duke University Press, Durham, NC.

MIT Press for permission to cite excerpts from Ray Jackendoff, *Consciousness and the Computational Mind,* copyright 1987.

The University of Chicago Press for excerpts from Sandra M. Gilbert, "Life's Empty Pack: Notes toward a Literary Daughteronomy," *Critical Inquiry*, 11, 3, copyright 1985 and Richard Moran, "Seeing and Believing: Metaphor, Image, and Force," *Critical Inquiry*, 16, 1, copyright 1989.

Ruth Nevo, the editor of *Hebrew University Studies in Literature and the Arts*, for permission to include in Chapter Six portions of my article entitled "Chaucer and Literary History" which appeared in Volume 16, 1988.

Less formally, I owe a great debt to my colleagues at Bar-Ilan University who have argued with me and encouraged me over the years: especially to Sharon Baris, Daniel Boyarin, Harold Fisch, Kinereth Meyer and Murray Roston. Ray Jackendoff was a great help, in spite of his claim that he doesn't know about literature. Deborah Salter's small but crucial contribution was to force me to tell her what this book is about in one sentence while she was choosing a raincoat at Macy's. I am most grateful, as well, to Philip Skelker of Carmel College, Wallingford, Oxfordshire, who gave me shelter, food, and good wine while I wrote the early versions of this book. Joel, Ruth, and Josh, helped more than I can express. My greatest debt is acknowledged in the dedication of this book to my husband, Bernard Spolsky.

Introduction

> Th'air...but for vacancy,
> Had gone to gaze on Cleopatra too,
> And made a gap in nature.
>
> —Enobarbus, in
> *Antony and Cleopatra**

The suicide of Cleopatra preempts Octavius Caesar's plan to lead her through the streets of Rome in triumph, and thus she makes of him an "ass unpolicied." Although Shakespeare's poetry identifies her with the movement of flowing water through most of the play, she finally achieves her triumph over Caesar—he is ungoverned—through her own firmness of purpose. As she approaches her death she declares that she is "marble constant." The claim of constancy is, however, only half true, for it is her essential fluidity that has allowed her to change water to marble; her infinite variety enables the apotheosis. When Cleopatra gives over the baser life to fulfill immortal longings, it is the polysemy within herself that permits the resolution of ambiguity. Antony, only slightly less than Cleopatra, dramatizes the possibility of change. Caesar recognizes this crucial similarity between the two protagonists: Antony "is not more manlike / Than Cleopatra; nor the queen of Ptolemy / More womanly than he." He has already undergone an alteration before the play begins: "the triple pillar of the world transform'd / Into a strumpet's fool."

It is because *Antony and Cleopatra* is essentially concerned with the possibilities of transformation that I have taken from it the metaphorical title of this book. In the epigraph above, the syntax of Enobarbus' sentence is a subjunctive, a counterfactual—he denies that

*All citations from Shakespeare are taken from *The Complete Works of Shakespeare,* Hardin Craig and David Bevington, eds.

there is a gap in nature. There might have been "but for vacancy," which fills in where there otherwise would be a gap. In spite of his denial, the emptiness doesn't disappear. Similarly, I will argue, in line with the cognitive speculation that motivates this study, as vacancy rushes in to fill the gap left by Cleopatra's departure, our minds seem to rush in to confront and patch the gaps in our understanding of the world, and to attempt continually to stabilize the dynamically unstable. But, crucially, the emptiness remains.

Although there is plenty of talk in literary theory about gaps,[1] it is not widely recognized that the gaps are neither occasional nor random. The hypothesis I propose to explore in this book is approximately this: the gaps in human cognitive structure—the vacancies between fragments of understanding—not only permit but actually encourage transformation and innovation and, furthermore, this state of affairs is the logical outcome of evolutionary development. Put another way, there is a level of cognitive structure at which brains can be said to bridge gaps creatively in response to failures in understanding, these failures themselves produced by the neurological equipment on which we depend for that understanding of the world. The work of coordination between only partially commensurate representations of the world is the daily business of all human minds. The nature of the system is such that satisfaction is only fitfully achievable, and bridges that serve a purpose for a time must sooner or later be rebuilt. Beyond that, however, I want to claim here that a culture's most powerfully imaginative texts are understandable as the heroic efforts of particularly responsive minds, goaded by the inevitable asymmetry and incompleteness of mental representation to vault the gaps in brain structure thus surpassing the limitations of the biological inheritance. The mind itself can hurt you into poetry.

This hypothesis is supported, if yet fragilely, by cognitive theorizing and some neurological data.[2] It needs not only a lot more of both of these, but also the attention of literary scholars. Only they can bring to the debate the familiarity with complex texts and sophisticated interpretive practice by which the hypotheses generated by cognitive scientists may be rigorously challenged.[3] The subject of my study, then, must be the written reports of the interpretive/critical reactions of experienced readers of texts, that is, of those readers whose reading and publishing performance is evidence, *eo ipso*, of their authority in the interpretation of complex texts. Literary theory, whatever pretensions it now and again makes, is ultimately founded on good reading—what it wants to know is what the experienced reader of a text does, and under what circumstances, in order to produce a satisfying reading. The answer to that question is that persuasive literary critical texts exhibit the same kinds of compensatory responsiveness that literary texts themselves do; they exhibit the kinds of gap-bridging that are what minds know how to do in order to make sense of the world.

I see this claim as a counterweight to current cultural materialisms, according to which the historical contexts of the production of meaning are both the constraints on that production and the sources of and forces for innovation or change in it. While research in many areas of the humanities and social sciences is concerned (and quite reasonably so) with understanding the power of culture to structure and constrain, it is worthwhile at the same time to investigate the role of biological materialism as co-legislator of human life and understanding. The inevitable slippage we have come to acknowledge between words and the world has at least an analogue, and presumably also a source, in the workings of the human brain.

In returning to the evidence of literary criticism, this study continues the larger project I began with Ellen Schauber in *The Bounds of Interpretation: Linguistic Theory and Literary Text* (1986) in its aim of exploring more closely the ways in which experienced readers make sense of texts. The earlier study was grounded in linguistic and literary theory, both of which overlap with theories of mind. In this study I depend on two of the cognitive theories, the first being the preference model, a version of the theory of fuzzy categorization that is already widely linked to issues in the philosophy of mind and thence to interpretive theory. Although it is the semantic theory of Ludwig Wittgenstein that has been most widely read by literary theorists, pathbreaking work on the subject has also been done by the cognitive scientist Eleanor Rosch and the theoretical linguist Ray Jackendoff.

The second cognitive theory on which I depend is the theory of the modular mind. Since the publication of Jerry Fodor's book, *The Modularity of Mind* (1983), the theory has provoked interest and argument in cognitive science and linguistics. It is now available in a spectrum of versions but has not yet been considered in connection with issues in literary theory.

The topic of fuzzy categorization, however, is familiar to a literary as well as a linguistic audience, and so I pause here merely to record that its importance in this study derives both from its grounding the argument for the pervasiveness of metaphor in all language and from the centrality of categorization to all thought.[4] My assumption, as argued in Schauber and Spolsky (1986), is that there can be no interpretive theory that is not at base a genre theory (i.e., a theory of categorization). Categorization itself, it will be argued, because it introduces a fundamental asymmetry and, thus, an instability into all interpretive processes, acts as a spur for both inference and recategorization. Mervis and Rosch state the issue baldly (with no intention, I presume, to cause a deconstructive frisson): "A category exists whenever two or more distinguishable objects or events are treated equivalently" (1981:89). The function of this inbuilt dependence on error is "to provide maximum information with the least cognitive effort.…It is to the organism's advantage not to differentiate one stimulus from others when that differentiation is irrelevant to the purposes at hand" (Rosch, 1978:28–29).

It is this functionalism, perhaps, this assumption that "the purposes at hand" must be taken into account, that links Rosch's theory at first glance to Wittgenstein's account of meaning as a set of family resemblances, and thus to the many current versions of contextualism. Both Rosch and Wittgenstein find the Aristotelian notion of categorization or definition by necessary and sufficient conditions untenable and present large amounts of data to prove its shortcomings. Ray Jackendoff's preference model (1983, 1987) suggests a formalism that can display the fuzziness without losing sight of the richness of the factors that make up meaning judgments.[5]

While the implications of fuzzy categorization may be familiar to the literary audience, even as those implications reach to undermine the notion of literal meaning, this audience is perhaps in need of an overview of the other cognitive theory I will be depending upon here. Modularity theory, like fuzzy categorization, tows a rather heavy load of cognitive instability in its wake; it virtually entails the same kind of tension, if not actual paradox, that Rosch describes for all categorization.

Modularity suggests itself to me as a productive way of looking at the epistemological issues within literary theory because of its assumption that the human brain takes in information about its environment through several channels simultaneously, each specialized for the reception of a particular kind of perceptual data. We hear, see, and feel, for example, through different systems, and we apparently also store information according to the modality of its reception. It is the evolutionary history of the species that has, in its wisdom, produced this set of distinctive perceptual mechanisms by which we respond to the pied beauty of our world. Our survival thus far is evidence that specialized modules seem to do the job well enough: the cells in the retina distinguish lines and colors, for example, while the cells in the ear distinguish sounds. From the point of view of the survival of the individual, having multiple receptor systems is a kind of insurance policy: if one breaks down, others may remain intact and can at least partially compensate.

While the mind is well described as modular when we are attempting to describe its distinct intake devices (eyes, ears, etc.), it also is clearly the case that, in order to be able to talk about what we see or respond to verbal instructions with muscular action, a modular brain must manage communication among the modules. This, the theory postulates, is accomplished by translator devices. It takes no sophisticated cognitive theory, however, to tell us that not all visual knowledge can be stated, nor can all tastes be described. These translators, apparently, do not connect every level of every module with every level of every other. Philosophers and poets have long noticed that language cannot entirely recreate what one sees or feels. Recent literary theory has emphasized not only the inadequacy of the verbal description vis-à-vis the visual or sensual experience, but also the power of the words to suggest (not only to hearers but to speakers themselves) images, sensations, and thoughts beyond those of their original context. Brain theory confirms that the inadequacies of language are not merely matters of local inadequacy—gaps that a larger vocabulary or a new metaphor could fill. The phenomenon of incommensurable readings is not accidental; it is genetically built into the brain.

The modular systems by means of which individuals understand the world and their place in it, then, are both independent of each other but also, and to differing degrees, interdependent. That they are not, however, entirely translatable one to another—that there are gaps—is the crucial point for hermeneutic theory. The first step toward recognizing the systematicity of the gaps in human understanding is to recognize that this state of affairs, this incomplete commensurability, is the outcome of evolutionary logic. If translation were total, there would be no need for the variety of windows on the world; one could do well enough with any one of the intake devices, and the others would presumably have atrophied or disappeared. Presumably, then, there is an advantage to the species in retaining the multiplicity of modules even without full translatability among them.

The gaps between modules over which information is not translated are so much a part of our experience of what it is to be human that they mostly go unnoticed. When I am sitting on the opposite side of the table from you, you cannot see my body below my waist. You are probably not aware of it, either. But it is not hard to imagine a situation in which you could become aware of it. From memories built up from kinesic experience it is even likely that you could envision, from the orientation of my spine and upper body, whether my legs were extended, crossed, or symmetrically bent at the knees. But although you can get far toward bridging the gap of occlusion by the application of memory and inference, you cannot actually see my legs without repositioning your own body. Memory and inference, hypothesis and mental imagery, are at work constantly to fill these gaps in visual knowledge. Visual representations themselves can fill in other gaps and, in large part, satisfactorily so. The combinations we can make are, after a certain amount of learning experience, habitual. They don't take any noticeable effort and they provide secure enough information for many purposes.

What is amazing is that the process works as well as it does. Here's another example: you smell smoke, remember that you have a cake in the oven, and picture it burnt—you jump up and run to take it out of the oven. The connections between smell, memory, visual imagination, and musculature work well enough, and thus conceal that these confluent structures of information are not first-class translations of what is really happening in the world. The smell may come from a neighbor's house, and you noticed it only because you have a cake in the oven. The image of the burnt cake may arise from a memory of your last such accident, or even from an old *I Love Lucy* show, but you certainly can't see it as you sit in your study and sniff. Functionally those gaps, or failures of translation, don't cause too much trouble: at worst you run to the oven for nothing and return to your study distracted by old memories. It's mostly good enough for us that sounds and smells call up scenes in our minds, such that we can act on them, and any image of burnt food will serve here.

Much more interesting to literary theory, however, are the occasions when the gaps are not filled habitually or conventionally but creatively, as in literary texts. These texts, and likewise the subsequent interpretive texts that read the earlier ones, are profitably understood as responses to gaps in understanding that are not amenable to repair in conventional ways. The resources for bridging gaps that are available to creative individuals are analogous, however, even homologous, with the daily struggles we all face to create links between the fragments of what can be known. This book, then, is concerned with exploring evidence in literary interpretation to support the contention that innovation in literary systems can be understood as evidence of the mind's responses to incompatible representations. It is in the nature of the beast, however, that unconventional innovation will be risky in at least two ways: it may not be understood, and it may not achieve more than local and temporary success. These two risks, in fact, go a long way toward describing what a literary text is.

The difficulties and advantages of assuming modularity of mind

One of the most contentious issues in the current work on modularity is just how much processing can be done entirely within a self-contained module, that is, a module whose representations cannot (by definition) be produced by (take advantage of) the interaction of incoming stimuli and memory or already-in-place representations. This is the cognitive version of the question of the power of the hermeneutic circle: how much can you come to know that you don't already know?

A certain amount of current neurobiological research is aimed at establishing just how much processing can be accomplished in impenetrable modules. A lot hinges on the outcome. To begin with, if there is very little accomplished automatically and stupidly in the module without the resources of memory, then the amount of interface that needs to be postulated between a central processor (i.e., the hypothesized site of intermodular communication) and the modules may be so great as to make any talk about self-enclosed modules trivial. On the other hand, there are reasons to think that, even if the amount of modular processing is small, it is theoretically and practically crucial to the survival of the individual, and thus still worth tracing. Modularity, for example, supports the ability to recognize and respond without prejudice to a situation outside of and different from an individual's previous experience, and this is of clear evolutionary advantage in protecting a body from unforeseen danger. We could generalize further from that ability and postulate that modularity is a necessary prerequisite to any changed understanding, new knowledge, or creativity. As I understand the modularity hypothesis, then, the impermeability of some of the lower levels of representation to information from higher ones is evidence against the hegemony of memory. It weighs, thus, against the power of the hermeneutic circle and for the possibility of change.

The neurological evidence, however, is far from conclusive. Of the many arguments that have been made (see Tanenhous, Dell, and Carlson 1987 for the methodological advantages of assuming systemic modularity of mind), the one most crucial to our concerns here derives from its potential to describe change. If the mind is made up of subsystems, then one can see how stability in one system, even temporary stability, permits inferences about the function or meaning of new structures in other systems. In language, for example, a new vocabulary item may combine new with familiar morphemes in an already-in-place morphological structure. That new word also belongs to a recognizable syntactic category. The familiar structures, then, provide a leg up for the one who is attempting to accommodate novelty and infer new meaning. If the mind is modular, new information might enter one module without being blocked by prejudices of that or another module. The higher-level central processor would then have the job of reconciling stored and new representations, but wouldn't get to work until the new representation already had a foot in the door.

Jean Piaget (1952) described this process as assimilation and accommodation and considered it to be the main way humans take account of new information (i.e., learn). Willard Quine (1960) compared learning by inference to climbing up the inside of a chimney. You can advance by moving your legs up only because your back is pressed to the solid wall behind you. The mix of familiar and unfamiliar structures distributed among separate systems similarly allows the human intelligence to cope with novelty in areas other than language. Eating a mango for the first time, though strange, is not a cognitive catastrophe. But too much change and too little to hold onto can be unwelcome and frightening, and in extreme cases can make learning impossible.

The literary system, which both authors and readers internalize and use to make meaning, is profitably examined as a collection of subsystems that function independently in part but that also are interdependent. A reader has a chance of inferring meaning from unfamiliar structures in any one of the various literary subsystems as long as there is some degree of concurrent stability in the other subsystems. We might think, for example, of the set of genre categories as a subsystem of the literary system; the set of ideologically motivated interpretive paradigms in use at any one time could be considered another, and periodization terms another. The chapters in this book examine change in these three distinguishable literary subsystems. In each case the modularity model suggests why change occurs in the forms that it does.

One advantage, then, of a modularity theory is as a hypothesis that identifies a systematic basis for describing change in literary interpretation. It commits us to recognizing that change is neither accidental nor fortuitous, but a result of the continuing attempt of the mind to deal with its own limitations, to make hypotheses that might move it beyond those limitations. The instabilities of literary systems, such as the birth and death of genres, the succession of critical movements, the revaluation of texts and thus of the canon, the shifting of borders between generic and periodic literary categories, are neither organic nor contingent aspects of literary systems, but are explainable within a theory of the human mind's ongoing project of constructive innovation. The exploration of some of these instabilities is the subject of this book.

I would make an even stronger claim, namely that the literary subsystems through which interpretation is accomplished are not only metaphorically similar to the modular subsystems of the brain, but are themselves evidence that the understanding of literary texts proceeds by the interaction of distinguishable processes. If we examine the different sorts of literary criticism that have been produced over the past twenty years or so and ignore the distinctive names readers have given their approaches, looking instead for evidence of underlying processing distinctions in their production of meaning, we will find that the distinctions between them can be seen to line up with the different kinds of processing that cognitive scientists have begun to describe. The mind allows different kinds of thinking, and while we surely need to use all the systems we can and need to work hard at aligning the outputs of the different systems, it is also true that in different circumstances different people will favor different strategies, will be seen to be building interpretations that look different because they take advantage of, or foreground the results of, different processing possibilities. In short, different styles of criticism can be seen as evidence of the existence of distinguishable, if interdependent, modes of knowledge, originating in distinguishable if interdependent modules of the mind.

Another advantage to be gained from the development of a theory of modularity in interpretation is perhaps even more momentous for literary and aesthetic theory, but can only be hinted at here. If we view the mind's innate incompatibilities and its attempts to compensate as a cognitive description of creative restlessness, then we have, here, evidence relevant to the discussion of the function of art. We would have support for the hypothesis that artistic production has cognitive value (i.e., can be considered as knowledge in whatever way we may postulate that other mental structures count as knowledge. Literary texts, for example, could be seen to serve a crucial cognitive function, namely as hypotheses about the coordination or enregistration among otherwise incompatible structures of knowledge. We would have the basis not only for an epistemology of art (its truth value), but for a pragmatics of art (its functional value), and probably for identifying the two as well.

Describing changes in literary systems

Renewed interest in the social contexts of literature and in understanding the power or powerlessness of literary texts in those contexts has made the issues of change more pressing. As long as change in literary worlds could be conceived as a sequence of archaeologies in which one merely replaced the other without changing much outside itself, the mystery of such change could remain unexamined. But the same social and political conditions that encourage the explicit hope of cultural criticisms that new ways of reading can bring about social change also make urgent the task of investigating how the biological constraints on human semiosis allow hermeneutic procedures to work in the world.

That the issue is not well understood is perhaps disguised by the routine assertions of new historicist and neo-Marxist critics that texts "work"—that is, actually produce rather than merely reflect or display social ideologies. Elaine Scarry, for example, tells us that "a materialist conception of language ordinarily has two companion assumptions: first, that language is capable of registering in its own contours the contours and weight of the material world; second, that language itself may enter, act on, and alter the material world" (1988:xi). There is no argument here—indeed one can learn that texts work from phenomena as different as cigarette advertising or Hitler's speeches. Most cultural materialists, however, are understandably diffident about making specific claims for the power of the pen to effect change. Raymond Williams, for example, although committed to the notion that ideologies are "not only received, they are also made and can be transformed," admitted the power of a disappointing "social reality" to "amend, displace, or deform any merely intended practice" (1977:204).

Williams is here recognizing that merely thematizing change, either in literary or critical texts, is alone unlikely to produce that change. The attempts of deconstructive language games (swerve, erasure, punning) to decenter the language of criticism seem to have failed to escape the established structures of authority, having by their very success undermined the kind of authoritative values on which any social critique must rest, and having also established at least temporarily a new authoritative critical language. I suppose it must be admitted, then, that there is a measure of desperation in turning to the discourse of cognitive science in the hopes of finding a material base in which to investigate questions of human potential and limitations. The field holds out the promise of providing a connection between the apparently systematic biological need and desire for change and the apparent openness to change of at least some aspects of cultural codes. The question we may ask of cognitive science is, then, how is it that discontent and desire for change do, in some situations, succeed in using rhetoric to tap into those structures of the human mind which are specifically built (or evolved) so that they can learn and change?

A further reason, then, for pursuing the modularity hypothesis is the bearing it might be revealed to have on the dilemma of causality currently pressing on literary theory and on criticism. If indeed the genetically inherited architecture of the brain determines it to be the source of subphenomenological (unconscious) negotiation over the possibilities of representation, and if the material structure of the brain is also, thus, the source of both human innovation and of the management of that innovation, it may also be reasonable to claim that the history of literature—both the production and interpretation—would exhibit a dynamic of change even if the cultural and political world were to remain static. Political utopia would lead neither to the withering away of literature nor to the installation of a permanent canon, unambiguously understood, because biological pressures for the revision of verbal representation would remain.[6]

In the meantime at least, the world being what it is, it doesn't seem likely that we will be able to test this claim. What can perhaps be investigated is how the postulated internal dynamic of the mind interacts with external pressures both producing and adapting to change within interpretive systems. This claim prompts a productive, materialist explanation of rather large amounts of metaphysical worry, from the reflections on the wall of Plato's cave to Paul de Man's paradoxical blindness and insight. This book argues that the difficulties, or perhaps the impossibility (mourned by romantics, celebrated by postmodernists), of maintaining the kind of unified perspective traditionally thought of as centered in an individual mind or soul are not logical or philosophical difficulties but are, in fact, material. They are an inevitable consequence of brain architecture and the structure of consciousness it produces. The inevitable striving toward coherence, then, drives interpretation from the inside, no matter what is happening on the outside.

How can these claims be investigated?

I am, ultimately, talking of Michelangelo. My claims about creative bridging are pertinent to the great imaginative literary texts as well as to critical responses. Exploring them directly through literary texts would, however, allow my own readings of this literature to become the focus of controversy, and that would be beside the point.[7] It was a methodological decision, then, to focus on the creativity instantiated in the encounters of experienced readers with literary texts as reported in published academic scholarship. I am interested in the ways in which old and valued texts can be read so as to retain their value in changed cultural circumstances and, as well, in the ways in which readers can revalue old texts or bring new texts into circulation. The differences between the different ways of accomplishing these tasks arise from the different mental possibilities with which we are endowed. I will attempt analyses, in some detail, of how experienced and innovative readers have read and reread in an attempt to chart both the internal and the cultural pressures doing their work.

As it is crucial to my hypothesis that the pressures for change are part of *all* readers' human biological inheritance, it seemed preferable to choose texts for study from among the more typical events in the history of literary criticism rather than from the atypical, the normal rather than the catastrophic or paradigm-changing. In each section of this study, therefore, I have taken as my examples literary interpretations that do not stand out as revolutionary, but as unusual only in their creative competence. By their publication in the institutionalized journals and publication lists of the academic literary establishment, they show themselves to have been, broadly speaking, authorized within the literary community. Some were less and some more startling at their appearance, but all were, in some way, innovative. The close attention paid here to critical texts rather than to literary ones is justified, as well, not by the arguments of Harold Bloom or Geoffrey Hartman equalizing the status of all texts, but by the overall goal of understanding the competence of the experienced reader of literature as demonstrated in the production of literary criticism. The project is, thus, not only a theoretical examination of change, but also an exercise in self-scrutiny, that is, a contribution to the history of the institution of literary study.

The chapters of this book are a series of excursions into the territory of modularity. Their unity, such as it is, comes from two sources. First, each study in itself is an example of a kind of change in a different literary system. Thus, on the assumption that literature consists, *inter alia*, of (1) a system of genres, (2) a set of interpretive procedures, or more likely a set of sets at any given time, and (3) a set of periodization categories, I analyze examples of genre change, methodological change, and historical change. The examples are chosen, each for the way it illustrates a way in which modularity can be discerned to incite, abet, or cooperate with innovation in the practice of experienced readers of literature. I claim further that these three subsystems are not accidental, but that they correspond roughly to the possibilities our brains provide for organizing intake and producing knowledge. The fundamentality of genre distinctions to literary studies, thus, is the literary manifestation of the fundamentality of the production of categorization judgments and of syllogistic logic within complex thought processes. The distinction between categorization and analogical and historical criticisms, then, are evidence of underlying distinctions between hierarchical/conceptual knowing, iconic/visual knowing, and chronological understanding, or understanding that attempts to account for seriality.

After a chapter in which I expand the methodological discussion in some further detail, Chapter 2 explores the production, in a small corner of the American literature establishment, of some new genre categories, apparently in response to the revival of pride in ethnicity in the 1960s. Chapter 3 examines some current criticism of *Hamlet* that aims more or less overtly at ideological efficacy. The explorations within the genre categorization system reveal, however, that the permanent inadequacy of our representations of categories and the concurrent need for such categorization are the foundation of the ability to make use of past experience in the production and use of inferences. The critical essays studied here argue for the centrality of categorization judgments, and thus of a genre system, to the production and revision of textual meaning. They display the links of literary categorizing with cognitive and philosophical theories of inference, reinforcing the cognitive claim that inference produces new knowledge. At the same time the essays studied here witness the interaction of text with social context and witness as well the importance of the distinction between context and conditions of significance.

Chapters 4 and 5 examine two stages in the development of feminist criticism: at first in response to the growth of political feminist consciousness, and later as an expression of analogical thinking. As distinct from the claims for logical rigor made for the procedures of matching and inference in the attempts to produce new categorizations, we see here how an analogical argument structure exhibits its responsiveness to the variety of personal experience more frankly. By adding analogical to logical possibilities, interpreters enlarge their repertoire of strategies by which to respond to change and to construct new meaning.

Chapters 6 and 7 take as their theme the writing and rewriting of literary history that, while clearly responsive to external pressure, turns out to be fueled by internal tensions as well. An argument between medievalists about how to write the history of medieval literature, plus an example of a recent attempt to solve a traditional problem with a nontraditional critical tool, provide exemplary matter for consideration of the kinds of social and mental forces that put up resistance to change. The multiplicity that insures conflict among conditions of interpretation at an unconscious level also slows down the reading, makes it "hard," unsatisfying in some way, and thus stimulating, challenging, but also attractive. In order to reduce the tension, literary historians narrativize, using stored knowledge to fill in gaps, causing their responsibility to the past to tug against present needs. Cognitive work on the visual module suggests that the conflict between an objective and a subjective perspective has a biological basis in the multiplicity of levels of vision of which human beings are capable. Historians benefit, as we will see, from a double coding that permits, alternatively, viewer-centered and object-centered understanding. In this way, then, the modularity hypothesis has implications for the kind of epistemology that would support historical criticism.

As I wrote these chapters I tried to maintain a distinction between the perennial hope for, indeed the felt need for, progress toward clearer means of expression and understanding, and the separate issue of whether that hope is futile. When the two issues are separated, it can be appreciated that the desire for something better does not disappear along with the surmise that it may never come. The evidence from cognitive studies suggests that individuals innovate out of a need for and in the hope of clearer understanding, although that goal is never more than fitfully and temporarily attainable.

Innovation in interpretive systems, I argue then, is doubly driven by the inevitability of disappointment in the cultural contexts of those systems and by the parallel difficulty that humans have in expressing in language all that they can conceive or feel or understand. This disappointment is deepened by the imaginative construction of how things could be better in the world, as well as by the human need for communication through language to be not only different but better. Where and when we find successful innovation in literary systems, we can usually find traces of the support structures—the other systems that, by providing relatively stable meaning, allowed the inferences to the new.

If the chapters that follow have any success, I would hope to persuade at least some in the literary theoretical community that there might be something to learn from an understanding of the cognitive grounds of epistemological change. At the same time, I would hope the linguists in my audience might be led to see the relevance of the discussion of cognition and figurative language to the issues of expressibility (i.e., the power and limits of language). Linguists have frequently expressed awe at what they understand to be the power of language: Zellig Harris liked to claim that language was much more powerful than humans recognized or, in general, had need of. He compared it to a dynamo used to operate a doorbell.

In addition to the standard praises of the complexity of human language and grammar that have introduced linguistics books and courses for the last sixty years, several aspects of its infinity have actually been points of dogma to scholars in the field. Generative grammar, as is well known, is founded on the infinity of sentences a human grammar can produce from a finite set of rules. The philosopher of language, John Searle, for his part, has argued for the infinite expressibility of a language: what cannot now be expressed, can, in principle, be eventually expressed (1969:68). My own thinking on this issue, however, owes a debt to the literary as well as to the language theorists. I don't think anyone writing about interpretive systems can disregard the pessimism of the French and American post-structuralists who are, willy-nilly, theorists of language failure.[8] This study examines the creativity that derives from failure and the new possibilities that arise from gaps in the system.

1 Minds, Modules, and Models

That which is now a horse, even with a thought
The rack dislimns, and makes it indistinct
As water is in water....
Here I am Antony,
Yet cannot hold this visible shape.

—Antony, in *Antony and Cleopatra*

Cleopatra's changeability, her infinite variety, is powerful enough to transform the triple pillar of the world into a strumpet's fool. But Antony's greatness, as well, consists precisely in his understanding of change and of the transforming power of the mind. He learns that only death, the deed that ends all other deeds, shackles accidents and bolts up change.

Shakespeare's *Antony and Cleopatra* is an exemplary exploration of how it is that people can renew themselves and reunderstand their world, even if heroic self-reconstruction through the force of Eros does not prevent death. Richard Dawkins' theory of the selfish gene (1989) is interesting in this connection. As part of an argument that the structure of mind results from evolutionary processes, it is widely acknowledged that modularity provides an advantage. Multiple modules can receive different kinds of information, producing the redundancy needed for disambiguation: better to hear, see, and smell an enemy approaching. But failing one of those modes, the others might be able to compensate, preserving life in changed circumstances for a little longer. Dawkins argues that the single goal of the species' germ plasm is to replicate itself; the human being doesn't have to live forever, but just long enough to reproduce. He argues, further, that a good idea works the same way. A successful idea reproduces itself and, just like a physiological advantage, may lengthen the life of the mind that has the good idea, thereby spreading itself (the idea) more broadly (1989:192).

If *Antony and Cleopatra* is a tragedy because the absence of issue prevents the superior genes of the two protagonists from continuance, the tragedy is nevertheless redeemed, on Dawkins' view, when those who learn from Shakespeare mate with others who have learned the same things, and pass on that understanding to their offspring. *Antony and Cleopatra*, thus, "works" in the world by spreading its understanding of flexibility, in the same way the selfish gene works to promulgate advantageous physical characteristics. In this chapter I will explore some versions of the modularity hypothesis in greater detail with an eye to deciding what aspects of the theory are crucial to describing the creative flexibility that readers of literature display in responding to change and also producing it.

The earliest and strongest version of the modularity hypothesis

According to the modularity hypothesis proposed by Jerry Fodor (1983), the mind/brain achieves its purposes, when it does, by a collection of relatively independent processing devices called modules that receive distinct kinds of information at peripheral levels (eyes, ears, fingers, for example), then operate over and produce successively richer (i.e., more integrated) structures of meaning. Fodor's theory is a computational and hierarchical theory. Building on the analogy of the brain as a digital computer, it describes the functioning of the perceptual system from peripheral processors to brain, in both its conscious and unconscious aspects, as the reception and manipulation of various structures of meaning or information. In order for this to take place, the separate kinds of information—say, that which arrives through the eyes and that which arrives through the ears—must be reduced or translated to a common language of mind, just as a computer can manipulate information only when it is made available in the form of binary numbers. The contents of his theory are thus conceived neither as "ideas" nor as neurons and synapses, but as mental representations, a theoretical fiction somewhere between the two, which are constructed and manipulated by mental processes.

That representations are constructed is not a new idea to many different sorts of literary theorists who have been, for a while now, assuming that some version of the model of the hermeneutic circle is reasonable. Modularity hypotheses, however, while assuming the contribution of experience to understanding, also argue that at least some of the equipment needed to construct representations of the world is hard-wired in the brain. It may be innate or grown, but not learned from experience. As Neil Stillings says about vision, for example: "The relationship between the visible physical world and reflected light is complex, and it is ambiguous unless the perceptual apparatus has various assumptions about the relationship built into it" (1987:387). Noam Chomsky's claims for an innate language module underlie Fodor's strong modularity. Chomsky argues that whatever the universal grammar contains, namely the "principles, conditions, and rules that are elements or properties of all human languages," they are present "by necessity...biological, not logical, necessity" (1975b:29).[1]

Even though Fodor's version of modularity is not widely accepted in toto, because he provided the descriptive terms that are the basis of subsequent argument and discussion, it is worthwhile to begin by understanding some of his claims.[2] In his version of the modularity hypothesis the modules in the brain are "intake devices" only. Their operations are stimulated from outside the body and cannot in any way be modified ("top down") by knowledge, experience, or contingent need. The operations of the modules are mandatory (one cannot chose not to organize incoming visual information), fast, and domain-specific (ears can't deal with visual input). The modules have fixed neural architecture and suffer characteristic and specific breakdowns.

Each module receives information at peripheral or low levels (the sensory receptors) and then processes that information by means of correspondence rules through several levels of selection and integration, ultimately making it available for whatever functions are required at higher or more central levels, that is, at the levels of greater abstraction, generalization, or integration. Information from the higher levels can then be made available to the motor system if a physical response is required. In order for a batter to hit a baseball, for example, the brain must, within a very short span of time, take in visual information, organize it, and translate it to a mediating level of representation from which it can be translated into instructions to the muscles. Similar translation processors make visual, linguistic, and motor information compatible so that we can talk about or sketch what we see or imagine, or read texts and infer mental images from the words.

Not all processing is as fast and efficient as those translation processes that allow an athlete to respond. Processes that require already acquired knowledge, experiences, or beliefs do not, in Fodor's theory, take place within the modules, but rather within a central processor that has access to the long-term memory. Compared to hitting a baseball, the interpretation of difficult or of novel language texts is processed over a much longer time and is often difficult to talk about. For Fodor, the central processor in which this kind of response would take place is what "thinks." It is there that the structures of information that have been constructed in the modules come together and meet up with each other and with memory. For Fodor, what happens in the central processor is what "we have in mind when we think of a cognitive process as paradigmatically intelligent" (1983:107). Here thinking and planning, imagining and creating take place. Here, however, the weight of the already known, categorized, or understood can work against openness to new information from the intake modules. Humans need modular (fast, unprejudiced) processing, but also slow considerate thinking in order to survive.

Argument is far from over, however, about how much of brain structure is innate and invariant, that is, set by the species' genetic inheritance. How much of the brain's work is modular as described by Fodor's adjectives? Specifically, how much processing is rigidly hierarchical, and how and where does feedback interrupt the chronological ordering of input? How soon, for example, do eyes need already stored information before they can successfully categorize? What kind of processes characterize post-modular processing, that is, the thinking that Fodor attributes to an underspecified central processor? Claims and counterclaims about innateness, for example, will clearly be important to the discussion of the possibilities of change because they delimit the kinds of interaction with the world that can conceivably be culturally determined. We need to know how and how early learned behavior enters and influences the process of interpretation.[3]

Jackendoff's modularity theory

Ray Jackendoff's revisions of Fodor's theory begin from agreement that understanding is modular. He claims that those distinctions in our interpretive capacity of which we are aware, such as the distinction between knowing what red is and interpreting a lyric poem, must be supported at least in part by corresponding distinctions among the representational structures of the mind. He calls this the hypothesis of computational sufficiency: "Every phenomenological distinction is caused by, or supported by, or projected from a corresponding computational distinction," or to put it another way, "the world we are aware of is just that which the brain/computational mind is capable of representing" (1987:24–25). This argument is a version of the evolutionary argument for a realist view of the relationship of human minds to the world. On this view, even though our minds manifestly deceive us and mislead us now and then, we wouldn't still be around as a species if we weren't at least well enough suited to respond to the real world around us to keep us alive until we reproduce. Here is Jackendoff's statement of the modularity thesis:

> The apparent heterogeneity of mental life is supported by a genuinely heterogeneous collection of psychological mechanisms....Seeing, speaking a language, thinking, and remembering, for example, are not simply diverse uses of a single general psychological mechanism (be it association, stimulus-response connections, generalized problem-solving, or whatever). Rather there are specialized mechanisms, or modules, that subserve each function, each with its own characteristic task-relevant adaptations. (1987:260)

Notice that this is already a valuable enrichment of the familiar hermeneutic assumption that we can only understand what our mind/brain or experience permits us to understand. According to the modularity hypothesis, the hermeneutic claim is right, but the faculties of the brain that can achieve understanding are multiple. We have more than one kind of intelligence, or understanding, and are thus suited to understand different kinds of things about the world. Important bits of our ears keep us upright with respect to the earth's gravity, our eyes distinguish safe paths from the edges of cliffs, and our ears tell us the direction from which a threat, or a friendly voice, is approaching. The resulting redundancy helps us to disambiguate, and thus keeps us from being misled by inevitable modular failures. The modularity of the mind, thus, becomes exemplary for theory: the model or theory of the interpretive system, which itself displays disunity, multiplicity, or modularity, thereby displays the disagreements or gaps that are the stimuli for change in that system.

Conversely, to the extent that a theory of making meaning, i.e., an interpretive theory, is generalized, unified, or totalized, it will not be able to account for change because disruptions or conflicts will be, by definition, disallowed or redefined from within so that they fit. This, you will remember, is the problem with the strong form of the argument of the hermeneutic circle: if all processing was always already contextualized by the already learned, new information could never enter the system. The more blind men there are, the better they'll understand the elephant—provided, that is, that they can communicate with each other to produce a single description. The theory that can account for not only successful understanding, but also conflict, failure, tension, mismatching, and misunderstanding has to be a cluster of theories rather than a unified theory because it is at the interfaces between systems, each of which is, on its own, understandable, that adaptation, re-representation, and mismatches occur.

Marvin Minsky catches the inevitable conflict between modular aspects of understanding in his metaphor describing the brain as a "society of mind." The emotions and reason, he postulates, develop separately in the infant brain, and only later do they learn to exploit each other. "But because they each evolved to use rather different processes for different kinds of purposes, they are each endowed with somewhat different ways to represent the knowledge that they acquire....[This] makes it hard for there ever to be good communication among the different protospecialists" (1988:172).

Axiomatic to any version of the modularity theory is the assumption that modules communicate at their output stages only. There has to be enough exchange to let people talk about what is seen, or respond physically to verbal and visual signals, etc. But if there were translation connections between modules at every stage of their processing, its advantageous speed would disappear. Jackendoff's attempt to infer which levels within modules communicate with which levels in other modules, then, is a step toward identifying points of cognitive blindness—those places at which translation into more complex understanding is taking place, but which are not available to our conscious awareness. We can understand the relationship of all the legs to the table, for example, even if we can only see one or two of them as we look at it. There are places at which the representations produced in one module cannot be communicated to a different module; they are representationally incompatible with information from another module such that calibration is impossible.

Jackendoff's view of the modularity of higher-level thinking is an improvement on Fodor's lack of interest in this aspect of the process. Jackendoff resists collapsing all thinking beyond the intake of stimuli into a centralized soup. He postulates that there is still some modularity in the foggy "central" regions of thought, that is, that the distinctions between representations are retained even at the more interesting higher levels. As evidence for this, Jackendoff notes that if one thinks about something one has actually seen or visualized (imagined), it remains identified as visual information at all levels of thought, even though an integrative processor regulates its interaction with (for example) language produced from the conceptual module. The job of this processor is to construct "the most coherent conceptual structure that can be maintained in registration with information arriving from other modules and makes this structure available for translation by other modules into action and into feedback to perception" (1987:266). The production and understanding of figurative language would, for example, testify that a process of information sharing or coordinating is taking place between the visual and the conceptual modules, with access to all the memory that is available. It is the integrative processor that effects the registration of two intakes which may or may never have been linked before.

Jackendoff hypothesizes, further, that the central integrative processor works according to a preference rule system, that is, a system that can handle gradience. Its function is not limited to linking various aspects of intake according to past links only, but links them in the most coherent conceptual structure possible (p. 252). It is the central locus of the judgments, as it were, that grant meaning to inexact, default, or nearest matches, even filling in chains of transformation and inference with other available material so as to produce as satisfying and coherent thought as possible. Here, then, is another hypothesis of interest to literary theory: the production and understanding of figurative language (language, that is, in which images and words are linked) depend on the ability of the central processor to arrange the interaction between two (or more) kinds of structures that the modules produce. The parts of a metaphor, for example, "make sense" together and yet retain their distinctiveness as words or images.

These collocations of figurative language are, of course, notoriously inexact. Think, for example, of Dylan Thomas's command: "Do not go gentle into that good night!" What do we see? What do we hear or know nonvisually? Indeed, the difficulty of producing satisfying equivalences between visual and linguistic data is not only the empirical situation to which we can all testify, it is also the foundational axiom of a modular theory: if the representations were not fundamentally incommensurate, there would be no reason for the existence of different modules. The system of enregistration, then, is inherently unstable. It is designed to seek the most coherent structure possible, but since information from different modules will never be identical, it can never get an entirely coherent match. Figurative language, we may then say, is a bridge between two ways of knowing that are, in that language and not without it, collated.[4] Innovative figurative language, for example, an original metaphor, is a collocation that is also a personal attempt to solve a representational problem. Dylan Thomas's line, presumably, solves a problem for him by proposing a collocation to express a previously unconventionalized structure. An image, when fresh, may be both a strikingly unusual structure and a pleasingly coherent one in the context of the poem.

The visual and the language modules

The two modules that have been described in greatest detail are the visual and the language or conceptual modules. It is, thus, not accidental that these two will figure most prominently in my discussion and it is their characteristics which will be explored through the analysis of critical essays. Whether these two are on equal footing as modules is, however, hardly beyond contention, and my extensive use of the distinctions between them requires some argument here. It must be admitted that, while there seems to be a certain naturalness in the candidacy of a visual module as the back-up system for the eyes, an aural module supporting the ears might seem the obvious parallel rather than a linguistic module that involves the capacity for speech production, and probably for semantics as well. Furthermore, the evidence of the visual module is the physiology of vision, while the evidence linguists have presented for the independent existence of the language module is, beyond the existence of specific areas of the brain that control speech, mostly what Fodor (1979) has called "speculative psychology," that is, reflections on aspects of language competence conceived in a generative framework.

The asymmetricality of this parallel has led Fodor to spend rather a lot of time in *The Modularity of Mind* arguing that the modules do not in fact correspond to the traditional distinctions of the five senses and that the linguistic module, with its centerpiece syntactic processor, is indeed a paradigm case of a module. Indeed, the traditional five senses are not necessarily the best way to divide up the different bodily avenues to knowledge, nor is there any reason to limit their number to five. Physiologists now add, for example, the vestibular sense (responding to gravity and controlling balance), and the neurologist Oliver Sacks in several of his books has popularized the proprioceptive sense, a separate sense of one's own limbs and their relationship to one's body from moment to moment. The kinesthetic sense, on which we depend for our understanding of how movement plays out in time and space, is another. I have argued that kinesic knowledge is a distinguishable mode of knowing (n.d.), and Stanley Cavell (1987) argues for a specifically sexual knowledge. Howard Gardner (1985) enumerates some others, among them a musical and an athletic sense. Peter Brooks (1984), citing Louis Mink, argues that the production and understanding of plot or narrative is the human way of knowing how one fits into the dimension of time, and Daniel Dennett (1991) makes this narrative ability the source of the sense of self. Some of these claims are more easily accepted than others, and overall there is no agreement on where the lines can be drawn between these different ways of knowing.

The distinction between saying and seeing, however, is hard to gainsay. The pretheoretical assumption that language is hierarchical, logical, and propositional, and that it structures thought in those modes while vision accesses a paratactic, analogical, and geometric way of knowing is argued by Chomsky's claim[5] that the purpose of syntactic structure is not primarily communication but rather to permit the organization of high-level thought—that is, communication with the self. The assumption here is that the particular hierarchicality of syntax is the paradigmatic structure out of which human thought can be built in a way that we normally think of as logical or propositional.[6]

The assumption that vision is an analogical, non-hierarchical faculty appropriately concerning itself with forms in space and not with sequential propositions was argued by G. E. Lessing in 1766, and by theorists before and after him.[7] Indeed, the differences and the interrelations between visual and conceptual capacities and thence between the visual arts and literature have a long history of critical attention in the West long before the modularity hypothesis. Jackendoff, however, explicitly associates the propositional with the linguistic module, and the geometric with the visual, thus verbalizing some familiar assumptions and integrating them into thinking about modularity.

The visual module, he tells us, works with representations that he calls geometric/spatial, while the linguistic module manipulates algebraic representations:

> In a geometric representation objects are necessarily represented in terms of their shapes and apparent sizes. By contrast, algebraic representations like logic, associative nets, or our conceptual structure represent an object by means of an arbitrary symbol that has no bearing on its physical appearance. (1987:181)[8]

As later discussion will bear out, while human minds seem to depend on both those kinds of thinking (and several others as well) for different tasks, cultures may variously allocate their appropriateness and value their capacities. Most famously, in the Western tradition of language interpretation, analogic reasoning is more acceptable for the interpretation of texts labeled as literary or religious than for texts categorized as scientific.[9] The critical discussion of postmodernism, to take another example, could hardly be conducted without the distinction between "analytical, referential" discourse, and a postmodern discourse that is conceived to be the opposite of that (i.e., open and inconclusive, nonhierarchical).

But here is where the extension of the general assumption of a distinction between analogical and logical thinking to the distinction between the language and the visual modules breaks down, revealing that the modules Fodor proposes are too large. As we will see in the chapters to come, analogical thinking is required for language use, and for inference as well. Similarly, no inference could get off the ground without having made categorization judgments—very possibly dependent on spatio/geometric analogy. One would not want to say that language is entirely propositional, nor that one's vision does not include hierarchical judgments. As substantial research on modularity has begun to demonstrate, the cooperation between modules begins much closer to the peripheral sense receptors than Fodor thought. Not very much can be accomplished without intermodular cooperation and reference to memory (already acquired knowledge).

On the issue of the interrelationships between the production of different modules, argument in literary and interpretive theory, however, is just beginning. W. J. T. Mitchell's *Iconology* (1986) is an important study of the relationship between words and images, but he errs, I believe, in dismissing centuries of theoretical worry about the ways verbal and visual thinking relate to each other simply as a mistake. He correctly asserts that "the history of culture is in part the story of a protracted struggle for dominance between pictorial and linguistic signs, each claiming for itself certain proprietary rights on a 'nature' to which only it has access" (p. 43). He comes close to the biology of the problem, asking why we have "this compulsion to conceive of the relation between words and images in political terms, as a struggle for territory, a contest of rival ideologies" (p. 43).

But he takes the political as his central concern and moves rapidly away from the issue of perception to ask what interests and powers are served by the split between words and images. In order to move from the history of ideologies to the possibilities for change, however, we must recognize a cognitive level of conflict as well, a level at which images and words compete even before their cultural appearance in art or in criticism. If we explore how the human mind struggles with not entirely compatible representations demanding to be correlated, then we may be able to advance an understanding of the potential relationships between representation and change. It is my claim here that both the cooperation and the frequent incommensurability of the representations produced by the different modules are relevant to the explanation we seek of creativity and innovation.

Gardner's modularity theory

Gardner's early discussion of modularity (the first edition of *Frames of Mind* appeared in 1983) is interesting mostly for its failures. He chooses the production of poetry as his example of linguistic intelligence because the sensitivities or abilities he considers to be the core operations of language are present and magnified, as it were, in the poet: "a sensitivity to the order among words—the capacity to follow rules of grammar, and, on carefully selected occasions, to violate them.... A sensitivity to the sounds, rhythms, inflections, and meters of words.... And a sensitivity to the different functions of language..." (p. 77). Although these abilities indeed are shared between the production of poetry and the production and reception of all language, Gardner unfortunately omits a necessary condition for the production and understanding of poetry: the ability to understand original figurative language, that is, nonconventionalized relationships between words and images, which by any definition must be an intermodular ability.

All language use requires conventional links between words and images; to make them is a necessary condition of knowing the meaning or reference of words. To imagine, however, what Robert Frost means by the "something" "that doesn't love a wall" requires precisely the kind of translation or annotation process by which the ability and experience of one module (the linguistic) must be brought into registration with those of another—in this case, the visual module (which Gardner calls the spatial intelligence).

Gardner, however, is repeatedly blind to the evidence of his own data as time after time he cites the linguistic performance of artists or scientists describing their work or their insights, or even their intermodular problems, for example, Van Gogh talking of the difficulty of reproducing color and Einstein talking of visual modelling of physical states (p. 196). He might also have picked up a clue from the difficulty he notes children have in representing their spatial knowledge of their environment in words or by drawing maps: "While children's spatial understanding develops apace, the expression of this understanding via another intelligence or symbolic code remains difficult" (p. 180).

The major weakness of Gardner's work, thus, is its assumption, despite his own evidence, that interaction between modules is, in most instances, miraculously trouble free: "In normal human intercourse, one typically encounters complexes of intelligences functioning together smoothly, even seamlessly in order to execute intricate human activities" (p. 281). Gardner uses the adjective "seamless" in at least three other places (pp. 87, 203, and 210) to characterize human mental functioning. My claim here, on the contrary, is that the seams are just what we need to notice. They are the sites of innovations resulting from the incommensurability between modules.

The crucial recognition of failure

Jackendoff (1987) took two crucial steps toward a recognition of the importance of the limits of understanding. He introduced the notion of gradience in understanding, providing a way to talk about better or worse cases. It was of course a giant step away from idealization to recognize that cognition is indeed a matter of stronger or weaker, clearer or fuzzier judgments rather than right or wrong understanding. He also made some interesting suggestions about sites of blindness in the system. His talk about enregistration between systems focuses the possibility of failures there, and that is also a move toward a more intuitively adequate description of our mental processes. Once we give up praising how wonderfully all the systems of human cognition work together and introduce the recognition of failure into the discussion, we can begin to search out human ways of coping at the borders of the modules.

It is here that the theory stakes its claim about change: it is the combination of distinct modes of representation and the limitations of the translators in entirely overcoming modularity which make every interpretation inevitably a compromise. All attempts to coordinate between modules, then, contain a certain inevitable instability or vacancy that will open up the need for or provoke further attempts at representation, that is, innovation. That the task of collation, annotation, or registration will never be entirely accomplished is a spur for trying again, trying another strategic combination perhaps, and is thus a continual impetus for change.

Cognitive scientists have in fact had a theory of what happens at the borders within the brain where different incoming stimuli must meet. The homunculus theory, as it is called (there's a little man in there), is actually not so much a theory as a placeholder for a theory, acknowledging its inadequacy by its silly name. What the metaphor of the little man does indicate is that what is still needed in these theories of brain function is an account of a centralized intentionality. If the modules are swift but stupid, who, what, or where is the little man who acts as border policeman, dispatcher, arbitrator, and general registrar? How do all the incoming data get arranged into coherent thoughts or propositions or plans of action? Who sorts and hierarchicalizes, who compares and chooses between competing claims on the attention of the mind/brain? Who is the "you" who you think runs things?

Parallel distributed processing models

In the work of some recent brain theorists, the perceived failure of coordination has come to suggest a solution to a problem, rather than to be the problem itself. Theorists interested in parallel distributed process (PDP) theories of mind are currently speculating that the less we attribute to a powerful central processor-supercomputer the better. PDP theories (see for example McClelland and Rumelhart 1986) offer a very plausible challenge to the mind-as-computer metaphor by suggesting that processing from the smallest perceptions to the grandest idea complexes does not happen in structured sequences building from smallest to largest, but by massive numbers of parallel (simultaneous rather than serial) and distributed (happening in more than one place at once) neuronal activations. This activity achieves what it does not because it computes according to programs that "know" what they are aiming to accomplish, but by highly redundant collocations of neuronal activity, some of which turn out to be adaptive. Heinz Pagels points out the consequences this model has for the notions of the representation of knowledge. In these theories

> *knowledge is distributed throughout the network;* it is not localized in a specific magnetic memory core or the position of a microswitch. The representation of knowledge, according to the connectionists, is distributed among the strengths of the connections between the units....Networks don't quite so much compute a solution as they settle into it, much as we subjectively experience our own problem solving. (1988:126)

PDP theories are still modular theories.[10] If Fodor's basic unit is the module, Gerald Edelman's (1989) is the much smaller neuronal group or population. A population of neurons is module-like in that it is a speedy primary processor. A particular population may be genetically suited, say, to cooperate in perceiving curved lines or in distinguishing a particular random noise from a human speech sound. The gene structure of the species, however, does not fully predict or determine the final form of the neurons and their arrangement in groups. That is done on site, as it were, in reaction to the actual stimuli with which the organism is confronted. The neuronal group has more and stronger synaptic connections among members of its group than with other populations, but communicates and coordinates with other groups as well. Two crucial innovations in the PDP version of modularity are important to our argument. Where Fodor described the modules as "hard-wired," that is, fully genetically determined, the PDP theorists see the neural architecture as genetically predetermined to grow the necessary fine wiring of axons and dendrites on site and in context, depending on what stimuli that context presents. It also can adapt as that context changes (as the body grows, for example).

The importance of this difference cannot be underestimated. It is the possibility of regrowth and restructuring of the neuronal groups during the life of an individual brain that allows the groups themselves, locally and adaptively, to accomplish the coordination that previously had to be attributed to that mysterious and unlocatable central processor. The second crucial advantage for our purposes of a PDP theory is that its parallel and distributed multiplicity—just the sheer number of competing attempts to meet local processing needs—produces a processor that is highly tolerant of error. It does not need to work with the kind of precision computer hardware demands of engineers and programmers. As Edelman describes it, "Perception leading to categorization is adaptive and not necessarily veridical" (p. 316).

Edelman's Neural Darwinism

The tolerance for error allows Edelman to make a truly revolutionary proposal in his theory of neuronal group selection, as set out in *Neural Darwinism* (1989): there is no central controller. The brain is a jungle of competing claims, and the strongest win out. The job gets done as best as it can, and as long as that's good enough for the survival of the species, it's good enough. The notion of a single correct or ideal response becomes irrelevant. The evolutionary arguments for brain structure and function have thus moved from supporting cast to principal players in the PDP theories of brain organization. The modularity of the brain, it is assumed, is adaptive: as a species, we have evolved sufficiently so that we've got what it takes to survive. Edelman, for example, like the other modularity theorists, begins by assuming that the neural system has many different parts, with different abilities, and that we need all those different ways of knowing because the world is polymorphous. His view of the epistemological tasks of the brain are explicitly Wittgensteinian:

> Objects do not come in predefined categories, are variable in time, occur as novelties, and are responded to in terms of relative adaptive value to the organism rather than of veridical descriptions. This lends a relativistic and disjunctive flavor to the categorization of objects by animals: things are partitioned according to those factors that are significant for and available to the perceiving animal. (p. 260)

Edelman does not deny that the world is organized and that its properties can be described by chemistry and physics. The individual, however, is not born with direct access to this structure. We do not receive sense "data," as the algorithmic theorists would have it, but just a lot of stimuli. The animals that have competed successfully are those that have been able to categorize these stimuli in a sufficiently clear way to make them into reuseable "data" or knowledge.

A large number of brain cells, far more than are eventually retained, begin life in the infant child's head. The stimuli that pour in through the infant's senses stimulate groups of cells, and if the organization of a particular group's receptors is fortuitously well adapted to, or can grow to adapt to, the needs of the infant in his or her environment, then the synapses within that group will be chemically strengthened by repeated use and will survive and even outbid other cell clusters for the job of mapping what the world out there is like for that child. These maps help the brain determine how to interpret similar kinds of stimuli in the future. Since every individual's experience is unique, the organization of an individual brain is unique—a consequence of that brain's experience under the kind of competition Darwin thought prevailed in the natural world. Relativity, here, is not a philosophical concept but a description of brain structure.

The process of adaptation toward stimuli is dynamic. The brain keeps up with the changes by extending new axons and dendrites as needed from the neurons already in place until a satisfactory arrangement is found and until the situation changes and a new arrangement is needed. The advantage to the organism of the brain's adaptability to a complex world in which a survivor must constantly be ready to encounter something new and previously uncategorized is clear. On this view, the precision coding Fodor wants to write into the brain on the assumption that it works like a digital computer is not only missing, but would be a distinct disadvantage because it would restrain adaptability. The brain is built, rather, without detailed instructions about how the nerve endings will connect with other neurons or with muscles, but rather with the innate potential for new growth. This is the only way, Edelman argues, that the animal would have evolved at all, because evolution selects for behavior which increase the species' chances of survival. The hypothesis of epigenesis, that is, that the structures of the organism are not all predetermined but instead grow toward effective behavior in response to the environment, is a leap of very great importance in the theory because it opens the way for an explanation of the way the physical structures and cultural ideas can interrelate. Some consequences of this possibility for interpretive theory will be explored in Chapter 7.

But we have moved away from the argument of the neurons, and because one of the good things about Edelman's work is how closely he sticks to the actual physiology of brains, let's get back to it. As he describes it, a population, or group of connected neurons, takes on a specific job, each responding chiefly to one feature in its environment, but responding, perhaps not as efficiently, to other similar features as well. Each feature then (say a line at a specific angle) stimulates several groups of cells. A population that can't grow so as to organize itself to cope with the task it was genetically designed to do will die off. There are, of course, limits to what kinds of epigenetic growth can be expected and to how quickly it can happen. The population of cells that might be expected to adapt was born already almost there, as it were. But there will be overlap. A population of cells may do a few jobs, some better than others, some that other populations do better. The overlap, like redundancy in higher-level cognitive systems, explains the organism's great adaptability and its capacity to recover after injury by reassigning necessary jobs to another group that had been doing it, if not so efficiently, or had been doing something nearly like it, until then.

Within the neuronal group, once a connection is made that can be successfully reused (i.e., that is adaptive in its context), that connection will be strengthened and become part of the map or representation of the world which the organism uses to predict and act. The map is continually updating itself as its member cells sample the environment through separate channels in the same modality or in different modalities. Each channel can sample a different part of the environment as a result of the body's movement and position, and according to the properties of the sense receptors can extract different features from the environment. Edelman calls this "disjunctive sampling." The resultant map does not provide a complete representation of the environment; there are plenty of gaps. On the basis of its samples, however, it achieves "adaptive categorization" (p. 231).

It is not coincidental, I believe, that the idea of doing without anything more than an internal drive toward cognitive closure or equilibrium as a governing intentionality has been recognized as a theory we could live with just as postmodernism has begun to be widely understood beyond the esoteric circles of its origins. The new theory is democratic in the way it allows all comers to compete, and it is centrally postmodern in its recognition and acceptance of a good deal of lack of communcation and muddling through as a reasonable description of mental life. The Darwinian arguments can be made to support this view. Evolutionary adaption is adaption toward behavior which allows survival of the species. The brain that can muddle through is good enough. The computer model of mind inherited from its founding metaphor the standard of elegance of program design, but when the metaphor switches to evolutionary adaptability, then survival, not elegance, is sufficient.

Edelman's theory makes a great leap forward from a literary theorist's point of view because it brings the actual cell populations in the brain within hailing distance of an individual's felt mental states and patterns of response. One can see that he could almost hypothesize a theory of a fragmented, contingent, necessarily opportunistic or pragmatic postmodern consciousness from the state of brain affairs that Edelman describes. In *Neural Darwinism* he does not take this next highly speculative step. But others have.[11]

Dennett's gappy consciousness

In *Consciousness Explained* (1991), Dennett suggests the kind of consciousness that would result from a brain that is not elegantly programmed, but sufficient, a brain in which there is no commander in chief but a succession of "coalitions of specialists" (p. 358). In order to make the leap from neuronal processing to a discussion of consciousness, Dennett necessarily returns to a reliance on metaphor, which Edelman was in large part able to avoid. Dennett's metaphor for human consciousness is a narrative that is available in multiple drafts. A lot of discrimination judgments are being made at different sites around the brain. They don't necessarily all get together anywhere. Some die out, unnoticed, and others connect with other constructions, sometimes building into a sufficiently developed and coherent chain to be called a perception, a feeling, an idea, or a spur to action:

> This multitrack process occurs over hundreds of milliseconds, during which time various additions, incorporations, emendations, and overwritings of content can occur, in various orders. These yield,

> over the course of time, something ***rather like*** a narrative stream or sequence, which can be thought of as subject to continual editing by many processes distributed around in the brain, and continuing indefinitely into the future. Contents arise, get revised, contribute to the interpretation of other contents or to the modulation of behavior (verbal and otherwise), and in the process leave their traces in memory, which then eventually decay or get incorporated into or overwritten by later contents, wholly or in part....At any point in time there are multiple drafts of narrative fragments at various stages of editing in various places in the brain....
>
> Since these narratives are under continual revision, there is no single narrative that counts as the canonical version, the "first edition" in which are laid down, for all time, the events that happened in the stream of consciousness of the subject, all deviations from which must be corruptions of the text. (pp. 135–136)

At this point, many scientists and philosophers are going to lose patience with Dennett. In fact, throughout the book he has felt the need repeatedly to reassure his audience that, even though it is a difficult concept, if they concentrate and follow his arguments and his evidence, they can learn to live without the assumption of a central command. Throughout his book, his metaphor for the central processor has been called the Cartesian theater: the place where you (the controlling self, the singular point of view) sit and watch the parade or performance of consciousness, the place where you see the scripted and organized results of brain processes, the site of your coordinated and coherent understanding.

A reader of Dennett like myself, however, finds his reassurance superfluous from the outset. His theory scans the territory that modernist literature has been exploring for almost a century now: it confirms the realism of those representations of mental life found in the stream of consciousness writing of James Joyce and Virginia Woolf. It is no news to students of literature that the experience of mental life is of a messy, disjoint succession of perceptions and connections, capable now and then of providing a pleasurable, if highly fragile, cohesion.[12] Dennett himself, apparently not having lived the last twenty years worrying about poststructuralism and postmodernism, needs these reassurances himself, but there is a hint in his book that the Berlin wall between disciplines may be falling:

> [The author speaks:] There is still one puzzle, however. How do *I* get to know all about this? How come *I* can tell you all about what was going on in my head? The answer to the puzzle is simple: *Because that is what I am.* Because a knower and reporter of things in such terms is what is me. *My* existence is explained by the fact that there are these capacities in this body.
>
> This idea, the idea of the Self as the Center of Narrative Gravity, is one we are finally ready to examine. It is certainly an idea whose time has come. Imagine my mixed emotions when I discovered that before I could get my version of it properly published in a book, it had already been satirized in a novel, David Lodge's *Nice Work* (1988). It is apparently a hot theme among the deconstructionists. (p. 411)

Dennett then quotes from Lodge the explanation of the nonexistence of authors outside of the texts they produce. While in Lodge's novel this may of course be read as satire, it is in fact a faithful paraphrase of Roland Barthes's and Jacques Derrida's own philosophical pronouncements on the nonexistence of the *hors-texte.*

I want to close my discussion of these brain theories with reference to Dennett's final commitment to modularity and the gaps between, because that, beyond the details and disagreements among the various theories, is what we need to work with. Dennett doesn't use the word *modularity.* He is, primarily, a philosopher, and his focus is on the phenomenology of consciousness, not the neurology of brains. He concedes that consciousness *seems* to be continuous, but he reads the neurological evidence that fills his book as argument that consciousness is not, in fact, a plenum. We make up (narrate) the connective material, the useful fictions that lend coherence to our understanding of our lives. But consciousness itself, he asserts, "is gappy and sparse, and doesn't contain half of what people think is there" (p. 366).

Summing up and hedging

Having begun with talk about creativity and change, this chapter has served, I hope, to change the terminology of the discussion so as to take advantage of recent advances in cognitive science. But I should state clearly that, although the most recent PDP theories have some attractive aspects to a literary mind, it isn't ultimately of great concern how the neuroscientists eventually describe the mind/brain. In fact, it would be surprising if there aren't new theories around by the time this book gets into print. What is important here is the assumption of the copresence of modularity and gaps in mental processes, and I am satisfied to continue thinking along these lines based on the fact that theorists who fall on different sides of the argument about how much of the brain's work is computational nevertheless assume a version of modularity.

Instead of saying that "necessity is the mother of invention," we can now say the more EC (evolutionarily correct) "brain modularity necessitates the creative and tolerant bridging of gaps." We may also begin to see that the fact that human minds have at least a partial awareness of the limitations of their own abilities itself contributes to the perpetual striving to fill in vacancies. In short, the assumption of modularity and the inevitable difficulties that arise from the multiplicity of modules allow us to see how the need for adaptation and change could be built into the structure of the brain itself.

It is, finally, the urgency of the issue of the relationship between culture and biology that drives my attempt to bring a materialist, biologically based cognitive science as a counterweight to current materialist historical scholarship. That materialism finds its accounts of both meaning and change solely in the rhetoric of the socio/cultural force fields surrounding an individual artist, but abandons the material almost immediately for a study of the discourses about the material. I have, thus, deliberately chosen for study here examples of literary change that seem to be driven by the social upheaval of the 1960s and 1970s in America. By displaying a prima facie relationship to their social contexts, they seem to beg for historical explanation; however, when the essays are read in tandem with homologous pieces of contemporary cognitive theory, they reveal the variety but also the limitations of the cognitive strategies that can be mobilized for the production of and the response to change. I would hope, by this procedure, to enrich interpretive theory by deferring, through the detour into cognition, the inevitable circularity of identifying text and context, and the textualization of context.

Let me admit at the outset two of the risks of this project. While it would be hard to gainsay the broad assertion that biological structure has a bearing on the possibilities of interpretation, I hope I am not, here, committing the common mistake of interdisciplinary studies by assuming that the hypotheses presented from the area in which I am an amateur are (somehow) more reliable than the more familiar, but embattled assertions in my own field. I do not intend to offer the theories of cognitive science as buttresses for theories of reading, only to explore what can be teased out of a confrontation of the emergent theories of cognition with a suspicious reading of innovative texts.

The second risk, perhaps more serious, is also connected to what Fodor has called the epistemic boundedness of the mind. What are the limits to what we can think? It can be stated perhaps as a problem of arithmetic versus significance. The complexities of brain processing being what they are, it may be the case that although there undoubtedly are some kinds of things brains cannot do, the sheer number of combinatorial possibilities of what they can do may be so great as to be able to produce, by circumvention and recombination, anything that may not be directly producible by the brain in a straightforward way. Thus, although my physiology prevents me from scratching my left elbow with my left hand, because I can achieve the same relief by using my right I would be an ungrateful wretch indeed to label that inability a "limitation." There is, indeed, a substantial amount of evidence demonstrating the ability of the brain to compensate for incomplete information in some areas and, as well, for damage to some specific areas of the brain by finding new pathways that will accomplish more or less the same task as is normally achieved in the now impossible way.[13] There is also evidence that different (normal, untraumatized) brains manage the same tasks in different ways, that different individuals have favored styles of problem-solving. Fodor considers the problem (1983:120 ff.) and concludes that in spite of the large numbers of things we can do, there probably are significant limitations on what a human being can think or know, and no amount of creativity will allow a Faustian vault beyond the brain's possibilities. The question, then, of what can be considered a genuine physiological limitation is at the heart of the issue of creativity. Is a truly infinite system of recombination a necessary and sufficient condition for us to speak about a creative brain, or is a very very large number of possibilities good enough?

2 New Genres

American Autobiography

> Every time serves for the matter that is then born in't.
>
> —Enobarbus, in *Antony and Cleopatra*

Of the three triumvirs, Lepidus is the one who pursues every opportunity for a compromise that will bring Antony and Caesar together and avert catastrophe. On Antony's first return to Rome from Egypt, Lepidus has a word with Enobarbus in hopes that Antony's friend will be able to influence his general toward moderation. Enobarbus's answer, however (the epigraph above), takes a deterministic view. He seems to be saying that he can't change Antony to match the needs of the moment: the fit of time and temperament can't be tailored by any individual. The tragic outcome of the play would seem to prove Enobarbus correct: time and that matter born into it come to terms, but not through the conscious intervention of any one person.

For my first example of how time and matter come together, how, that is, literary critical practice is ultimately served by the interface of cultural change and cognitive possibilities, we may look at a set of essays about autobiography. These essays display the struggles of some literary critics to make meaningful genre distinctions—that is, to use category labels so as to highlight significant similarities and differences among texts. The result is the emergence of two new categories or genre labels where the earlier single one, autobiography, has come to seem insufficiently descriptive. In one essay a new category name is suggested, as familiar and canonical texts are reconsidered in a changed political context. Ten years later, the political situation that had influenced the first categorization has elevated the status of a group of previously noncanonical texts. The genre name that was new ten years ago is now under pressure from the newly relevant texts, and another change is forthcoming. The essays are examples of genre criticism, but my reason for bringing them to your attention is not for the excellence or particular importance of their claims about genre. I claim them, rather, as exemplars of the interconnections between social history, conventional procedures within the systems of academic literary interpretation, and the specific adaptive powers of the human mind/brain. In literary genre discussion we can witness one of the ways in which the conventional strategies of literary systems take advantage of the brain's ability to categorize and to readjust to new situations by recategorizing.

In an essay entitled "Autobiography and America" (1971), James M. Cox presented a proposal for a new subgenre: American autobiography. His examples are Benjamin Franklin's Memoirs, Henry Adams's *Education*, Henry David Thoreau's *Walden*, and Gertrude Stein's *The Autobiography of Alice B. Toklas.* In works of this specifically American kind of autobiography, Cox argues, the act of writing the story of the self seems intentionally to instantiate the self-creation of the new American nation.[1] Cox acknowledges the function of his own context as a spur to his new categorization: The recent importance of autobiography is, he writes,

> a result of, and a response to, the revolutionary political attitudes and feelings which have fully emerged in the last five years. For when politics and history become dominant realities for the imagination, then the traditional prose forms of the essay and the autobiography both gain and attract power, and the more overtly "literary" forms of prose fiction—the novel and the short story—are likely to be threatened and impoverished. As such a process takes place—as politics and history tend to claim dominion over the imagination—then the literary imagination tends to respond by denying the generic distinctions which are both powerful and convenient categories in periods of stability and peace. (p. 144)

Autobiography, then, is no longer the right term for the texts Cox wants to understand. It is, on one hand, too generalized: it fails to indicate a crucial distinction between American and European autobiography. European autobiographies such as that of Jean-Jacques Rousseau, are more personal memoirs in which the individuality of the speaker and the speaker's estrangement from the surrounding culture are emphasized. Cox argues that in America, however, autobiography is "the form which would realize the revolution and thus stand for it....[It is] the life of a self-made, self-governing man written by the man himself" (p. 151). Cox's American autobiographers do not separate themselves from the community. Of Adams, he says, "He knew he had to make life art...he dared to identify his history with that of his country" (p. 163). *Walden* is then also shown to be a revolutionary's plan for America—the self-made book by the self-made man for the self-made country.

The traditional category of autobiography is also too small for Cox's texts, too clearly limited by the assumption of facticity. There are several ways in which "autobiographical narrative falls between history and fictive narrative" (p. 146). His American autobiographers are fictionalizing their lives in tandem with American revolutionary history. Cox thus proposes a new category to be added to the set of literary categories already in place to enable a reader to fill a perceived gap. The single available category, "autobiography," is felt to describe both too large a class and too small a class of texts. The literary critical recategorization recorded here allows recognition and discussion of differences in the texts that became culturally significant to the context of reading during the 1970s and 1980s.

Cox's rule of American autobiography (as inferred from his discussion) can be described by a preference rule, that is, a set of well-formedness and preference conditions. The difference between the conditions of the old and the new rules displays the adjustments he has made in the system of genres. As a set of discreet and differently structured conditions, a preference rule displays a sense of what is a central and what is a peripheral descriptor. As a formalism for describing the conditions for category membership, a preference rule is capable of displaying both the gradience of representativeness among category members (since all members of a category are not equally representative of it), and the fuzziness of category boundaries. (See Mervis and Rosch 1981 and Jackendoff 1983.) When a sufficient number of the conditions of a preference rule are met, the reader feels satisfied in characterizing a text as, say, American autobiography. "Sufficient" here is defined circularly, as in the Gestalt rule of Prägnanz originally formulated in Wertheimer (1923): if the reader feels secure about the category judgment, then ipso facto a sufficient number of conditions have been met. When a reader feels less secure with a judgment, we assume that an insufficient number of the conditions have been met. Here, then, are the well-formedness conditions (WFCs) of Cox's rule, that is, his absolute and necessary but not sufficient conditions for a satisfying categorization:

WFC 1: American autobiography has to be a narrative history.

WFC 2: The author, writing the story of his or her life, is revealed to be a self-made, self-possessed, or self-educated person.

WFC 3: Just as the text is self-written; the self-invention is in some way revolutionary, i.e., analogous to the national (American) sense of revolution or change.

WFC 4: American autobiography "proposes a model life,...not presented as a model to follow but one to equal." (pp. 155–156)

Cox's discussion also turns up a set of gradient necessary conditions (GNCs) that must be met by texts if they are to be called American autobiographies.[2] American autobiography shares properties with the novel and with histories in these ways:

GNC 1: It takes as a central interest the characterization of a person.

GNC 2: It does this in a way that counts as being imaginative.

GNC 3: It is a rhetorical (formal) gesture.

GNC 4: Its writer imaginatively identifies his or her life with the revolutionary possibilities of America.

In addition, Cox recognizes a set of typicality conditions (TCs), that is, features typically found in American autobiography:[3]

TC 1: It is like those of Franklin, Thoreau, or Henry Adams.

TC 2: It is written in America by an American.

TC 3: It is written by the character it is nominally about.

These conditions also divide between TCs, which do not admit gradience, and gradient typicality conditions (GTCs), which do:

GTC 1: It becomes "more possible" during periods of political upheaval. (p. 155)

GTC 2: It is confessional (an account of a private life).

GTC 3: It is like a memoir (an account of a public life).

GTC 4: It finds women irrelevant to the pursuit of the model life.

GTC 5: It receives serious critical attention.

GTC 6: It is currently highly marketable.

It isn't important to decide whether or not GTC 2 and GTC 3 present a real contradiction, since it is the nature of typicality conditions that they can enumerate contradictions. In no text will both be present, even though either may be considered typical of the genre. The conditions of a type are not a logically structured set, although neither are they entirely arbitrary (see Rosch 1978). They are, rather, the furniture of an experienced mind, which accepts conditions of meaning from a variety of sources. An individual text that meets all necessary and a subset of the typicality conditions will be categorized as an American autobiography by Cox, and by you if you accept his argument.

Western American autobiography

Ten years after Cox's essay first appeared, Arnold Krupat published "American Autobiography: the Western Tradition" (1981). Obviously impressed by Cox's linking of American autobiographers as self-creators with their self-created land, he nevertheless quarrels with him. Our interest in their disagreement is in the example it offers of how different inferences about function can express themselves as differences in categorization. In order to argue for his own category against Cox's, Krupat has to name two more categories: European autobiography, which he will describe in such a way as to emphasize the similarities of European texts to Cox's texts and their differences from his own, and Eastern American autobiography by which he grants genre status to Cox's texts while differentiating them from his own.

Krupat challenges Cox for "accepting traditional foreclosures of a sectionalist, racist, or sexist kind" (p. 317); that is, for considering only the canonized texts. He himself, while calling attention in footnotes to the autobiographies of American blacks and women, focuses in the body of his article on a series of narratives written about Westerners such as Buffalo Bill Cody, Davy Crockett, Kit Carson, and Sam Houston, none of whom actually wrote his own autobiography (Carson was apparently illiterate) but actively encouraged or cooperated with the authors who wrote their life stories for them. Krupat's new category thus makes explicit what had until then remained implicit—the well-formedness condition of autobiographies: that they are written by their subjects. Never having been a distinguishing feature among texts, it had never had any place as a descriptor. Now it is a heavily weighted condition.

Krupat, furthermore, has two gradient necessary conditions. One he calls *historicism,* that is, the text is a description of the self in relation to the conditions of the historical period. The second is *egocentric individualism.* According to Krupat, then, Franklin's autobiography is an exemplar of historicism, that is, it presents the perceived identity of the subject and the history of his country. Thoreau, for his part, exhibits the European trait of egocentricity: he perceives himself as separate from the multitude of men, even to the extent of pursuing an obscure style of writing. They are all, of course, written texts. These three conditions, according to Krupat, identify Cox's autobiographies with what he calls the European polarity in Eastern American culture, a tendency specifically different from a collocation of conditions he calls the native American Indian polarity.

What is presented here as a disagreement about a categorization judgment is also a difference in inference from structures to function (e.g., Cox reads *Walden* as intended to represent a typical American experience, while Krupat sees it as purely self-expressive). Krupat's new category gives voice to what he infers to be the opposition between a culture considered to be adult and civilized because it is literate and a culture perceived as childish and barbaric because it is oral. Eastern American autobiographies are all "old-world oriented" because of their self-conscious literariness even when they are American in their identity of American subjects with American history. "Civilized" authorship, which represses phonological presence and sublimates the voice into the sign, invents the self through letters. In America, Krupat claims, even the identity with American history is lost through the emphasis on making through writing, as opposed to the uncivilized Indian who makes through doing. After Franklin, he says, "the scriptive act is all; there is no America, only the making of Americans" (p. 309).

Krupat is thus postulating a detachment from history and an attachment to civilization as writing that pushes Eastern autobiography in a crucially different direction from Western autobiography in which the rejection of writing was decisive. That the Western American autobiographies were not written by their subjects is not just an accident of educational opportunity, but a deliberate rejection of Eastern/European culture. Krupat's ultimate quarrel with Cox is not that Cox's category of American autobiography isn't large enough to include Western autobiography, but that in fact it is only in the Western texts that the genuine American article can emerge, free from the pull of European standards: the texts Cox reads will not fit.

Thus, Krupat's gradient necessary condition for the genre of Western autobiography is:

GNC 1: The subjects of Western American autobiography identify with the Indian polarity in clear and conscious distinction from the Eastern, or European polarity.

The next major divide involves the issue of writing itself. Krupat challenges half of Cox's claim (WFC 2) that the self-made text is a well-formedness condition: "The Western autobiographer," he claims, "lives his life apart from writing, going so far as to entrust its actual inscription to another" (p. 311). Note here the advantage of the decomposability of category judgments: in the same way as a rule is made up of a set of conditions, so a condition is made up of other conditions (Mervis and Rosch 1981). In principle, a condition can be infinitely further specified since each word, indeed each morpheme of meaning, is itself a set of conditions of meaning that could be expressed in words that themselves could be specified ad infinitum. So Krupat challenging one part of Cox's WFC is a challenge to the clustering of several different conditions. He would in fact keep many of Cox's conditions. Since he acknowledges that experience must be transformed into artifact in order to count as autobiography, Krupat accepts that it must be a written text. His category, then, begins with the following WFCs:

WFC 1: American autobiography is a narrative history.

WFC 2: The author is revealed to be a self-made person.

WFC 3: The self-invention is analogous to the American sense of self-creation.

The Western autobiographer, however,

> does not settle down long enough to establish his text in writing, which, as an act, he largely scorns; he invokes instead the "natural," "oral" tradition of the Indian...reciting his part in the "history" of the nation with which he identifies, or even acting it out upon the stage. (p. 310)

For a subject who couldn't or wouldn't write his own narrative, the solution according to Krupat was "submission to degrees of collaborative composition" (p. 311). Thus another well-formedness condition:

WFC 4: There are always two authors of Western autobiography: the subject and the writer or editor who makes the story into a written narrative.

And a gradient necessary condition:

GNC 1: The two authors collaborate. In some cases the book is entirely written by someone other than the subject; in some the editor just edits.

Another necessary condition accounts for Krupat's refusal to accept that his category of Western American autobiography is simply biography: Krupat agrees with Cox that the particularly American trait of both the Eastern and the Western life stories is the way the subject identifies him- or herself as self-made in a self-made nation. To be self-made, and then to arrange to have a book written about you, is tantamount to writing it yourself. Thus:

GNC 2: As long as the hero identifies with the self-making project of America, and there is evidence that he actively wanted his story told as an exemplary narrative, it is American autobiography. A self-promoted or intended book of a self-made, exemplary life is an autobiography.

This condition implies another:

GNC 3: The subjects of the Western books are, if not stereotypes, certainly types: Cody, the good scout, Boone the stalwart pioneer. (p. 313)

The Western subjects are specifically not egocentric individualists; they are individuals only in that they did extraordinarily well what everyone was doing. On this condition, Krupat distinguishes his text from many of the Eastern autobiographies, such as those by Thoreau and Adams, because their subjects "go against the grain," struggling against dominant tendencies they identify and reject in the American life around them. Krupat infers from his autobiographers, in spite of the "Indian polarity," a self-effacing identity with the birth of a nation. All end their narratives, he notes, with the "inevitable triumph" of white civilization, some even going so far as to recommend how the Indians may most easily be exterminated (p. 314).[4] This identification with the American experience combined with what Krupat identifies as the absence of egocentricity leads Krupat to suggest that stories such as Thoreau's and Adams's may even be stories of failure to identify with the community, and this in turn leads to one further gradient necessary condition of Western autobiography, and that is its emplotment as a comedy:

GNC 4: "The structure of Western autobiography strictly follows the 'emplotment' (in Hayden White's term) of American history as the nineteenth century generally conceived it." Down to the triumph of the white man over the Indian, it "progresses firmly toward a 'happy ending', where justice prevails." (p. 314)

This last necessary condition would not be met by Thoreau, Adams, or Stein if, as Krupat suggests, we accept William Dusinberre's characterization (1980) of these lives as failures. In addition to these necessary conditions, Krupat suggests a series of typicality conditions and one gradient typicality condition that are often found in Western autobiography:

TC 1: The subject expresses his refusal "to accept the act of writing as the mark of manhood and civilization." (p. 310)

TC 2: The subject of a Western autobiography is not a preacher or a farmer but a hunter or a warrior.

TC 3: In many cases, the subject had experienced Indian captivity or had voluntarily gone to live among the Indians.

GTC 1: The subjects were nearly or wholly illiterate.

None of Cox's canonical texts fit Krupat's rule. The title of Krupat's article, however, "American Autobiography: The Western Tradition," suggests that he meant merely to indicate a branching of the American tradition that could be expressed by considering as necessary conditions only those that can be shared by texts expressing both the European and the Indian polarities. The necessary conditions of Western autobiography, such as the avoidance of writing and the comic emplotment, could be understood as typicality conditions of the larger category of American autobiography. Since typicality conditions need not be fulfilled, the list of them can include contradictory features. American autobiography, a category readers of both essays are now in a position to reconstruct for themselves, thus can be said to include as typicality conditions all four of these conditions:

TC: The writer aims at a sophisticated, even an obscure prose style as a mark of his civilized or educated state.

TC: The subject eschews an elegant prose style, refusing "to accept the act of writing as the mark of manhood and civilization." (p. 310)

TC: The writer and the subject are the same person.

TC: American autobiography can have two authors.

In some ways, the example of new subcategorization rules for autobiography is a "success" story of a certain kind of literary change. A "neglected" genre, autobiography had by 1985 moved closer to the center of readers' attentions, and two scholars had observed the change and had written new rules to describe it. Cox and Krupat were claiming a connection between the past political realities of a culture and the generic and rhetorical forms (as opposed to the themes) of the written texts of that culture, and readjusting the literary genre system to accommodate that understanding. They were, as well, themselves participating in a change that was to become manifest over the 1980s. They were not only correcting the historical record: making the words of literary history fit the world, but were demonstrating by their criticism that perceived and recorded changes in the literary system seem to originate in changes in their own context which, in the 1970s, newly valued the differences between American and European culture and, as well, the differences among Americans. Further than that, their new categories also provided new possibilities for future readings of texts that could now be based on the new rules they had evolved.

Cox has added the following two conditions to the general rule of significance[5] by which he interprets:

> GTC 1: Prefer the interpretation that acknowledges the power of revolutionary times to impinge on the literary imagination.
>
> GTC 2: Prefer the interpretation which recognizes the merging of nonfictional narrative with some aspects of literary creation in autobiographies of revolutionary periods.

The second spells out just how a revolutionary period might impinge: it might blur the distinction between genres so that literary imagination of the kind usually found in fiction can be recognized as well in autobiography.

As a consequence of Cox's new conditions of significance, aspects of earlier interpretations of his canonical autobiographical texts will no longer be found satisfying. Autobiography, traditionally conceived, does not have a structural or functional condition that embodies a historical distinction; since the 1960s, however, the historical period during which an autobiography is written has almost inevitably been weighed in the category judgment.

Cox's ultimate choice of "American autobiography" as his new category rather than "revolutionary autobiography" is a result not only of the considerations represented by his two new conditions of significance, but as well by his perception of the analogy between the earlier revolutionary period in American history and his own. His categorization makes explicit the relation he perceives between revolutionary America of the eighteenth century and revolutionary America of the 1960s. He sees in both periods the cooccurrence of nation-building with the flowering of autobiography and the building of the American self as an independent and self-made creation. This analogy is authorized by the general aesthetic rule:

> GNC: Prefer that categorization which distinguishes the texts being interpreted from others by conditions which are valued *in the context of the interpreter.*

This condition is, ultimately, catastrophic for the literary historian in its reversal of the hierarchy of value between then and now. The full power of this rule will be explored more fully in Chapter 6 and Chapter 7, where it will again be seen undermining what literary historians understand themselves to be doing.

The category fits the time

Although weaknesses could certainly be found in Cox's analogy between revolutionary eighteenth-century America and America of the 1960s, the proposal nevertheless was harmonious with the project of Americanists at the time. Their announced goals were the discovery or development of just such ideological patterns projected simultaneously from historical events and imaginative literature. The Americanist Leo Marx, for example, had described his work *The Machine in the Garden* (1964) as "about the region of culture where literature, general ideas, and certain products of the collective imagination—we may call them cultural symbols—meet" (p. 40). R. W. B. Lewis had hinted at why this kind of interdisciplinary work was particularly exciting in the field of American studies: the origins of the ideas had not yet disappeared into a remote past, but were, as it were, almost within reach. In his introduction to *The American Adam* he explained his search for "a native American mythology," for "the representative imagery and anecdote that crystallized whole clusters of ideas" (1955:1).

In the scholarly atmosphere suggested by these programmatic statements it can easily be imagined that a categorization that distinguished American autobiography from its European forbearers would not be caviled at by a community dedicated to identifying the genuine American article. The question remains, however: why should a categorization that was innovative and satisfying in 1970 become vulnerable in 1980?

Part of the answer is that, just as Cox's own conditions of significance had allowed his innovation, Krupat had his own conditions of significance that came to him through his political and academic context. The revolutionary 1960s had made itself felt in the academic world by the late 1970s, particularly in the changing population of the universities. The new academic reading public was more heterogeneous than it had been: each group with a strong sense of ethnic identity had succeeded to some extent in challenging and revising the established canon of texts taught and studied.

Cox had actually referred, in his opening remarks, to the popularity of *The Autobiography of Malcolm X,* but so strong had the exclusionary power of the canon been for him at that time that he had not, after that single mention of the book, gone on to consider it further as an American autobiography. His closing revolutionary gesture had been to refer to Gertrude Stein. Estelle Jelinek, however, noted in 1980 that had Cox seriously considered women's diaries and autobiographies along with men's he would not have been able to make the generalizations he made about the cooccurrence of revolution and self-invention. Thus a new and heavily weighted condition of significance, present in Krupat's and Jelinek's context but not Cox's, was:

> GTC: Prefer an interpretation (including categorization) that recognizes the values and literatures of women and minority ethnic groups as important to the definition of American categories.

The reweighting of conditions of significance and the introduction of new ones has increased the audibility of other voices and had, thus, by 1981 made Cox's choice of texts seem unreasonably limited, displaying, before the subject of autobiography ever arises, a competing paradigm of who is an American. A white Northeasterner no longer is the only one who matches the category. Inevitably, however, Krupat has his own inconsistency. His Western autobiographers are all male. We had to wait until 1982 for Lillian Schlissel to publish women's diaries of the westward journey.

Another important difference in Krupat's context, a change internal to the academic community, was the widely disseminated post-structuralist critique of language. One effect of this critique was to make the hitherto straightforward notion of writing much more complex and interesting. Krupat does not, in fact, make sophisticated use of the critique of logocentrism, but just as Cox, himself no revolutionary, did not remain untouched by the revolution around him, Krupat, no deconstructor, is aware of issues that had not, ten years before, been problematic.

Krupat's TC 1 (the subject expresses his refusal to accept the act of writing as the mark of manhood and civilization) thus ironically does double duty: it can be understood not only to claim an antiestablishment heroism for his autobiographers, but also to claim his own connection to a prestigious literary establishment. Thus, where Cox had no reason to question the well-formedness condition that an autobiography was written by its subject, Krupat is able to separate that well-formedness condition into two conditions: "the intention to have the story told" remains a WFC; the act of writing it then becomes a typicality condition. He then can argue that although these particular Americans could not agree that writing is a serious creative act, they nevertheless wanted their exemplary American stories told.

Eleven years later, the popular press testified that Krupat had correctly seen the demotion of the previously necessary condition that an autobiography be authored by its subject to a typicality condition. The American newspaper, *USA TODAY*, in its edition of 21 May 1992, reported on the continued popularity of the Buffalo Bill genre. We learn that Knopf has signed a contract for the autobiography of television talk show host Oprah Winfrey who "will work on the book with writer Joan Barthel." Whoever is interested in updating Krupat's description of American autobiography will probably want to include a condition describing the interconnection of money and co-authorship. The newspaper reports that "publishers' rosters are groaning with big-name autobiographies. The two biggest: H. Norman Schwarzkopf's *It*

Doesn't Take a Hero, written with Peter Petre, for which the general reportedly received $5 million, and Magic Johnson's *My Life*, written with William Novak, for which Johnson reportedly received more than $4 million in a multi-book deal."

The second major expansion of interpretive possibilities in which the recategorization participates is the consideration of the fictional aspects of autobiography. Cox's GNC 1, which admits the novelistic and imaginative aspects of autobiography, allows for a complex series of inferences about the texts. By 1980 argument seems not to be needed on these conditions; we see, for example, an assumption that the borders of fiction and nonfiction are changed in William Spengemann (1980).

Spengemann not only assumes Cox's GNC 1, namely that autobiography "shares properties with the novel" and is an imaginative and rhetorical gesture, but goes farther, describing two texts conventionally categorized as novels, Hawthorne's *The Scarlet Letter,* and Dickens's *David Copperfield*, as "poetic autobiography." According to Spengemann, autobiographical form has changed "in response to changing ideas about the nature of the self, the ways in which the self may be apprehended, and the proper methods of reporting those apprehensions" (p. xiii). Remarking on the change by which "the boundaries of the genre have expanded," Spengemann is particularly interested in the variety of structures that can be considered functionally autobiographical: "there is now virtually no written form that has not either been included in some study of autobiography or else been subjected to autobiographical interpretation" (p. xii).

In 1983, Gordon O. Taylor began the preface to his book on American autobiography by quoting what he referred to as Cox's "still-seminal essay." He acknowledges its importance not so much for its re-sorting of autobiographers as for its recognition of a "new alignment and alliance among autobiography, historiography, reportage and the novel which have emerged in this century" (p. ix). Taylor thus chooses to replicate Cox's attention to another aspect of categorization, that of functional genre: the genre as defined not only by the form but by the inferred intention of the author to make his or her form perform a specific task. Thus, Taylor studies, for example, Michael Herr's narrative of his experiences as a journalist in Vietnam, *Dispatches* (1977). He infers Herr's purpose to be one shared with other writers about the war:

> Over the past ten years or so...American writers in increasing numbers have attempted to distill images of the war's private as well as public meanings, images which might fix those meanings in the national consciousness with the force of art as well as entering them in the documentary record....Extending an autobiographical narrative into certain kinds of close encounter with the war, the efforts of these writers...have come to constitute a process of ongoing inquiry as to the appropriate terms of literary treatment. (pp. 121–122)

Cox's innovation, then, recognizes that the writer of an autobiography may, as Taylor says, attempt to use his words to influence the world—to "fix those meanings in the national consciousness." Paul John Eakin, two years after Taylor and four after Krupat, is also able to take for granted some of the innovations first made explicit by Cox and Krupat. His model of autobiography analogizes the acquisition of language particularly as it develops into the power of storytelling, and the development of self-consciousness and self-invention: "In this developmental perspective, the autobiographical act is revealed as a mode of self-invention that is always practiced first in living and only eventually—sometimes—formalized in writing" (1985:8–9). His clear separation between the experiential and the communicative aspects of self-invention suggest that Eakin would not be worried by Krupat's double-authored autobiographies. These reaffirmations of the rules proposed earlier by Cox and Krupat need not be attributed to a direct and conscious line of development between scholars. Taylor cites Cox, but Spengemann and Eakin cite neither Cox nor Krupat.

Although Cox's four gradient necessary conditions of autobiography belong equally to history and to novels, he retained the distinction between an autobiography and a novel by a gradient necessary condition that the former be history, by which he meant something like referentially true at least in major incidents. For Eakin, however, this condition is no longer a necessary condition. An autobiography is still clearly distinguished from a novel, however, by its focus on the psychological task of self-invention that the writer undertakes as a necessary condition of the genre. It may be a typicality condition of the novel, but it is neither a well-formedness condition nor a gradient necessary condition.

It is, thus, the expansion of the functional conditions of the genre that allow Spengemann to claim that autobiographical form has changed in response to changing ideas about the nature of the self, but this is of course true of all genres of discourse. More to the point is Spengemann's demonstration in his own work that what has changed is the category of texts the critic is willing to read as autobiographical. This change, its source outside the literary community, affects nonacademic readers as well, so that the community of readers prepared to understand the psychology of the self as an imaginative invention grows.

Finally, one of the most significant changes which readers in their various communities are still working through is the revaluation, begun in the 1960s, of the individual self in relation to a community. This revaluation is not at all straightforward, involving as it does the dynamic between the individual within the community as well as the immediate ethnic or gender community with which the individual identifies within the larger community. In contrast to the exemplary autobiographers of early America, the new American autobiographers are exemplars of exclusion, dispossession, and lack of identity with a single abstraction called America. This of course removes the necessary condition which began the new genre, the identification of the writer with the nation.

In the flowering of American autobiography, then, ideological conditions of significance can be discerned to have an impact on the literary system. What began as a monolithic idea of what it means to be an American has been replaced by a collection of ethnic and gender identities. This new America is federal in a way unanticipated by Thomas Jefferson: to be individual, to be self-invented, is American in being at the same time unique and representative. "Black autobiography," writes Elizabeth Schultz, "like the blues, expands the solo; [yet] the voice of the single individual retains the tone of the tribe" (1981:111). This new situation could be attested in the production of innovative genre classifications because, as a crucial and yet inherently unstable aspect of the cognitive system, categorization is both permanently necessary and permanently open to reformulation.[6] All the genre critics here, as has been obvious, had more in mind than categorization, but the cognitive importance of categorization is evidenced in their efforts to produce satisfactory genre labels. Furthermore, changes within this system have, as we will see, created new epistemological problems while solving some old ones.

3 New Inferences
Reading Hamlet and the Politics of Genre

Age cannot wither her, nor custom stale
Her infinite variety.

—Enobarbus, in *Antony and Cleopatra*

The epigraph here applies equally well to Cleopatra and to Hamlet; it needs no ghost come from the grave to tell us that the tragedy has been open to an infinite variety of interpretations. We have begun to see, however, in the American examples, and we will again recognize here, that the process of drawing inferences from categorizations can reinforce old patterns of thought as well as allow the emergence of new understanding.

The innovative and enriched understanding of the category of autobiography evidenced in the last chapter was apparently understood by its first proponents, Cox and Krupat, as an attempt to make the words of the descriptive system, that is, of literary history, better fit the way the world of texts actually was or had been. Even further, it enabled the writing of new texts and the rereading of old ones as American or as Western autobiography. We saw, furthermore, that the cultural turbulence of the 1960s influenced not only the systems of academic literary interpretation, but swayed the publishing world as well; by the time Krupat's article appeared he could discuss no less than five noncanonical texts, all of which had been edited for the first time or reissued after the appearance of Cox's essay. He is able, furthermore, to footnote a bibliography of Native American autobiographies (1981), three studies of African-American autobiography (two in 1974 and one in 1979), and a collection of essays on women's autobiography (1980). The availability of these texts is both a result of change and a prerequisite for its diffusion and for further change within the literary system.

As we have begun to see, then, a new categorical possibility provides more than a new name. It is productive in that it allows and also encourages the generation of new chains of inference. The possibility of the production of new inferences is particularly important to those critics, for example, neo-Marxists and feminists, who hope to escape being merely historians or reflectors of the ideologies that surround them, and who would like to make academic criticism influence ideology in the broader social context. An examination of some aspects of that possibility is the subject of this chapter.

Back in 1978, in a landmark feminist study of American literary texts, Judith Fetterley expressed her belief that the recognition of literary versions of repressive ideologies would lead to their defeat: "To create a new understanding of our literature is to make possible a new effect of that literature on us [which] is in turn to provide the conditions for changing the culture that the literature reflects" (pp. xix–xx). It is assumed among cultural critics that influence can indeed flow from words to the world, that the work of the literary critic can make what Terry Eagleton calls a "contribution to the construction of a counterpublic sphere" (1984:113). Elizabeth Meese, to take just one of many examples, argues that "the motive of feminist criticism...must be resistance in the interest of social transformation through interpretation" (1986:14). When it comes to explaining how influence flows within a society, or what magnitude of change can be expected, literary critics are for the most part realistically modest, but not hopeless.[1] Change, as Frank Lentriccia notes correctly, is enabled in part by the inevitable and fortunate heterogeneity of social life: "Ruling culture does not define the whole of culture, though it tries to, and it is the task of the oppositional critic to re-read culture so as to amplify...marginalized voices" (1983:15).

The essays to be examined in this chapter suggest that the extent to which critics who are committed to social change are able to enact the power that interpretation theoretically grants is often a question of how the inferences that conventionally attach to literary genres may be subverted and remade. I will ultimately conclude something like this: while the invention of new categories trailing new inferences is one way to represent innovative ideology, leaving the conventional categories in place and inferring new meaning from them can also be a subversive critical act. If the goal is not just adjusting literary history to better reflect social change, but instigating or, in Lentriccia's term, amplifying the voices calling for that change, then one of the ways to attempt to reach that goal is in cooperation with the mind/brain's ability to innovate chains of inferences conventionally connected to already-in-place categories.

A set of recent readings of Shakespeare's *Hamlet* makes an interesting test case precisely because of its genre. The genre of tragedy itself exerts a pressure against ideological revision, both through its age and dignity within the genre system, and by its specific functional conditions. Because the conventional genre assumptions have a powerful hold on the literary imagination, failure to engage them—failure, that is, to respond to the entailed inferences of the traditional category of tragedy—lames the attempt to make criticism work for change. Even in the presence of what they interpret as an author's good intentions, it has been difficult for critics to understand revenge tragedy as other than retrograde—its action always leaving the situation worse than it was before. These inferences, however, though conventional, are not logically entailed by the structures—inferences never are. Even tragedy should be able to teach us amendment of life. The examples here argue that those critics who have, after all, managed to produce readings which offer alternative visions have done so by taking advantage of the strategic power of creating new inferences for genre categorizations.

The power of the genre conventions to dominate any interpretation of a tragedy has been detailed in many studies. From the structural conditions of English Renaissance revenge tragedy, that is, its typical (but not inevitable) pair of antagonists and its plot structure, twentieth-century critics have repeatedly inferred a struggle to reverse any potentially meliorative movement. Michael Neill's description is exemplary:

> The opponents in this struggle are the politician (tyrant or usurper) and the revenger. The first is a new man whose drive to possess the future requires that he annihilate or rewrite the past: the second is a representative of the old order, whose duty is to recuperate history from the infective oblivion into which his antagonist has cast it. (1983:36)

A consequence of this reading is that, even when the revenger intends to restore the moral status quo ante by killing only the evildoer (real or imagined), it seems to be a necessary structural condition of the genre that the revenger cannot, in the event, limit the violence. As Catherine Belsey notes, "wrath always exceeds justice: that is its nature" (1979:140). Typically, the protagonist or revenger, seeking to restore the traditional values of the community, uses the same violent methods as the destroyer of those values. The expression of the inevitable return to evil, then, is widely understood to be a necessary condition of the genre, that is, an entailed inference about the meaning of its structure. The revenger's action simply repeats the original error.[2]

David Leverenz (1980) and Jacqueline Rose (1986), both feminist critics, and Terence Hawkes (1985), a cultural materialist, are among those who might have been expected to find new ways of reading the play. Their various perspectives ask new questions and produce patterns of response that differ markedly from those of formalist criticism, yet at the end of the day they read the play as conserving old values. In spite of the great difference between their view of what matters in a text from the views of many of the readers of *Hamlet* who preceded them, they don't produce the alternatives one might expect. Their readings find the play delivering the conventional tragic message of the inevitability of failure.

Leverenz's reading focuses on Hamlet's failure to build an adult personality that satisfactorily combines masculine and feminine aspects, and thus he sees the tragedy as resulting from the rejection of the feminine in favor of the rule of strong arms and no tears. By the play's end Hamlet has resigned himself to the male public role: "He mouths its language and assumes its stance of male combat....All the women are dead" (pp. 123–124). *Hamlet*, in Leverenz's analysis, demonstrates "the destruction of good mothering" (p. 111),[3] and his essay, then, is constructive cultural criticism presumably in that it helps audiences draw the lessons from the play that Hamlet himself fails to learn. Although Leverenz blames both parents for Hamlet's dilemma, he blames Renaissance patriarchal social structures for the fact that Hamlet himself blames only his mother. His view differs from T.S. Eliot's (1951:98) view of Gertrude's insufficiency in, among other things, its claim that the problem is not a flaw in the drama, but in the "patriarchal order, which has cracked all the mirrors for self-confirmation" (p. 126).[4] While one can appreciate the delicacy with which Leverenz attempts to avoid the sexism of Freudian theory and to distance himself from the sexism of a good mothering theory, the implication of his reading is something ironically like this: if it weren't for the patriarchy, mothers could bring up their children properly.

Small wonder, then, that Rose found Leverenz's essay little help when thinking about *Hamlet* six years later.[5] In search of a theory of femininity that isn't bound to "blame the mother," Rose surveys some of the most influential psychoanalytic readings of the play: those of Freud, Ernest Jones, Jacques Lacan, and André Green. Although she finds them all wanting, she concludes from the number of times the same issue is reopened that the play "unleashes an anxiety which returns to the question of femininity" (1986:47). This anxiety, she postulates, is just as likely to be a result of the psychoanalytic discourse itself as of the text of *Hamlet.*

Questioning thus the values of the society which so esteems a play that "enact[s] such a negative representation of femininity, or even such a violent repudiation of the femininity in man" (p. 47), she implies that we must simply stop reading the play. If consciousness is any kind of power, however, and if therefore Rose's critique of the psychoanalytic theories available for text interpretation makes a real contribution to her readers' greater awareness of their own lives, then perhaps not reading *Hamlet* may, after all, be a small price to pay.

Terence Hawkes has written, expanded (1985), and reprinted (1986) an article called *Telmah,* which displays his understanding of the effects of the political contexts in which critical positions are taken up, and by so doing adds an important dimension to the study of Shakespeare. He forces us to see the various readings we inherit as related to their own contexts of production as much as to the scholarly arguments to which they address themselves. His essay and his work as founding editor of an important journal of cultural criticism (*Textual Practice*) have helped along the important task of debunking the view of scholarship as a march of progress conducted by disinterested soldiers in the crusade for truth. Nevertheless, even Hawkes fails to suggest the kind of new reading that would justify, in his own eyes, continuing to read, produce, and teach the play. His article includes a brief analysis of *Hamlet*, in which he details the argument that the play, like all revenge tragedy, is backward-looking, cyclical, and recursive. (Hence his renaming it *Telmah—Hamlet* in reverse). Hawkes's identification of the structure of *Hamlet* as self-defeating is congruent with the genre of revenge tragedy: the sin that was to have been purged is replicated, and no healing occurs. His own interpretation, thus, also fails to escape the grasp of retrogression.

The more ambitious part of Hawkes' essay is an interpretation of an earlier reading, that of John Dover Wilson (1935), which is described as embedded in Dover Wilson's relationship to the Russian Revolution. The overriding goal of Dover Wilson's reading, Hawkes suggests, is the search "for unity, progression, coherence, and, if possible, sequential ordering...as part of a ruthless and rigorous process of domestication" (p. 324). Dover Wilson's ruthlessness is conspicuous in his ingenious but, to Hawkes, unconvincing naturalization of the problem of the dumb show presented before the play-within-a-play. Dover Wilson's proposal that Gertrude and Claudius are engaged in conversation during the dumb show and thus don't see it responds to W.W. Greg's 1917 essay in which the problem had first been raised of why Claudius and Gertrude don't react to a mime of murder, but then do react a few minutes later when the play itself is acted. In Hawkes's account of Greg's argument, Claudius's nonreaction shows that the ghost has failed the test, and thus we have no choice but "to choose between giving up Shakespeare as a rational playwright, and giving up our inherited beliefs regarding the story of *Hamlet*" (Greg 1917:400; quoted by Hawkes, p. 319).

Hawkes then argues that Dover Wilson couldn't face "giving up Shakespeare as a rational playwright" and that he produced his solution out of a need to defend the orthodox and rational Shakespeare against Greg's insinuation. Having inferred this need, Hawkes then argues that it is consistent with Dover Wilson's politics. As Hawkes reconstructs the situation, Dover Wilson had been a supporter of the October Revolution of 1905 but had, over the years, changed his position. In 1906, Hawkes reports, Dover Wilson in an article that appeared in *The Independent Review* had supported the Social Revolutionaries, including their position on the necessity of terrorism. A 1914 article is then cited as evidence of his having changed his position to one of support for the Russian autocracy (i.e., the Tsar).[6]

Dover Wilson's attack on Greg, his "literary tsarism" (p. 324), according to Hawkes, is thus a defense of England against Bolshevism in a "displaced Shakespearean form" (p. 325). Hawkes then develops a suggestive generalization about English criticism in this century which, he claims, can be seen to produce a standard response to national crisis: Dover Wilson's response to Greg is compared to E. M. W. Tillyard's "well known war-effort, *The Elizabethan World Picture* of 1943—a discourse which, seeking for the final, confirming presence of authority, nominates the linchpin of the political structure as 'God's representative on earth.'" Each of these two interpretations, according to Hawkes, is "less an accurate picture of the world it purports to describe, than an intimate, covert measure of its author's fears about the fallen world in which he currently lives" (p. 324).

Having argued, then, that Dover Wilson's reading of *Hamlet*, like Tillyard's interpretation of the Elizabethan age, was a function of and analogous to the critic's understanding of the political necessities of his day, Hawkes exempts himself from the generalization. His own reading is the conclusion of a clear-sighted and tough-minded postmodernist reader who can no longer be lulled into accepting an interpretation which assures the audience that all's well with the moral systems of the world. His is an honest willingness to accept the depressing meaninglessness of a stage full of corpses, to resist attempts "to resolve, to domesticate...contradiction" (p. 330). Hawkes's political reading is, of course, itself a demonstration that he is correct in arguing that interpretations, his own as well as Dover Wilson's, reflect political or cultural needs in the context of the interpreter. He does not get beyond his own context of postmodernist anomie, fragmentation, and relativism any more than the earlier critics get beyond their need for order and wholeness. Might we have hoped, however, that he could help us find a way to read *Hamlet* without the determinism of classical tragedy?

Resisting genre

The essays of René Girard (1984) and Stanley Cavell (1987) take another approach. Also embedded in the issues of their own times—and what interest would they have for contemporary readers if they weren't?—they do manage at least a step beyond their own contemporaries' rejections by rejecting, rather, the conventional moral lessons of the genre of tragedy. By addressing the generic structure of *Hamlet* and substituting a new view of moral possibilities for the fatalism of the inferences traditionally invited by the genre, Girard offers a way to read *Hamlet* that makes it an antirevenge play—a plea for an end to violence.

It isn't necessary to accept Girard's own claims for the power of his theory of scapegoating to describe all of the history of humankind (White 1978a) to see that his reading of *Hamlet* does find a way to teach the rejection of the violence of revenge. He begins by noting that in the structural condition of the genre, which pairs two protagonists as antagonists, there can be read a pattern of similarity where others have seen only mighty opposites. Girard argues that although Shakespeare makes his villains distinctively evil, he builds on the recognition that Shakespeare often shows his victims "behaving and thinking exactly like their antagonists" (p. 159). In *Richard III*, for example,

> we are in a world of bloody political struggles and not one adult character in the play has not committed at least one political murder or benefited from one. Most have acted in the past just about as Richard now is acting. Given the slightest chance, they would act again in the same manner. (p. 159)

Something similar happens in *Hamlet.* Although a revenge hero must believe in his revenge, Hamlet often acts as if he were indifferent, as if he has been dragged onto the stage of the wrong play. Girard reads the bedroom scene in which Hamlet compares the two portraits of Gertrude's two husbands as an attempt to convince *himself* that there is indeed a difference. Gertrude's allowing herself to pass so easily from one man to the other also allows the inference that there is little to differentiate the two.

From this new pattern ("new" in the sense that a genre reading that accepted the conventional view of tragedy would not validate it) which Girard calls the "equalization of villainy" (p. 161), he infers that Shakespeare meant to convince at least parts of his audiences (as Girard hopes to convince his whole audience) that revenge is illogical as a moral position because victim and revenger are indifferent honest.

"The demise of the villain is never the victory of right over wrong...nor the triumph of wrong over right which our perverse and inverted pessimism now seems to require" (p. 166). It is instead a "hostile convergence" on a victim, indifferently guilty (since everyone is), which amounts to a "general ganging up...as a scapegoat effect, a kind of moral or even physical lynching, fundamentally irrational and arbitrary in spite of the superficially rational and moral motivations which are exhibited by the lynchers" (p. 166). The ritual satisfaction that the victimization of a scapegoat brings depends on the equal guilt of both victim and pursuers.

Girard argues further that Shakespeare knew very well that since it is precisely the reciprocity of the relationship between the cat and the mouse that keeps the wheels of the dramatic machine turning for five acts, the structures of revenge tragedy couldn't be abandoned entirely. Shakespeare's genius, then, shows in his juggling two tasks: "Shakespeare...is more interested in the undifferentiation of revenge than in the differences of character portrayal. But the amazing thing is that he can emphasize the one and the other almost simultaneously" (p. 162).

Girard concludes that this combination of the revenge plot and the scapegoat ritual produces a double play: it provides the *katharsis*, the purge of emotion that large segments of Shakespeare's audiences would have felt at the downfall of a satisfactory scapegoat, while at the same time it can speak to the more sophisticated in Shakespeare's audience of his great "weariness with revenge" (p. 173). For Girard, *Hamlet* is, and was intended as, a meditation on the need to escape from revenge in which Shakespeare subverts the genre as he uses it to please the groundlings.

If Girard's mythical/anthropological discussion is vulnerable to criticism as an oversimplification, we may still appreciate his attempt to move beyond complaining about tragedy. He is trying to find a way to make it work, to make it address, even exhort, ultimately teach its audience not to fall into the madness of revenge, especially given the nuclear threat of self-destruction so palpable during the years that he was developing his theory.[7] He reads and asks us to read *Hamlet* as a negative exemplum.

Stanley Cavell's reading of *Hamlet* is similarly framed by the demands of the intellectual world in which he attempts to construct a moral response, and his approach accomplishes its renaming by wrestling with the generic angel. The weapon that worries Cavell is not the nuclear one, but rather the philosophical skepticism that threatens to explode the possibility of continuing to do philosophy—that threatens the possibility of knowing anything. When he reads *Hamlet* he sees a new analogy: "Skepticism already [bears] its own marks of a tragic structure" (1987:5). He thus produces a response to a present ideological dilemma by reading one aspect of that ideology, namely philosophical skepticism, into the genre itself, as Girard did, and then inferring new moral meaning from the newly constructed generic pattern.

Cavell claims that Shakespeare's tragedies are tragedies precisely because their protagonists reject or resist the "best case" for knowing the existence of others (1987:11). Skepticism, on this view, rather than being a laudable though "misguided intellectual scrupulousness" (p. 6), is a denial of or withdrawal from the world, a refusal to meet what is not philosophically (logically, verbally) certain. The denial produces, in Cavell's words, "a self-consuming disappointment that seeks world-consuming revenge" (p. 6). Cavell's response is to claim that what he calls ordinariness or everydayness, thematized most frequently as love, specifically as married love, is often the way out of tragic denial. *Hamlet* presents him with a variation of this problem. First, he asserts that "what philosophy registers as uncertainty in our knowledge of the existence of the world is a function of, say an intellectualization of, the child's sense of loss in separating from the mother's body" (p. 13).

Now he must describe this sense of loss in *Hamlet*, something that is fairly easy to retrieve from all the psychoanalytic criticism about the relationship between Hamlet and his mother. Cavell in fact takes his cue from the same 1917 essay by W. W. Greg mentioned earlier in which it was first proposed that it is Hamlet's imagination (a hallucination, not a truthful ghost) that provides the details of the old king's death scene—the poison poured in the ear. While Greg suggested that the source of Hamlet's imaginative reconstruction of his father's death scene is a play familiar to Hamlet called "The Murder of Gonzago," Cavell prefers to pick up Greg's suggestion that the play within a play and the dumb show with which it begins "is such a play as Hamlet might have dreamed" (Greg p. 405) and claims he *did* dream it, or fantasize it along Freudian lines. He argues that Hamlet's memory of a primal scene of parental intercourse figures itself as his fantasy; what disturbs the tragic prince is, thus, not only imagining Claudius as his father's murderer, but as his mother's lover.

Cavell's argument here depends on substitutions of the kind Freud describes as occurring in dreams: the powerful pouring poisoner here is the woman. Cavell then claims that "Hamlet divines that his father experienced Gertrude's annihilating power before him" (p. 185), and because he cannot be free of his mother, he cannot be successfully born into the world as an independent person who is secure in his own existence:

> On this deciphering of the dumb-show as primal scene—enciphering young Hamlet's delayed sense of Gertrude's power to annihilate all Hamlets—I see Hamlet's question whether to be or not as asking...how he...lets himself be born as the one he is....To exist is to take your existence upon you, to enact it, as if the basis of human existence is theater, even melodrama. To refuse this burden is to condemn yourself to skepticism—to a denial of the existence, hence of the value of the world. (p. 187)

"The play's name," says Cavell, "for the thing that debars Hamlet from existence is revenge—revenge...as the destroyer of individual identity" (p. 188). Here Cavell's Freudian view of the unnatural relationships within the royal family joins with what has already been noted about the genre of revenge tragedy: its pull backward toward an old world. The revenge action is read here as a metaphor for Hamlet's psychological situation. If parents should, properly, be mourned and separated from, then one who must reenact old quarrels indeed lacks advancement. If Cavell had stopped here he would have achieved something like what Leverenz and Rose did, having shown the cause of the tragedy to be in the psychological hold of the past over the present. But the crucial point for my argument is that he goes beyond them to reject the conventional inferences from this central genre condition.

In Cavell's reading, the knowledge necessary to avoid the tragedy of being unable to get beyond—free of—one's parents (i.e., the knowledge needed to resist revenge), is present in the play itself. The process of mourning in which Hamlet is engaged at the beginning and at the end of the play is a process of detaching himself from memory, from an object that has passed, of burying one's dead. G. Wilson Knight noted (1949:19) that Claudius in fact gives Hamlet good advice when he tells him to forget his father's death. For Cavell, the interruption of Hamlet's mourning, itself understood as the necessary separating from both father and mother, is the cause of the tragedy. But it is not only the audience who can learn this moral: Hamlet's presentation of the play within the play is proof, for Cavell, that Hamlet himself has dreamed, or divined, the need to escape his mother's power as well as that of his father.

In opposition to the conventional inference, then, that tragic heroes are destroyed by fates larger than themselves, outside, and beyond their understanding, Cavell claims great understanding and perception for tragic heroes and heroines. Their tragedy lies in their rejecting what they know. Hamlet in fact has "the power, or the fate, to perceive objectively, truly" (p. 186). The possibility of refusing to reject this knowledge is thus offered as the teaching of Cavell's reading. Like Girard, he too, then, offers us a negative exemplum.

In conclusion, we might note the analogy between the classical notion of Fate, the fate of the gods of the Greek tragedies, and the cultural paradigms of today's cultural criticism. The examination of these essays suggests that even in the midst of a critique of ideology, submission to received functional genre conditions is all too easy. If the multiple deaths at the end of *Hamlet* preclude either Claudius's or Hamlet's emerging as the new man who can dictate the terms of future events, the essays of Leverenz, Rose, and Hawkes suggest that it is not so easy for the critic to take on that role. One need not agree with the conclusions of Girard or of Cavell, however, to recognize that their essays succeed in ways that the first three fail.

The possibility of separating the structural conditions of a genre from the functional conditions so that new inferences can be produced is inherent in the genre system itself and has always provided the possibility for irony, hypocrisy, and parody.[8] Indeed, after Harold Bloom, misreading has taken on a positive coloration, by its association with power, and is no longer considered failure.[9] Given Hamlet's rush to erase from his memory the moral teachings of the "old saws and books," there is perhaps some poetic justice in Rose's erasure of *Ham-*

let. What Girard and Cavell show us, however, is that critics can read the text so as to realize its revolutionary possibilities and, like Horatio, live beyond tragedy.

Categorization and inference

With the essays on autobiography and on Hamlet as examples, we are now in a position to link the critical ability to make use of genre categories to the general argument about the crucial epistemological status of categorization. The examples of the recategorization of autobiography and the reinferences from tragedy demonstrate three aspects of categorization that enable interpretive flexibility: its inherent instability, its decompositionality, and its close relationship to inferential processes.

If, as I have claimed, a categorization is always unstable because it is always a compromise, always only more or less satisfactory, it is, then, always open to a more satisfactory categorization, should one suggest itself. The dynamic of categorization balances the need to understand something new in terms of something already familiar, so that old responses can be helpfully invoked, against the need to recognize and perhaps benefit from the peculiarity or specialness of the new experience. In principle, then, a categorization judgment about anything that isn't exactly identical with its type, that is, a categorization judgment about anything even slightly novel, will be a compromise, will be inaccurate, will be, thus, unstable. Making a categorization judgment, then, is always conditional, the making of the judgment itself an invitation to remake it.

Concurrently, however, with the general cognitive tendency to reduce the number of categories needed to organize a perceptual field, richer categorization provides cognitive flexibility that may justify the extra effort. Occam's razor holds: categories are not multiplied beyond usefulness; however, the ability to produce new ones is often quite useful.

The dynamic is in principle always open. All things being equal, the possibilities of categorizing something as a familiar type or of opening up a new category of which it is the founding member are always equally available. In the event, however, all things are usually not equal. For many purposes, including animal survival, being able to recognize a given token as a example of a type is presumed to be an advantage. Fitting new tokens into old types produces efficient storage of information and thus reduces the reaction time needed to deal with a new phenomenon. How long would a mouse live if it could not recognize all kinds of cats as the same kind of enemy?

High culture, on the other hand, has the luxury of play. Voluntary activities of animals farther along the evolutionary scale are often arranged so that the reductiveness in categorizing new tokens as known types can be a dispensed with in favor of the stimulation of fine distinctions. What changes the dynamic, of course, is the value to the categorizer of the distinctions. A mouse is happy to have escaped the cat, whether it was a Siamese or a Manx that pounced. One of the conditions of the literary system, however, is that experienced readers consider themselves rewarded when their reading and genre assignment are slowed down by the difficulty of deciding which of a set of possible categories a text most nearly fits. The literary system puts no value on saving time. Morse Peckham (1978) and Barbara Herrnstein Smith (1978:44) both make this appreciation of cognitive dissonance a defining feature of high art. In literary interpretive situations the inability of a reader ever to make a definitive categorization judgment is the sign of the value of both the text and of the interpretation. As Geoffrey Hartman allows, "The critical spirit does not automatically place itself on the side of reason, enlightenment, or demystification" (1980:40).

The second aspect of categorization that gives it such an important role in interpretation is its decompositionality. Minds apparently have no difficulty understanding the hierarchical composition of units (e.g., a text) such that something which can be named with a single category name can also be understood as having individually nameable parts, and a relationship between the parts can be understood. All this is just to say what Wittgenstein (1958) has taught us, namely that a text can be recognized as like another text in one way and different in others, and that categories do not impose both necessary and sufficient conditions for membership. If the determination of genre were a simple look-up or matching procedure in which a token text was matched to a monolithic type already stored in memory, then no new text could ever be categorized, because only one text would exactly fit the prototype. So if we want to describe the system of literary categorization that apparently obtains among experienced readers, the system, that is, by which they categorize new texts as more or less like familiar ones, the genre concepts in the system must be described as consisting of variously decomposable and variously necessary or dispensable parts. Either a type or a token is most usefully considered not as an unanalyzable whole (e.g., a platonic ideal) but as a set of conditions. Not all conditions need match the type or token to which it is being compared for the categorization to be considered successful.

The third aspect of categorization that makes it so cooperative an accessory to revision is its close connection with linguistic inference. It has not been widely realized that making judgments about genres of texts and drawing inferences are closely connected interpretive operations.[10] Greater specification of the linguistic module will help us explore this aspect of the flexibility of processing further.

In Jackendoff's description, the peripheral levels of the module receive the sounds of speech, integrate them, parse them, and prepare a preferred reading of their meaning (including preliminary categorization selections) for integration further up in the system where information from other modules is available. The central processor, working algebraically, eventually produces what Jackendoff (1987:121–159) calls the *conceptual structure*. The highest level in the language module, conceptual structure is the representation of what we think of as the highest level of verbal organization, including chains of inference and deduction. These chains are produced from representations provided by the lower processing levels, and if this is a fair picture, much of inference is a direct result of the categorization judgments that have already been made at lower levels. But the processes work in two directions. This is how Tverski and Gati describe the interaction of categorization and inference:

> Similarity plays a dual role in theories of knowledge and behavior.…Indeed, similarity is as much a summary of past experience as a guide for future behavior. We expect similar things to behave in the same way, but we also view new things as similar because they behave in the same way. Hence, similarities are constantly updated by experience to reflect our ever-changing picture of the world. (1978:98)

Categorizations, then, although basic, are also tied to high-level understanding because implicit in a categorization judgment are all the premises that can be logically deduced and inferred from it. Furthermore, the cognitive function of a category label such as a genre designation comes from the mind's ability to use it to produce inferences. To identify a text as a token of a type, then, is nothing less than to make available all the inferences that can be derived from the given set of assumptions, that is, all the well-formedness and the preference conditions that describe the genre.[11] The conditions of the new genres suggested by the interpreters of autobiography show how far what may seem like a simple categorization can take one. There is, in principle, no end to the chain of possible inferences and deductions that can emerge from the logical properties of the conditions of a category.

To be able to categorize, therefore, is to be able to predicate, to claim a set of qualities or conditions for something. To predicate a series of categorizations about *B*, then, is to be able to know, think, or say pretty much whatever one wants to about *B*: American autobiography is narrative history, is a story about the author's life, proposes a model life, etc. Conversely, any condition of *B* will suggest its membership in some category: Girard argues that a play which signals the similarity of revenger and victim is an antitragedy. Since type/token (or type/type) categorization depends on the compositionality of the conceptual units in our understanding (or to be more precise, the decompositionality of concepts), then to be able to predicate is also to be able to exclude by negation: a play for which one can imagine a better ending is not a tragedy. Also, two texts can be compared by inclusion and exclusion: *B* and *C* are both like *A* in *these* ways but not in *those* ways. Cox says of Walt Whitman's *Song of Myself*: "If autobiography is narrative and history, then it is not poem and prophecy" (p. 159). It is this decompositionality that allows Girard to argue that, if *Hamlet* has antagonists which resemble its protagonists, it is an antitragedy, while its standard revenge motifs make it a revenge tragedy as well.

Since categorization also allows types to be related to types, hierarchies can be inferred: Type A is included in Type B. This is most clearly seen in generic categorization sentences such as

> "Western autobiography is a kind of American autobiography."

Jackendoff shows that it also governs the logical relationship between verbs and modified verbs as in this pair of sentences (invented for the sake of example):

> "Franklin writes about his inventions."

which includes

> "Franklin writes elegantly and in a belle lettristic tradition about his inventions."

Writing elegantly is included in writing. The model can be extended to show relationships between other parts of speech as well. Knowledge that can be inferred from a categorization is also used by Krupat in his argument. When he challenges the usual necessary condition of an autobiography (that it be written by its subject), he is forced by the categorical logic of his statement to invent a higher category of autobiography which includes writing, speaking, or having someone write for you.

Krupat needed this logical move because he wanted to include in his canon life stories that are not written by their subjects. His position would be strengthened if he could actually exclude from the category of American autobiographers a group of Easterners who not only wrote their own books, but wrote them elegantly. But since, as we have seen above, writing elegantly cannot be excluded from writing, he tries another tack, namely, to activate the category that was implicit but unnamed in Cox's article—European revolutionary autobiography. He proposed some conditions for this category beyond the two simple ones that Cox had depended on, and argued that there are three necessary conditions found in European autobiography after the eighteenth-century revolutions: *"egocentric individualism, historicism,* and *writing"* (p. 307). Cox's canonical American autobiographies meet all three of those conditions and are, therefore, excludable as "old-world oriented and self-consciously literary" (p. 308). Krupat thus implies that Easterners shouldn't be categorized as American; their cultivation of old world "belles lettres" sets them in self-conscious opposition to the native American tradition he claims is Indian and oral. For Krupat, it is the category of European revolutionary autobiography that includes the Eastern American autobiographies.

The conclusion must be that arguments against old categorizations and proposals of variant genre categorization are far from being quibbles but are, in fact, potentially vastly productive. A categorization judgment actually generates new conceptual structures (equivalences, hierarchies), which can themselves, recursively, be the basis of further inference. Looked at from the other end of the telescope, a genre categorization is no less than a way of organizing a competent reader's ability to pattern inferences about a text and its relations to other discourse. Precisely because genre categories are, in the mind of an experienced reader, so flexible, they are a fertile source of innovation. Every repatterning of conditions, while it will include previously excluded texts, is also likely to exclude some that had previously been included. Cox excluded Rousseau and Whitman; Krupat excluded Franklin and Adams along with Rousseau.

These exclusions, the supplementary, rejected terms, may sometimes disappear from the canon, but they may also hang around, putting pressure on the dynamic of categorization for the periodic opening up of new categories when the implications of the old have been satisfactorily, if not exhaustively, explored. This projection into the future defends categorization against the claim that it is no more than an academic exercise which simply re-sorts what already exists. The project of drawing new inferences from a genre, of misreading it, as it were, by refusing to accede to what E. D. Hirsch called a text's "intrinsic genre," is logically productive as well, as the Shakespeare readings have shown.

It is perhaps because the category name *tragedy* has such a long and dignified history in literary criticism that neither Girard nor Cavell suggests renaming. They both, however, have identified new categories. Girard, having identified a new pattern—the equalization of villainy—in revenge tragedies, finds that *The Merchant of Venice* also fits. We might call his new category 'plays which teach the foolishness of revenge.' Cavell also finds a Shakespearean comedy, *The Winter's Tale*, to be profitably categorized as a tragedy of disowning knowledge, one however in which the redemption is not only implied, but actually staged as Acts IV and V of the play. One of his new categories, then, is something like 'Shakespearean dramatic explorations of skepticism.'

If, as I argue, literary categorizations enact chains of inference, then the need to work through the implications of a new categorization proposal is part of an answer to the question of why Cox's categorization could initially be satisfying (i.e., well-received), then not satisfying, and its replacement ten years later also satisfying. Although a challenge to an interpretive proposal such as Cox's may immediately be mounted by interpreters in a competitive literary community, such a challenge, if based on a competing set of conditions of significance, will not, itself, automatically be taken as definitive. I suggest that what it means for scholars to entertain a proposal for a new category such as Cox's, over an extended period of time, is like what Thomas Kuhn (1970) called doing "normal science." Those scholars agree, in effect, to explore the implications of the new categorization and the possibilities for further ramification, that is, for subcategorization.

For example, Cox's student, G. Thomas Couser, published a book called *American Autobiography: The Prophetic Mode* describing a subset of American autobiographers who "like Old Testament prophets interpret the history of [their] community in the light of God's will" (1979:3). All category names may eventually be replaced, not because they are wrong, since that isn't a functional standard, but because their usefulness is exhausted. The same process can be seen in all kinds of literary naming, whether the names are of periods, methods of study, or styles.

The account of recategorization is thus enriched, because it now describes not only how new categories are responses to changed social awareness, but also how readers decompose complex texts, weigh separately the conditions that make up the set, make gradient distinctions among conditions, and distinguish between conditions necessary to the success of the categorization and those which are typical of, but not necessary to, such a categorization. It acknowledges and describes how the ties between genre and inference are multiplied arithmetically by the number of conditions in any genre rule, and thus displays how virtually infinite chains of interpretive inference can be produced. The genre system, including the possibility of renaming, conceived of in this way, is not a handy oversimplification, but rather a reflection of the complexity of the readers' construal of the world and the ease with which that understanding can learn and change.

If, then, to change a categorization is to open all those possibilities anew, if recategorizations entail new inferences about texts, and new inferences can also be produced from old categorizations; if the drawing of inferences about textual meaning overlaps significantly with the judgment about the genre of a text, it is, thus, not surprising that revisionary inference often presents itself in critical discourse as a suggestion for a new genre category, or as an argument about the viability of one or another genre in a given cultural context. What has often been described over the past one hundred years of literary history as the "birth" or "death" of a literary category, is more productively seen as an expression of the human ability to draw new inferences and then recategorize in the presence of new conditions of significance.

The proposals for new generic categories which were the source texts in Chapter 2, emerged within the turbulent political climate of America in the 1960s and 1970s. They are claims for change made, in John Searle's phrase, "in the direction of words to world" (1976:3). Even as they acknowledge the power of their own political contexts as provocation for their recategorizations, the implied goal of the literary historians in all these studies of autobiography is to try to understand "distant times"; their job, as they see it, is to be open to the old text in such a way that their critical assertions reflect the state of that world. The critics, thus, suggest revisions in literary historical descriptions, claiming that the new categorizations and attendant inferences are truer accounts of the way the world actually was, and that the new category names and the implications they propose are better descriptions of the generic intentions of the authors of the texts involved than were available under the old category names.

The world is further acknowledged as having influence on the words of literary history in that the world of the interpreter has provided the trigger for the suggested recategorization and new inferences. Most of the critics claim that the conditions of significance in their own contexts have encouraged sympathetic identification with authors of old texts. This connection between social climate and new literary history is advanced as a way of explaining why critical perceptions, specifically new categorization judgments, if they have always been true, had not always been apparent to critics.

There is, however, also influence in the direction of words to world: revisionary literary history itself produces changes in the literary systems of the interpreters. Since changing genre terms is not simply a reassignment of a text from one category to another, but is rather the opening up of a new chain of inference, it is likely that what may be presented as modest repair to the historical record will in fact change the interpretive rules sooner or later. Once old rules are replaced and new categorization distinctions introduced, all texts may then be read according to the newly installed categories or rules, and in light of the newly possible chains of inference. The changes that claimed to be backward-looking thus become part of the system determining future interpretation.

Word-to-world influence seems to be possible, then, the difficulties of productive textuality notwithstanding, through the assertions about the world made by the functional conditions of literary genres. The production of assertions, however, is not generally held to be the raison d'être of literary texts. They have wider interests, as does literary criticism. In the next chapter I turn from essays which innovate primarily through language and conceptual structure, to examine the development of feminist criticism as an example of a mode of literary analysis that privileges the value of knowledge available through modules other than the conceptual/linguistic.

In its beginnings, for all its shock value and in spite of its raised consciousness, feminist criticism was, from a cognitive point of view, more of the same. Eventually, there emerged a style of criticism that earns the description "radically new" because its force indeed seems to be driven by the operation of a different module. Feminist criticism first presented a serious challenge to interpretive theory as a whole in its attempts to explore and develop ways of knowing that are analogical rather than logical. If Jackendoff is right in his claim that "every phenomenological distinction is caused by, or supported by, or projected from a corresponding computational distinction" (1987:24) then it might be claimed that this kind of thinking has its roots, if not its expression in the visual rather than the linguistic module. Having argued for the possibilities of the visual module as a source of literary knowledge, I will then admit that it would be impossible not to use both kinds of thinking, though one or another may seem to predominate in a given style of reading.

4 Women readers and women's rules

'Tis paltry to be Caesar.
—Cleopatra, in
Antony and Cleopatra

To watch the development of feminist criticism over the last fifteen years has been to watch the growing recognition that women can set their own priorities for the strategies of reading they feel most congenial, just as they were choosing their own ways in other areas of social life. At the beginning, some of the new rules were simply pragmatic rules moved into the literary system. Judith Fetterley's *The Resisting Reader: A Feminist Approach to American Fiction* (1978), in many ways representative of the founding phase of feminist criticism, documents the transfer of a pragmatic rule already functioning in the social context of the reader to that reader's literary system. Unwilling to trust men's analyses of character or situations in her culture, Fetterley decides to distrust them as authors and narrators as well. This immediately produces a conflict with an established literary rule, namely the reliable narrator rule. It also produces longer-range consequences: if male narrators can't be trusted, there isn't much reason to read books written by men. This change rather quickly has the effect (though not in Fetterley's book) of raising a demand for a revision of the canon.

The second text considered here, a 1985 essay by Sandra Gilbert,[1] represents a later stage of feminist criticism. It takes the step virtually entailed by Fetterley's distrust of male authors, reading texts only by women. Gilbert joins to her study of George Eliot's *Silas Marner* an analysis of a noncanonical novel by Edith Wharton and a fairy tale.

In one way, Gilbert rejects Fetterley's lesson: she does not mistrust some of the male writers who have been significant to her intellectual past, namely Freud, Lévi-Strauss, and Lacan. But in another way Gilbert goes further than Fetterley, and that is in the shift toward a style of argument that can be identified with the search of feminist critics for an appropriate language for the expression of their revisionary readings.[2] A central feature of that style is a preference for arguments based on analogy and transformation rather than on assertion and inference. In her article, conditions of significance in the context of interpretation deriving from psychoanalytic and poststructuralist theories revalue the process of making transformations or analogies so that it is more highly valued than the processes of producing inferences and deductions as a method of thinking and of talking about literary texts. The analogical style has, at least since the romantics, been considered appropriate for poetry but not for academic criticism. The revaluation of argument style leads Gilbert, as we will see, to rewrite rules of genre appropriateness as well.

Together the essays of Fetterley and of Gilbert show how literary systems respond to innovation in nonliterary systems and in other literary systems, and how a change in a single heavily weighted rule can eventually produce a style of criticism so different from the earlier discourse that it splits the reading community: many male readers will find themselves so strongly resistant that they will not read women's literature or criticism at all.

Fetterley's reading and Fetterley's rule

Fetterley argues that reading American literature is a self-defeating activity for an American woman. Angry at Hemingway's *Farewell to Arms*, for example, it seems to be her kinesthetic sense that rejects having to cooperate with the narrator by imagining herself bleeding to death after a botched Caesarean section stillbirth. Catherine's death, she argues, is logically necessary to Hemingway's plot so that Frederic Henry can "survive, free of the intolerable burdens of marriage, family, and fatherhood, yet with his vision of himself as the heroic victim of cosmic antagonism intact." (p. xvi)

In her discussion of Hemingway's construction of his romantic heroine, Catherine Barkley, Fetterley notes that not only must she die in childbirth, but that she must, as well, apologize frequently for "making trouble" both to her lover and to the doctor. She is the heroine only because her death preserves Frederic's tragic heroism. Her continuing life was unimaginable to Hemingway (p. 66). Fetterley knows, of course, that she isn't the first reader to have noticed the inconsistencies in Hemingway's characterization of Catherine. She claims, however, that male readers of the book, in their attempts to harmonize various aspects of the characterization, have not faced the real problem: "their need to explain [the characterization of Catherine] suggests that to accept and confront her contradictions might be to discover something rather unpleasant in Hemingway's handling of women" (p. 65). They don't seek this confrontation because it might force them to recalculate Hemingway's brilliance in the galaxy of modern American writers.

The point of Fetterley's book, however, is that women readers have only to gain from such a confrontation. Even though they can read as if they were men (they have been doing so for all the years they have been students of literature in patriarchal institutions) and can agree to share Hemingway's hostility to women and to shed tears for the men in the book, finally, to agree that "the only good woman is a dead one" (p. 71), is to pay too high a price for entertainment.

What Fetterley demonstrates is that women readers can also refuse to agree to an interpretive situation in which their intellectual life as readers of literature is at odds with the rest of their lives. The resisting readings Fetterley presents emerged from her reactions and the reactions of her women students to a group of canonical texts. Fetterley claims that her resisting readings are, for women, the preferred readings: natural and reasonable. They would have been expressed in university seminars and in print if they hadn't been repressed by women's need to conform to standards set by men but labeled "objective" and "universal." It is, thus, a major claim of her book that women readers have traditionally had to learn a preference rule by which they identified with male authors, narrators, or heroes.[3] The rule outweighed their own instinctive understandings in favor of the male readings which were valued within the academy and the institutions of literary criticism.

Fetterley herself has been educated in the establishment reading she resents and thus has no trouble understanding why male readers see Catherine as a burden to Frederic: as a representative of domesticity and smothering possessiveness. Yet her book also demonstrates that her competence is flexible. It seems that readers can learn to resist and reread. The central focus of Fetterley's resistance is a gradient necessary condition of narrative called *the reliable narrator rule.* As Wayne Booth has taught, the narrator is the reader's main link with the world of the novel. In Schauber and Spolsky (1986), we wrote the rule as follows, the wording largely having been taken from Booth (1961):

> GNC: Prefer to assume that a narrator will
> a. provide reliable access to relevant information,
> b. define for readers the ordering of values on which their judgments should depend,
> c. relate those values to established norms, and
> d. generalize the significance of the work as a whole.

Fetterley argues that for a woman reading *A Farewell to Arms* to prefer to assume what the preference rule asks her to, that is, to trust the narrator in these four specific ways, is to allow herself to be drawn into powerlessness, to submit to the "enactment of the drama of men's power over women" (p. xiii). But if she consciously distrusts the narrator, assumes his unreliability, and then identifies and corrects for the bias he introduces, her reading provides her with both coherence and satisfaction.

A reader infers the reliability of a narrator from the consistency of his or her attitudes, actions, and words. Fetterley, however, infers the untrustworthiness of Frederic's self-portrayal as idealized honesty and romantic goodness from a rather complicated series of inferences: the head nurse at the hospital, for example, describes Frederic as "domineering and rude." Instead of disapproving of her for disliking him, as Frederic himself (and presumably Hemingway), does, Fetterley agrees with the nurse's judgment: the nurse "sees herself as morally superior to Frederic and is critical of him, seeing in him a selfish egotist, as insensitive to the concerns of others as he is to the larger issue of the war" (p. 54). Fetterley presents what she infers to be Frederic's attitude from his invention of a reason (in her view, a conventional, sexist reason) for the nurse's hostility: "Frederic disarms [the nurse's] criticism by implying that the basis of her hostility toward him is his sexual relationship with Catherine....He insinuates that her hostility results from rejection while his is the result of contempt" (p. 54).

From this and other examples of his relationships with women other than Catherine, Fetterley reads Frederic's character not as a hero but as a coward evading his own motives and aims, which are, "by eliminating the agent that threatens to force adulthood upon [him,...to remain] forever a boy in an asexual world without women" (p. 47). By setting herself at odds from the beginning with a narrator whom Hemingway presumably intends to be reliable, Fetterley immediately frees herself to judge for herself what he reports. Her goal (not the narrator's) is to show that Catherine's death is inevitable—caused, in fact, by Frederic Henry's and ultimately Hemingway's attitudes toward women.

Fetterley acknowledges that Hemingway goes to some effort to separate Frederic's attitudes toward Catherine from other men's attitudes toward women. His friend, Rinaldi, for example, discusses all women in only coarse sexual terms, and by contrast Hemingway seems to be showing Henry to be more moral than other men. Indeed, Fetterley notes that Frederic Henry's hostility to or fear of women is never directly shown in his relationship with Catherine, yet it can be inferred from his own reports of his behavior towards the nurse, towards the asexual priest, from Catherine's worries that she is boring him, that she is not pleasing him, and from her guilt about her sexuality expressed in her feelings that she is only "good" when she is pleasing him. Frederic's contempt of women, she argues, is not only reprehensible, *eo ipso*, but actually requires the negation, even the death of the heroine, while simultaneously idealizing her in a story of self-glorifying romantic love.

Collusion with the reliable narrator rule, and with its collateral rules about how to reinterpret the tale of a narrator the author has deliberately made unreliable,[4] had not yet been widely questioned in the community of male readers.[5] However, this challenge, that is, the recognition that one needn't be bullied into trusting a narrator who exhibits sexist values, was an important founding and enabling move of feminist criticism. A new rule in direct opposition to Booth's was invoked. Instead of preferring to trust a narrator until presented with sufficient evidence of his or her untrustworthiness, Fetterley's rule would say:

GNC 1: Don't ever trust a male narrator; resist his attempts to "define the ordering of values on which judgment depends," etc.

Booth's rule was found inadequate because the conditions of discourse on which it was based had changed. Fetterley had first changed her rule about trusting men, and then her literary rule. This change in a gradient necessary condition eventually gathered weight within a section of the reading public sufficiently large enough to become visible as a new critical community. It thus split the community, which had previously seemed unitary, into two groups of readers on the basis of which of these two rules they followed.

In Fetterley's argument, this one change does not entail a change in other rules about narrators. In fact, Fetterley follows the rules Booth lays out for coping with unreliable narrators. If, as she says, Frederic Henry's hostility to women is deep in spite of his superficial romantic attachment to Catherine, and if, thus, he cannot be a reliable narrator, then Fetterley must correct for his bias. We can now watch her either substituting her own metaphorical transformations for those the narrator suggests (which she attributes to Hemingway, but which she cannot accept) or building additional transformations onto the suggested ones so as to arrive at her own interpretation of the romantic pair. Note that she can read the "male" inferences as she has been taught to. She saw her job as a feminist critic, however, as demonstrating that the rules of literary competence can be challenged and changed, as the rules of pragmatic discourse had been.

As an example of her repatterning of references already provided by Hemingway, we may look at what she makes of Catherine's teasing remark to Frederic that he is "Othello with his occupation gone" (p. 257). Hemingway, she presumes, may be suggesting the following two meanings: Frederic is abandoning the army because he is too gentle to be a soldier, and/or he is a passionate lover, but one who is too gentle to strangle the woman he loves. Fetterley notices another match, however, besides these two. She matches the association of Othello and strangulation with Catherine's dead baby, of whom the nurse reports: "They couldn't start him breathing. The cord was caught around his neck or something." Frederic thinks to himself: "Poor little kid. I wish the hell I'd been choked like that. No I didn't. Still there would not be all this dying to go through..." (p. 327).

Fetterley repatterns, joining the two references to strangulation. She says that "Frederic sees himself in the dead fetus which emerges from Catherine's womb" (p. 53). She then matches this identification of the father with the dead infant rather than with other instances of the idealized sensitivity that has been attributed to Frederic, that is, not with noble feelings of parental sacrifice (the match that she presumes Hemingway intended his readers to make), but with the feelings of resentment against the threatening ("strangling") power of women she has seen Frederic demonstrate elsewhere in the book. From these two substitute patterns Fetterley infers that Catherine's death, "however much it may be shaped as biological accident, is in fact the fulfillment of his own unconscious wish, his need to kill her lest she kill him" (p. 53).

Even when a resisting reader accepts metaphorical transformations others have made, he or she may demonstrate resistance by choosing a different stopping point for the transformation. Fetterley reports that an earlier reader of Hemingway, Robert Lewis (1970), sees Catherine's very adaptability, her willingness to put up with Frederic Henry's passivity, as the source of his hostility toward her. Catherine indeed, it is widely agreed, caters to Frederic's juvenile desire to avoid responsibility and commitment. By indulging him, according to Lewis, she fails him.

Fetterley accepts Lewis's reading as far as it goes, but distrusting him for blaming Catherine, she continues to transform. She claims that Frederic needs to feel betrayed because betrayal justifies his self-pity and supports his mammoth ego (a similarity to Othello, she notes) while he evades responsibility, e.g., by deserting his comrades-in-arms. Thus "the killings the novel details are those of Italians by Italians, and Frederic makes a break for the river because he is about to be shot by his own army" (p. 61). Furthermore, Catherine's body betrays her, and she betrays Frederic, promising "no complications" but then entangling him emotionally and abandoning him by dying. "Catherine cuts off his life as effectively as she strangles her own son inside of her" (p. 62). These betrayals are Frederic's justification for his act of betrayal—his desertion from the army.

What Fetterley has done by repatterning some of the imagery Hemingway provides and by extending the chain of transformations another critic began is to make the transformation meet her own conditions of satisfaction and coherence. She shows, as she had intended, that Hemingway has set it up so that "no matter what Catherine does she is bad for Frederic" (p. 62). Whether she indulges him or dies, she betrays him. Either way she earns Henry/Hemingway's hostility, so that ultimately dying is just about sufficient punishment for her. Fetterley concludes that Hemingway's heroine is not so much a consistent character as "a scapegoat whose ritual death allows the hero to survive" (p. 67).

As was the case with the readings of Cox and Krupat, changes in the cultural context of the reader are among the enabling conditions of the changes in patterns of reading and interpretation that Fetterley's book demonstrates. Changes in the conditions of significance had by 1978 allowed the recognition and the expression of reader's reactions that, according to Fetterley, had existed unconsciously all along but had never before been valued in the academy or expressed in print. Her book's title, in fact, alludes to the two related cultural phenomena that had changed the intellectual stage on which literary criticism was enacted, namely, the spread among Anglo-American critics of reader-response criticism, which had already provided the focus on the implied reader and the ideal reader, and the growth of the feminist movement.

The effect of either, and certainly of the two together in literary criticism, was a revaluation of the weight of the identity and concerns of the reader vis-à-vis the identity and intentions of the author such that the reader no longer assumed that a conflict between the two had to be resolved in favor of authorial intention. We have seen that Fetterley scrupulously followed the heavily weighted preference rule that encouraged the reader to recover, insofar as possible, the author's understanding of the characters he created and the meaning of the plot patterns in which they participate. She interprets exactly as her teachers did, speculating about the characters' unstated or unconscious intentions as well as about conscious ones as if they were not fictional constructs. The conflict between rules arises only over the narrator.

It is this conflict between rules, then, that produces a resisting reading. Fetterley's reading is not a substitution of her feminist reading for her masculine one; it is, rather, the tension between the two. The traditional masculine reading is present in her recognition of her claims to have recognized authorial intentions, conventional references, and many of the inferences and transformations; the feminist is present in the few significant revisions she does make. Most early feminist criticism testifies, thus, to the bilingualism of the critic who is speaking according to the rules of two languages. She has replaced some rules but not all. Rules learned within a patriarchal interpretive community are present, more or less explicitly, in early feminist criticism, and their presence very soon becomes an issue in feminist metacriticism. (See for example Showalter 1979 and Kaplan 1985.)

Until relativity in reading was reweighted by the conditions of significance in the critical world, Fetterley's readings were labeled subjective, unscholarly, and valueless in the academic marketplace. Indeed, until the reweighting, the experience of women had shown that for the majority of women themselves, such readings hadn't even emerged into consciousness, and when they encountered them in feminist critics they found them uncongenial.

If we ask why Fetterley, her women colleagues, and her students in the 1960s and early 1970s were reading the offensive American texts at all, the answer would be that the books were the canon. Resisting reading doesn't make sense in relationship to any but canonical works. As a reading strategy for understanding the canon, it provided women an alternative to cooperative or trusting reading (as patriarchal reading might be called) of books written by men.

Although the success of the early feminist criticism shows clearly that resisting reading can provide both coherent and satisfying interpretations, it soon became clear that outrage alone cannot long provide satisfaction. The cost to women of reading the American canon, if this is the only coherence obtainable, soon becomes too high. The resisting reader has an alternative however, and that is to stop reading Hemingway. Although Fetterley herself does not mention it, implicit in her resistance is the revision of the canon. The project has been taken up by other feminist critics, and by Fetterley herself in later work (e.g., 1984). In the context of this activity, the feminist critic of the 1980s assumed she had to turn to reading texts by women exclusively. (See for example Robinson 1983 and Greene and Kahn 1985.)

The passing years, and the growth of theoretical studies in general and feminist studies in particular, have vindicated early feminist readings like Fetterley's in some ways and revealed their limits as well. In the 1990s Fetterley's attack on Hemingway may seem to be aimed at too obvious a target. But it may also be that we now see Hemingway as an "easy target" because of the success of the early feminists. Elaine Showalter (1981) discusses the differences between the earlier feminist criticism and later versions. She notes, for example, that "all feminist criticism is in some sense revisionist, questioning the adequacy of accepted conceptual structures....But in practice, the revisionary feminist critique is...built upon existing models" (p. 183).

Jonathan Culler (1983), however, points out that early feminist criticism (like Fetterley's) has demonstrated the possibility of a literary equivalent of linguistic code-switching: if women had for so many years been reading as men and now could learn new rules of reading, so presumably men can also read as women, or Chicanas as Native Americans for that matter. Culler optimistically believed all readers could benefit from being multilingual readers. But neither Fetterley nor subsequent feminist scholars have been willing to concede this point. The appropriate analogy to reading by someone else's rules may not be the speaker with a repertoire of stylistic registers, but rather the left-handed child who has been forced to learn right-handed penmanship.

The distinction between "natural" reactions, interpretations, and readings, and "culturally constructed paradigms" is a crucial one, assumed in feminist criticism and theory (Greene and Kahn 1985:1) but debated as problematic in other epistemological discussion (e.g., Lévi-Strauss/Derrida and Chomsky/Piaget). Fetterley claimed that her resistance was natural. She was doing nothing more than exposing "a different reality and a different vision...a different subjectivity" (p. xi). Her complaint was that male writers and readers had successfully been passing off as universal what was in fact partial or lopsided, and the balance needed to be righted by bringing to consciousness the interpretations that women would naturally arrive at had they not been miseducated—had their own powers of understanding themselves not been distorted by the patriarchal culture.[6]

The claim that it is natural for women to read "as women," that different biological, social, or cultural groups have naturally different ways of reading, is the ideological condition of significance on which Fetterley's rule is constructed. The claim of naturalness validates the alignment of pragmatic and literary systems so that a rule can be transferred from one to the other, as Fetterley's rule was. The theories Fetterley was resisting had denied this, and will be seen again to deny it, claiming that scholarship and interpretation require a separation between an idiosyncratic reaction and an educated response.

However, the opposite claim for the relevance, even the centrality of the readers' life experiences remains a heavily weighted condition of significance in feminist criticism.[7] Fetterley also claimed that the novel patterns of interpretation that women following their natural inclinations could produce would have the power to induce further change, not only in literature but in culture:

> Consciousness is power. To create a new understanding of our literature is to make possible a new effect of that literature on us. And to make possible a new effect is in turn to provide the conditions for changing the culture that the literature reflects. To expose and question that complex of ideas and mythologies about women and men which exist in our society and are confirmed in our literature is to make the system of power embodied in the literature open not only to discussion but even to change. (pp. xix–xx)

Fetterley's single rule change had, as we have seen, left in place many of the old rules of New Critical reading which were, in the 1970s, being challenged from many directions, making Fetterley's reading soon seem naive. Fetterley's rule by itself, without additional changes in the interpretive rules, seemed to feminist critics insufficiently strong medicine for the sick patient, and to others, pointlessly angry as well as naive in its faith that a change in consciousness could change the world. If Fetterley is, then, naively bilingual, one might have predicted that an evolving feminist discourse would eventually overcome the dependence on the interpretive rules of a predominantly male literary community. I now turn to the work of a feminist critic who, seven years later, demonstrated again the value of remaining bilingual.

Gilbert's reading without Fetterley's rule

By 1985 the optimism Fetterley had expressed about the possibility of change had waned somewhat as the complexity of feminist issues had begun to emerge. The revelation of the difficulty of the questions of how exactly women's writing and reading might be distinguished from men's writing and reading was due in large part to the creation of an alternative canon—an exemplary body of women's writing.

Gilbert's essay, "Life's Empty Pack: Notes Toward A Literary Daughteronomy" (1985) is an investigation of the literary heritage that influential women writers have provided for their descendants, their literary daughters. She understands herself forced to report (as she did with Susan Gubar in *The Madwoman in the Attic,* 1979) that changing the canon is not enough; the enemy is within. George Eliot and Edith Wharton, according to Gilbert, preach the same message as Hemingway and Norman Mailer: submission and resignation to the will of the father. In the plots of *Silas Marner, Summer*—"a sexy story of an illicit love affair" (p. 366)—and a fairy tale patterned with a Freudian theory of incest and Lévi-Strauss's theory of the exchange value of daughters, Gilbert recognizes "father-daughter incest as a culturally constructed paradigm" (p. 372).

She describes her own essay as both a creation of a myth of female psychosexual development and a reading of texts written by women. She discloses "a dark, indeed problematic, pattern" (p. 356) that denies that consciousness is power, at least not in the simple way Fetterley hoped it was. It claims that when a woman writer like George Eliot (a powerful "female precursor"—a literary mother who should be able to teach her daughters truths different from the repressive ones they learned from their patriarchal precursors) achieves her greatest success, she betrays her daughters in spite of herself.

> Her power becomes self-subverting: in the moment of psychic transformation that is the moment of creativity, the literary mother, even more than the literal one, becomes "the stern daughter of the voice of God" who paradoxically proclaims her "allegiance to the law" she herself appears to have violated....Human culture, says the literary mother, is bound by rules which make it possible for a woman to speak but which oblige her to speak of her own powerlessness. (pp. 357, 358)

Gilbert's unstated assumption seems to be that George Eliot, having herself evaded the conventional Victorian pattern of female life and beginning, by the time she was working on *Silas Marner*, to be something of a critical and financial success, would never, had she been able to avoid it, have preached acceptance of "life's empty pack." (The metaphor from Emily Dickinson suggests both the burden of a pack and the lack of reward for carrying it that comes from its being empty.) Such moralizing, then, must somehow be inevitable, at least culturally if not biologically, and Gilbert sets herself the job of demonstrating that inevitability. If Fetterley's book, then, was important because of its position as a founding moment of feminist criticism, Gilbert's is similarly important because it makes explicit another crux in the feminist exploration of women's writing. Gilbert recognizes the next challenge:

> [*Silas Marner*] broods on events that are actually or symbolically situated on the margins or boundaries of society, where culture must enter into a dialectical struggle with nature, in order to show how the young female human animal is converted into the human daughter, wife, and mother. (p. 359)

My leap directly from Fetterley's book to Gilbert's essay, without a look at the wealth of feminist writing in between, highlights a surprising situation: Gilbert herself does not resist a cooperative, patriarchal reading of the stories about women told by Freud, Lévi-Strauss, and Lacan. Her speculation, she tells us early on, "rests on syntheses of Freud and Lévi-Strauss that psychoanalytic thinkers like Lacan and Juliet Mitchell have lately produced" (p. 358).[8] By adding the name of Mitchell, a feminist psychoanalyst, to the catalogue of her male sources, Gilbert indicates that she is not accepting Freud naively, as it were, but in full awareness of the feminist issues involved.[9]

From her own, Lacan's, and Mitchell's syntheses of these texts, Gilbert brings to the study of the texts a set of categorizations that match the mother to nature and to childish neediness which (in the myth at least) is always satisfied. Father, then, is equivalent to law, culture, social organization, maturity, responsibility, and of course power. Gilbert's way of interpreting is to seek further matches between aspects of Eliot's text that can be patterned with these opposing poles.

The irony this produces is painful: setting out to investigate various aspects of the "coercive cultural construction" of patriarchy (p. 381), Gilbert is herself coerced by her own interpretive procedures to arrive at the conclusion she claims to regret, and which her own life as a successful professional disproves. Gilbert, as we will see, clearly aligns herself through the rhetoric of her essay with a post-empirical epistemology. The story of Silas Marner "broods" on its themes, and so does she. She eschews the kind of logical argument Cox favored in which categories are kept as distinct as possible, evidence is presented, and conclusions inferred. In order to describe what she calls Silas's "transformations of role and rank" (p. 360), that is, from male to mother, from social outsider to insider, her procedure is to construct a series of more or less developed transformations by means of which she is able to fill in what seem to her to be textual gaps, that is, unstated assumptions on which the narrative depends, with aspects of other mythological, theological, anthropological, and psychological texts important in her intellectual tradition. Her own brooding, then, hatches a series of transformations that achieve the goal of producing the necessary reversals.

As will be abundantly clear, the series of transformations is not an argument in an Aristotelian way. It is, rather, a list of partial matches that Gilbert perceives between aspects of Eliot's novel and other highly valued texts. All of these matches are in some way promising: they present intriguing similarities and enough differences to encourage the imaginative mind to bring them closer together by further analogizing. The matches, of course, are only partial: more or less important dissimilarities remain to challenge their reader (i.e., Gilbert) to substitute terms, images, or concepts until the patterns that can be constructed from the matches are satisfying and coherent.

As it turns out, Gilbert repeatedly finds coherence and satisfaction in transformations that reinforce the "dark, indeed problematic pattern" (p. 356) in which "the text itself discovers no viable alternative to filial resignation" (p. 378). Now the mental process of producing transformations is an unbounded one: like free association or, better, Freud's dream work, transformation is a nonhierarchical process of making matches or finding substitutions, which can go on endlessly.[10] The stopping point of any chain of transformations will always be external, imposed upon the process from the outside. It is thus odd, given the separation of the process from the stopping of it, that Gilbert always stops her transformations at the point where they affirm the cultural pattern of patriarchy—at the point where they prove that indeed fathers ultimately succeed in possessing their daughters as child brides in spite of daughterly resistance. Before continuing the exploration of transformations in the abstract, it would perhaps help to have some examples. Let us follow some of Gilbert's transformations.

The start of the chain of transformations here is motivated by an analogy explicitly pointed to by Eliot, namely, the match between Eppie's golden curls and Silas's hoarded gold. The shared features of the color and the shape, and eventually of the value of curls and coins, launch the transformational process. The chain can be mapped, grossly, like this (→ = is analogous to, shares some conditions with, is like):

> gold curls → gold → money → spending money → means of exchange for goods → means of social exchange → participating in reciprocal human relationships

An inference (also consistent with the traditional interpretation) can now be made:

> If gold is a social link, then a person who has gold has social links. Its negative also has relevance: a person who has gold or money but doesn't spend it doesn't have social links.

The tie of kinship and social links and Eppie is a promising beginning for Gilbert's further transformation: her goal is to continue the chain of analogy until Silas is a mother. This is an exemplary pair of units for transformation because the partial match (Silas = Mother) is so bad (a mother is quintessentially a woman), yet can still be true since he raises Eppie. Although neither the biological parent of Eppie nor a female, nor experienced at personal relationships as mothers are said to be, Silas can be transformed into the "mother" slot. Gilbert begins by transforming Silas into the representative of nature, especially as it is opposed to society. She notes, for example, that he is "liminal" with regard to society, living near abandoned quarries on the edge of town; he accepts no religious law and won't even drink a pint of ale at the local tavern. Even his gold, because it is only hoarded, does not represent for him a means of exchange within society. It gives him no power.

Gilbert suggests that his marginality makes it likely that Eliot herself identified with him (as well as with Eppie), and by analogy this identification helps us agree to see Silas as female, at least in the beginning of the book. But Gilbert's goal is more complex: by the end, of course, Silas has to be the father. Gilbert concludes that "his transformations of role and rank, therefore, suggest at least one kind of redemption a fallen literary woman might want to imagine for herself: becoming a father" (p. 360). A further analogy or partial match suggested by Gilbert links Eliot's own marital nonstatus, and thus her marginality in her society, to Silas's status as an outsider. And another: at the time she was writing *Silas Marner*, she was "becoming a "mother" to George Henry Lewes's children" (p. 360) and finding it awkward.

Notice that Gilbert does not argue, in any usual sense of the word argue, that because Silas's money does not bring him economic power he is a woman, or that because George Eliot's living arrangements were unconventional Silas represents mother nature. On logical grounds, such an argument could not be convincing. This essay, however, is not built on inferential logic. Neither is the reader expected to accept one premise before going on to the next as we were in Fetterley's argument. On the contrary, Gilbert's procedure is simply to present a collocation of related, analogical images, details, excerpts, ideas. Thus, we have these additions to the chain of transformation:

> gold → social relationships → relationship to Dollie and Aaron → relationship to society at large → marriage of Aaron and Eppie

Note here that, whereas in the last chain of transformations hoarded gold could not produce social relations, here the golden-haired child leads to the relationship between Dolly and Silas. This is no contradiction in the logic of transformation. Analogy and transformation (as will be argued later) are significantly like (and rather mysteriously dependent on) visual imagination and memory; that being the case, the grammatical concept of the negative, an important logical operator in conceptual structure but not a part of visual competence, has much less weight here. (One cannot look at something and decide not to see it.) This chain, then, produces an inference:

> Human relationships are more important than hoarded gold.

So far the transformations are the traditional ones, which Gilbert adopts from the history of the literary interpretation of the novel. Eventually, however, by the accumulation of their own weight, the chain of traditional transformations, with the innovative meaning Gilbert infers for them, and some new visual analogies give her revisionist claim about patriarchy a kind of inevitability. You are not expected to see yet why Silas's identification with the mother will lead to the imposition of patriarchy—the picture emerges slowly.

Note, however, before we get into her original transformations, that Gilbert does not challenge the central and explicit image of the novel—the substitution of Eppie, the found, golden-haired child, for gold guineas that have been stolen from Silas. Yet she might have resisted. She might have complained at once about the sexism of equating money and a girl child, objected to Lévi-Strauss's equation rather than accepted it, and refused thenceforth to trust and to remain sympathetic with the narrator, rather than waiting for the Freudian confirmation of the objectification of the female. Where would that have led her? Would she have transformed otherwise, or would she have decided not to read Eliot?

Gilbert, however, having accepted this transformation, then finds others. Her feminist principles, that is, her conditions of significance, encourage her to explore further the terms of that familiar transformation of gold to curls. What had been a satisfying interpretation generates its own extension. She enriches the traditional interpretive pattern with her own series of transformations so that her essay as well as her conclusion will explicate her hunch that Eliot had something specific to say about daughters beyond her humanist universalist plea for mutual responsibility in social life. She now proposes an extended chain of transformations starting with gold. The negatives that belong to gold when it is hoarded, get transformed into other negative abstractions (the words are all quotations from Gilbert, p. 360):

> Silas's gold is empty of signification → meaningless → dead-ended → halted → static → regressive → currency that does not flow → nothing goes out into the world and nothing returns → retentiveness → anality

The negativity of this chain is extended by a pun: "Silas's history is thus a history without a story because it is without characters—without, that is, both persons and signifiers" (p. 360). This assertion masquerades as an inference ("thus," "because"), but if we were forced to make the assertion explicit here, it would have to be that a miser, to whom many negative characteristics are attributed, is not a "character." We are not, however, asked to agree with this assertion. The premise is based on the match between negativity and miserliness, and the claim wins consent, insofar as it does, as a suggestive analogy rather than as an inference.

Gilbert makes a further transformation between Silas's emptiness and the gold: "Its terror [the terror of Silas's history] consists not merely in the absence of meaning but in the presence of empty matter: the shining purposeless heaps of coins" (p. 360). Gilbert has now added a metaphor of her own to those she repatterns in the text: the useless empty coins are portrayed as blanks. She now identifies her second term in the transformation that governs the assertion and will bind up the transformations and her essay: she will stop transforming when "this mass of lifeless matter...[is] imprinted with vital signification" (p. 360). It will be Eppie's job to reconnect her father to society, to give him meaning. The image of the minting of coins suggests another to Gilbert, related again by transformation:

> Silas' transformation from fall to fatherhood is symbolized, in a kind of upside-down myth of Midas, by the metamorphosis of his meaningless gold into a living and meaningful child, a child whose Christmas coming marks her as symbolically divine but whose function as divine daughter rather than sacred son is to signify, rather than to replace, the power of her newly created father. (p. 360)

Each additional term in the chain of transformation, brought to it through other transformations and inferences, can also be patterned with others in the text. It is, thus, a potentially productive trigger for other chains of transformation and inference. The Midas connection is not pursued—it is no more than one of many sparks that contributes light because it can be matched with other texts: it involves daughters and fathers and gold, and its source in mythology weights it heavily for Gilbert. But Gilbert weaves gold from straw as the idea of a Christmas parody is followed through in more transformations. Gilbert now elaborates the pattern of potential matches between Silas's story and the Christmas story. One of the transformations she offers makes the pattern even more abstract: "dead matter must be kindled and dead flesh made Word if culture is to survive" (p. 361). More important is the inversion that produces Holy Father and Divine Daughter in the place of Holy Mother and Divine Son linking the story again with the Freudian family drama. The Divine Son, in the Christmas story links his mother to heaven, "but when the divine child is a daughter...she is a treasure, a gift the father is given so that he can give it to others, thereby weaving himself into the texture of society" (p. 361).

Given the weightings assumed in Gilbert's essay, specifically the preference for associative over propositional thought, it is not appropriate to quibble by noting that the child comes to Silas on New Year's Day, not on Christmas. Gilbert hasn't erred. What we have witnessed in this reader's reading was a decision, conscious or not, not to record explicitly an additional transformation she has assumed: New Year's Day, being the height of the twelve-day Christmas season, shares the Christmas symbolism. The reading is emerging by the accretion of transformations, not by argument, so if you are not satisfied with any of them, just read on—there will be many others; no one by itself crucial to the reading.

Transforming the idea of the Christmas gift of Golden Eppie, Gilbert uses the language of treasure and of weaving as a way of including in her patterning Claude Lévi-Strauss's claim that "a daughter is a treasure whose potential passage from man to man insures psychological and social well-being" (p. 361). Families match for Gilbert with Silas's mother and sister, both named Hephzibah (Hebrew for "my delight is in her"), and she then matches the regaining of female kin with "a promised and a redeemed land," which the meaning of the name "magically signifies" (p. 362).

The chain of associative transformations continues; sometimes the shared conditions of the partial match are numerous, sometimes few. Puns or verbal resemblances have the same weight as mythological connections, presumably on the authority of Freud's assertion that puns and slips of the tongue are meaningful. Talk of the promised land of milk and honey reminds Gilbert of an etymology for the word *daughter* that once interested Eliot, connecting the Indo-European root *dhugh* with *milking*. Weddings are discussed (a central issue of course), and the problem of whom Eppie is actually marrying comes up. I hurry quickly over these transformations, some of which Gilbert also gives scant attention to, skipping many, but will stop at just one more pattern. A reference to Eliot's being nicknamed Deutera (second) because she was like a second daughter to the man who so named her is matched by Gilbert with the law of Moses and the prohibition against incest, repeated in the Book of Deuteronomy. God's law patterns with God-free (Godfrey) Cass, Eppie's biological father, the discussion of whom is transformed into a meditation on Eppie's dead mother. Here, in order to match the Freudian story, Gilbert transforms Eppie's abandonment by both father and mother (the father rejects mother and child, and the mother dies, both thus failing to care for the infant) into Eppie's abandoning and burying her mother:

> Haunted by the primal scene in the snow when she was forced to turn away from the body of the mother, the emblem of nature which can give only so much and no more, and seek the hearth of the father, the emblem of culture that must compensate for nature's inadequacies...."'Father,'" says the girl "in a tone of gentle gravity..., 'we shall take the furze bush into the garden'"—for it was against the bush that Molly died. Now, fenced in by the garden of the law, the once "straggling" bush will become a symbol of nature made meaningful, controlled and confined by culture. (pp. 364–365)

It is hard to avoid asking whether, by accepting Juliet Mitchell's view that feminists must accede to Freud's story of the development of sexual identity and by (thereby) rejecting Fetterley's rule, Gilbert is not reenacting Eliot's betrayal of her literary daughters. A tenured professor, her work on this study having been supported by the most prestigious foundations of the establishment, this very essay read repeatedly in front of authoritative audiences, why is Gilbert preaching resignation? How can submission to the patriarchy seem inevitable to her when she, like George Eliot, seems to have turned its power to her own benefit?

Could it be that Gilbert has not learned Fetterley's lesson? That she is trapped by having agreed to set the limits to her transformations according to Lacan's opposition between masculine and feminine access to language in spite of her claim that she is unhappy to find them there? As Schauber and Spolsky (1986) argue, however, the process of producing transformations is independent of the decisions about which transformations will be considered satisfying and coherent. In fact, the stopping points Gilbert accepts for her transformations are hardly the only stopping points; her transformations could well have been different, had she not preselected Lacan's.

It isn't necessary to rewrite Gilbert's reading entirely to illustrate how differently she could have transformed had she sought different matches, that is, had she chosen a different goal or functional stopping point for her reading. A resisting reader might assemble all the same reversals or near-matches that Gilbert finds—those she calls parodies, such as the substitution of the Holy Father and Divine Daughter for the Holy Mother and Divine Son, the exchange of the Midas myth in which the miser father's child turns to gold or the child replaces the father's gold, Eliot becoming a substitute mother to foster children while writing about a father learning to mother—and then pattern all these partial matches so that she could draw an inference about reversibility, about the possibility of inversion. The slippage between mythical or anthropological patterns could be seen to imply exactly the possibility that Gilbert denies, namely, that women can, through their creative powers of transformation and inference, evade the patriarchy: either turn it on its head, or escape its power.

The crux in this interpretation would be Eppie's rejection of her natural father (Godfrey Cass) for her nurturing father Silas (Solace), which could be read as the heroic triumph of free moral choice over biological and/or social necessity. Eppie's planting the furze bush in the garden can be read as her settlement in her promised land of milk and honey, reached after the release from slavery. Harold Fisch (1986) makes a very similar argument to this, noting further that Eppie's choice of Silas evokes the Biblical Ruth's choosing to stay with Naomi. This would indeed have been a good way to argue the power of a woman's choice. According to Fisch, Eppie "challenges a social structure based on class and inherited privilege," signifying nothing less than transcendence and redemption since Ruth's fateful choice makes her the ancestress of the messianic house of David (pp. 348–349).

Gilbert, however, did not resist, but apparently concluded that the price of Fetterley's radical rule change, that is, abandoning the texts of a male canon, is too high. Having proven to herself that not only the literary canon written by men, but also by women, teaches the submission of women, to give up reading books that taught so would mean to give up reading. Giving up Washington Irving, Norman Mailer, even Hemingway is a possibility, but when Eliot, Wharton, Freud, and Lévi-Strauss must be abandoned as well, the cost might indeed seem too high. Intellectual and/or academic survival cannot base itself on the rejection of the whole canon of Western written knowledge. Fetterley's rule, then, is a typicality condition rather than a necessary condition of Gilbert's feminist criticism.

Categorization and transformation: Leaving room for the improbable

Gilbert's innovations are produced in the wake of her weighting of analogical patterning over logical inference. By producing masses of suggestive transformations, she has tapped a source of mental re-representation every bit as powerful as the process of inference. The first advantage of analogical thinking and reading can be seen more clearly through a specification of the similarities and differences between the structure of a categorization judgment and the structure of a transformation. Both depend on the matching of representations in order to identify similarities and differences. Both, as well, interact with inference. Analogical transformations such as Gilbert produces are not dependent on logical inference although, as we will see later, some logical inferences may be dependent on transformations. Because category judgments, like transformations result from (or are evidence of) a process of matching the sets of conditions of two units, we can describe the structure of a transformation as consisting of two units. There may be two references (one already in memory) or a reference and an inference. Both units include the matched condition or conditions.[11]

There is a crucial difference, however, between the match that accomplishes a categorization and the match that is a transformation. In a categorization the number of conditions shared between the new unit and a stored memory is very high. In a transformation, however, there may be very few matching conditions, perhaps only one. The creative power of a transformation is precisely that it posits a connection on the basis of a very partial, indeed minimal match. The match may be conventional and familiar:

> My love is like a red, red rose.
>
> —Robert Burns

Or original:

> The orphanage of possibility has had to be
> expanded to admit the sea mouse.
>
> —Amy Clampitt

But in neither case is the number of shared features (between lovers and roses, orphanages and sea mice) large.

Transformations, like categorizations, are relational, but where the latter identify close relationships, even identities, transformations make partial matches meaningful when complete matches cannot easily or immediately be achieved through reference, or in genres where reference is not valued as highly as the proposal and exploration of original connections. Where transformations produced by original matches are valued, they can produce an infinite number of new representations. Here, improbability is not a barrier to re-representation.

The following distinction thus emerges: the best categorization is the one in which the largest number of conditions in the text can be matched to (are shared with) the condition of a single unit in memory. The best inference is the one produced by the mental logic using the fewest premises, or by the comparison of constructed representations requiring the fewest number of representations. But in literary and some other genres (e.g., some religious/mystical writing) those transformations are valued as the most imaginative when the number of shared conditions is few but when those few produce even more transformations. Thus the best transformation is much more interesting because it is not governed by *probabilities* of meaning, but is richly productive of *possibilities* of meaning. Separating out a category of transformation, then, creates a place in the interpretive system for improbability, for the original, the unforeseen, the uneconomical. The novelty is valued either for itself or because it solves a problem for which a solution was otherwise unavailable.

We may note here another way in which transformations provide the flexibility necessary for reinterpretation, and that is that they are not substitutions. Once made, the twinned units both remain available, in fact are interchangeable in the further interpretations of the text. Neither part of the match is lost. Thus T. S. Eliot, having established in the first lines of "The Lovesong of J. Alfred Prufrock" the linkage of "the evening" to "a patient etherized upon a table," has not replaced "evening" with "sick patient" but has both for use in further patterning. He can thus expect us to see the passivity and the sickness in the social "evening" Prufrock attends. This matching and rematching functions as analogical argument, as it does in Gilbert's reading.

The process of transformation, furthermore, is valued in literary interpretation because it is not limited by the first match that occurs to a reader. Neither is there any sense that there is a strongest or closest match—a match of the highest number of conditions. It is, rather, an open-ended chain of associations. The process itself has no natural stopping point. Transformation will presumably stop when the two parts that began the process are linked in a match that the reader judges to be satisfying and coherent. As Gilbert's essay demonstrates, what counts in any given situation as satisfying and coherent is determined by conditions of significance within the prevailing system of literary interpretation, and in the local context of the interpreter.

Just as the process of drawing inferences creates new propositions and categorizations, innovative transformations allow new inferences as well and are thus indirectly responsible for more innovation. Furthermore, these new inferences are created out of error, mismatches, or compromise, as was the case in categorization. The result, as with categorization, is that the meaning inferred from a transformation is permanently unstable, permanently open to revision and re-representation.

Indeed, according to Robert Langbaum, much romantic and modern poetry aims to be the record of the kind of processing I have been calling transformation and to be specifically sensitive to the split between the transformation and the inference from it. A poet such as Wordsworth, he claims, is keenly aware of the distinction between the experience of a match or a connection which has a kind of primal validity and the ideas about that experience which are subsequently produced (1957:43). The poet, in this view, values the open-endedness of the perceived connections more highly than the inferences that may ultimately be derived.

Several generations of students of modernism have learned to grant the apparent independence of transformations from any inferences one might subsequently derive from Ezra Pound's own description of the composition of his poem "In a Station of the Metro." Parts of his letter were reprinted in the widely influential New Critical textbook *Understanding Poetry* (first edition 1938, fourth edition 1976) by Cleanth Brooks and Robert Penn Warren:

> Three years ago in Paris I got out of a "Metro" train at La Concord, and saw suddenly a beautiful face, and then another and another, and then a beautiful child's face, and then another beautiful woman, and I tried all that day to find words for what this had meant to me, and I could not find any words that seemed to me worthy, or as lovely as that sudden emotion....A year later I made the following sentence: The apparition of these faces in the crowd; Petals on a wet, black bough. (p. 71)

Hugh Witemeyer, in a discussion of Pound's poetics, says that

> the heart of the poem lies neither in the apparition nor in the petals, but in the mental process which leaps from one to the other. "In a poem of this sort," as Pound explained, "one is trying to record the precise instant when a thing outward and objective transforms itself, or darts into a thing inward and subjective." This darting takes place *between* the first and second lines. In the simplest possible verbal equation (a = b) the adventure lies in the unstated relation *between* the elements. (1969:34–35)

The shared condition between faces and petals, according to Brooks and Warren, was that both were, to Pound, "a glimpse of something beautiful, fresh and pure," a sudden revelation of beauty. A reader's process of transformation will pick out the matched conditions, and by doing so will be producing a new unit to be used in the building of a new pattern in which the faces and the petals do not just incidentally share a condition, a condition that is one among many in each unit, but in which the shared condition as a new unit has a new weight. That condition is now a necessary condition in the new pattern and may even be the head of it. The new pattern generates other inferences and transformations in a recursive and open-ended process. The main point here is that the making of inferences is independent of the transformation and can be devalued, even blocked, as it was by the conditions of significance of the Imagist movement.

Witemeyer has described how Pound's theory of poetry recognized that the difficulty of writing is the difficulty of finding words for "psychic experiences." A poem, to Pound, is "an objective verbal *equation* for a basically incommunicable experience." Witemeyer notes as well that the expression of the psychic experience itself is what was valuable to Pound, not any revelation of "an objective, transcendental order" (1969:24). Pound was interested in the psychology, rather than in the ontology of the sudden transformations he perceived, and was not therefore interested in the inferences that might be drawn from these experiences.

Complex interpretations such as Gilbert's are, of course, built by both analogical and logical processes. Different literary critics at different times, however, seem to rely on the two in different proportions, and what Gilbert's essay demonstrates is how representations produced analogically may be allowed to virtually swamp the conceptual or logical possibilities for interpretation.

Yet another advantage to Gilbert of an analogic/transformational style is that it does not require her to deal with a male or a female narrator's intended meaning, conscious or otherwise. As in the psychoanalytic monologue, the activity, productivity, and creativity of the interpreter's mind itself becomes the focus of interest. Exploration of indeterminate possibilities is, according to Mary Hesse (1988b), the goal (and the payoff) of analogic reasoning.[12] Although Gilbert's analogical thinking isn't always full-fledged analogical reasoning, its tentativeness would not be compromised by any implied conclusions, since they would themselves be only new hypotheses in need of confirmation. This mode of interpretation, furthermore, had an advantage over feminist criticism written according to Fetterley's rule in that it remained congenial to the feminist reader but was, as well, readable as a form of poststructuralist criticism. Its linguistic homologizing, disregard of genre distinctions, assumption of the centrality of the structured unconscious, and disinterest in classical definition and argument were all features of the critical styles of Derrida, de Man, Hartman, and Bloom. Gilbert thus found a way to remain bilingual: she speaks a language understandable within the male establishment, and yet one which, by its focus on her own readings, remains authoritatively feminist.

Gilbert's work here demonstrates that the question of what one has to be conscious of is more complicated than Fetterley thought when she declared that consciousness is power. She shows that it is the processes of making meaning themselves that need to be understood, questioned, even distrusted. The problems of what is a natural reading and how exactly a culturally imposed paradigm imposes itself (how much it demands and how we can see around it) remain in need of investigation. What is still needed is a better understanding of the relationship between mental processing, that is, the interpretive operations of the mind, and socially and subjectively selected conditions of coherence and satisfaction (i.e., between the transformations and the patterns produced from them). If Fetterley's change seemed too destructive, Gilbert may have given up too soon—failing to see the possibilities implicit in her own rhetoric. In the next chapter I will further examine the potential of analogical thinking to produce innovation in light of the modularity hypothesis. The evidence of Gilbert's essay will be used to explore the availability of alternative representations produced from, for example, the visual module.

5 Intermodular Competition
Transformation and Inference

> He was dispos'd to mirth; but on the sudden
> A Roman thought hath struck him.
>
> —Cleopatra, in *Antony and Cleopatra*

The essays on American autobiography and on *Hamlet* make their innovative literary claims primarily through chains of inference set in motion by, and/or resulting in, categorization judgments. Sandra Gilbert's significantly different style of reading suggests a significantly different cognitive support, that is, a different module. The basis for this claim is Jackendoff's hypothesis of computational sufficiency: "Every phenomenological distinction is caused by, or supported by, or projected from a corresponding computational distinction." Or to put it another way, "the world we are aware of is just that which the brain/computational mind is capable of representing" (1987:24–25).

This argument is a version of the evolutionary argument for a realist view of the relationship of human minds to the world; it is an entirely materialist theory. If we do not accept this hypothesis, then we have something more difficult to explain, namely, how a single brain mechanism can produce phenomenologically different kinds of knowing: why is knowing that something tastes like chocolate different from observing that it looks like chocolate? An answer to that question would *at some point* have to introduce differences, and thus we would have confirmed Jackendoff's hypothesis.

It is, then, assumed here that the hypothesized modularity of mind underwrites different ways of knowing, recognizable as different styles of interpretation. If there were no phenomenological consequences of modularity distinctions, then the hypothesis would be of no use in literary theory. If, however, there is a correspondence between interpretive style and the predominant processing and, furthermore, if a relationship can be noted between cognitive style and ideology, as I believe it can be, then the theory will demonstrate its value, having helped to map the boundaries at which culture and mental processing meet.

It may be worth repeating here just what benefit is to be gained from understanding the differences in interpretive style as differences between modular processes. Because modular processes entail instability as a result of the incomplete enregistration between modules, then identifying those differences is the key to locating the instabilities in interpretation that are *not* the result of contextual/historical pressure but are created by the mind's own search for stability. Gilbert's essay, then, displays evidence of competition between modular processes: she has been successful in producing interestingly new interpretations by analogy. Her chains of analogy are not defeated, indeed are barely threatened, at least in Gilbert's reckoning and in the estimation of those who found her reading worth publishing, by their insufficiency as logical arguments. They simply do something different. Cooccurrent contextual pressures had at least two detectable effects. As we have seen, by providing a preset stopping point they limited her innovative chains of transformation. At the same time, other contextual factors authorized the reweighting of analogy so that the logical insufficiencies were not weighted heavily enough to override it. The modularity hypothesis here provides clarity in mapping and in retaining the evidence of both the cooperation and the conflicts between processes and the interpretations they produce.

In this chapter I will try to exploit the distinctions I have displayed between the outputs of the different modules by claiming that interpretations which depend more heavily on inference and propositional argument are largely products of the conceptual/linguistic module, while the transformational/analogical style of Gilbert's essay was produced under the dominance of the spatial/visual module. It must be emphasized at the outset that this claim is an overgeneralization: no interpretation of any interest could present a pure example of single modular processing. Furthermore, although I have categorized the Gilbert essay as markedly analog, not all the analogies are visual. She joins figures such as curls and gold to abstract terms that are not primarily figurative such as "participation in reciprocal human relationships" or "regressiveness," and she sometimes makes logical inferences to link the images and invest them with significance.

Neither are the earlier, "inferential" essays without evidence of analogic or visual understanding, as when Judith Fetterley recognizes the strangled baby as an image of the potentially strangled Frederic Henry or, even more starkly, when she rejects what she identifies as the text's demand that she "imagine herself as Catherine," bleeding to death after the stillbirth. It could be argued, although she herself did not articulate it in this way at the time, that the founding motive of Fetterley's essay is a rejection of the required bodily identity of female reader and male writer's female heroine. The categorization resisted might not have been conceptual/propositional at all, but visual and kinetic—a match between the pain of the literary character and of the female reader.

It is important to note here, in distinguishing the styles of the different modules, that even if the different readers' reactions to texts were originally produced in different modules, they have all come to us through the medium of written language. Thus, even if readers have different cognitive styles, the language medium must at least partially occlude them. Furthermore, an entailment of the assertion of the mind's modularity is also an assertion of its ability to coordinate between the different kinds of representation, and this also makes it difficult to see what happens where. That a literary interpretation hatched primarily in the visual module comes to us in language is a demonstration of multiple processing or multiple coding and is an argument for modularity, but at the same time at least partially occludes that modularity.

The contribution of different modules is, nevertheless, distinguishable in an interpretation the same way as it is distinguishable in experience. You know whether you are seeing something that looks fuzzy or feeling something fuzzy. If processing were modular only at the lowest levels of perceptual intake, as in Fodor's theory, then modular distinctions would presumably disappear long before meaning was at issue, and we would not be able to label distinguishable aspects of complex representations as visual, aural, conceptual, or kinesthetic. Yet we can do this. This is consistent with Jackendoff's version of the hypothesis in which modularity is still phenomenologically present. Experience, in fact,

> is sharply differentiated by modality. There is no mistaking visual awareness, for example, for auditory awareness, or either of these for tactile awareness. They are vividly differentiated in experience. To be sure, one may be able to determine by either sight or touch that some object is square, say—and at a later time one may not remember which [way one came by that knowledge]. But in the experience itself there is no doubt whatsoever. (1987:51)

Another argument that various kinds of knowledge retain the label of their origins within composite literary interpretations can be inferred from the different weights different kinds of interpretations are granted, apparently according to the evaluation of their modular sources in their cultural contexts. Examples of this can be seen among the essays we have already studied. Fetterley's 1975 essay is perhaps the earliest one here that depends on a powerful bodily analogy. One of the reasons that feminist criticism was ignored, rejected, or scorned in its early years was because the kinesthetic mode to which it appealed was not widely considered an authoritative source of knowledge. The highest status was granted to the interpretations produced predominantly from the linguistic/conceptual module. The visual and aural modules were allowed authority in poetic texts, and kinesthesis (for example the appreciation of rhythm) was also allowed as a source of poetic value but rarely as a source of value or knowledge in the interpretation of prose. Freudian literary criticism, like Freudian theory in general, suffered neglect for the same reason. Even though Freud and his followers insulated their expression with many Latinate transformations toward abstraction, many readers did not trust arguments made on analogy from bodily knowledge.

By 1987, when Stanley Cavell published *Disowning Knowledge in Six Plays of Shakespeare*, the status in critical discourse of both analogy and discussions of the body had risen so high that his claims for bodily knowledge were widely acceptable. The issue had become clear enough, presumably through the work of feminist critics (as he acknowledges), so that he was able to recognize and assert his reliance on kinesis and bodily experience in a way that Fetterley had not been.

Recently the issue of interpretations and bodies has gained even greater status from the public embarrassment of the late Paul de Man. When de Man's past as an essay writer in Nazi-controlled Belgium was revealed, his linguistic idealism was widely reread as a self-serving and perhaps self-deceptive belief rather than as the clear-eyed, if tragic, vision it had once seemed. This reinforced a suspicion feminist and African-American critics, for example, were beginning to express more clearly, that language is not playfully nor harmlessly nor even tragically disconnected from the world, as some of the poststructuralists had claimed. It had been known to and still might cause grave bodily pain to those who do not control its power.

Thus, both experience and inference suggest that the coordination between modules is not ultimately concealed by language; if we look carefully, different ways of knowing can be discerned in verbal texts. Sometimes the evidence from one module supports that from another, as when Fetterley's inferences that Hemingway cannot be trusted to condemn his hero's selfishness confirm her resistance to identifying with the dead body of his heroine.

But the existence of knowledge from two sources is even clearer when, in Gilbert's essay for example, one finds a conflict between them. The chains of analogies produced from the visual/analogical module, valued by Gilbert at least in part as a rejection of a too-heavy reliance on propositional logic, are, as I have noted, themselves controlled by some rather too-powerful patriarchal conceptualizations and assertions. The interpretation as a whole suggests the presence of at least these two modular sources of knowledge; we see that language has not only failed to cover over the evidence of visual processing, it has also failed to hide the evidence of competition between the two.

If it is granted that different modules are producing different representations and retaining the traces of their origins, as in the Gilbert essay for example, we may still ask which modules are producing which effects. If we associate (as I have) propositional, hierarchical, or logical thinking with the language module, can we unequivocally claim that spatial/analogical thinking is produced in the visual module? What keeps me from answering an unequivocal "yes" is the issue of whether all metaphor (taken in the broadest sense to include metonymy, etc.) is figurative, that is, includes a visual element. And how visual does visual have to be? Does it have to be an image, in the sense of a picture, or is spatial/geometric awareness (say, awareness of distance and depth) also "visual?"

Metaphor and vision

Richard Moran (1989) offers a discussion of the traditional association of metaphor and visual imagery in the course of a thoughtful and sophisticated challenge to Donald Davidson's view of metaphor. Moran provides an interesting hypothesis about why it should be the case that metaphor is repeatedly identified with figuration, pictures, and vision, even though not all metaphors involve images. Moran claims, with striking originality, that metaphor (or metonymy, or any other trope) acts, in crucial ways, as if it were visual. It has, for example, the same force as something that is seen. Even if we do not agree with the metaphorical assertion, he notes, we cannot help "seeing" the terms of the metaphor. Because the metaphor is grasped through our imagining it visually (i.e., seeing it with the mind's eye), there is always part of it that remains irrecoverable in a paraphrase.

Further evidence of its similarity to an image is that it is still visualized even when denied. Moran presents the example of the metaphor that contains a negative: we find ourselves picturing a man and an island even when the statement tells us that no man is an island. Neither does grammatical or semantic conditionality effect the force of our seeing: "Grammatical mood and the distinction between assertion and "mere" mention simply don't apply to pictures" (p. 102). What allows Moran to make this claim is his separation between the assertiveness of a metaphorical statement and what he calls its perspective, or framing of images and of concepts:

> There are two dimensions of metaphor, the dimension of effects, which I've referred to in terms of framing or the adoption of a perspective, and the dimension of the beliefs that prompt the comparison in the first place, and which are necessary for the framing-effect to be something other than mere juxtaposition. (p. 108)

Here Moran supports my claim that different modules are at work: the metaphor gets its force from a level of knowing that is invulnerable to conceptual censorship: the grammatical particles have no effect on it. "Part of the dangerous power of a strong metaphor is its control over one's thinking at a level beneath that of deliberation or volition. In the mind of the hearer an image is produced that is not chosen or willed." (p. 90). This argument fits well with the modularity hypothesis. The visual module indeed is the paradigm of irresistibility: human evolution for survival assures that we can see even what we did not expect to see, such as when we react to the appearance of unforeseen danger.

Language, especially abstract language, does not automatically compel assent the way images do. Talking about Yeats's "Leda and the Swan," Geoffrey Hartman (1980) is recognizing this power of images to force themselves upon us when he questions "the poet's imperious assumption of a visionary mode, as if it were self-justifying. His exotic and erotic subject matter," Hartman says, "displaces the question of authority. For Yeats may be a voyeur rather than a visionary: we do not know where he is standing, or how ancient his eyes are, or if they glitter" (pp. 21–22). If Moran is correct, Yeats's ability to force our consent to his vision is less a matter of the prophetic authority of the poet or of poetic convention and more a matter of the irresistibility of the products of the visual module, even, it should be noted, when delivered verbally. In contrast, and in support of Moran's claim, no matter how clearly we picture the rape of Leda, we will not know, nor does Yeats even try to assert—he leaves the question open—if "she put on his knowledge with his power."

But Moran wants to claim (and is able to cite a tradition of scholarly argument on this) that metaphors need not all be pictures. If a metaphor isn't a picture, can we say that it arises in the visual module? This would leave the modularity hypothesis at a loss to explain why, in cognitive terms, something that is not a picture should act like one, or how else it could act. One of Moran's arguments for why a metaphor is not like a picture is just wrong. His claim that a "metaphor is semantically articulate in a way that a picture is not, that it has parts that perform different functions" (pp. 92–93) could not stand up to analysis. The art historian's stock in trade, after all, is describing just how the different aspects of a painting work together or against each other, in tandem or in hierarchies. Nevertheless, I would want to concede that there are metaphors that seem, at least at first, not to involve imagery.

If so, then I would argue that, in just those cases where imagery is missing or minimal, the metaphor does *not* have the irresistible force Moran claims for strongly visual metaphors, does not have the compulsion that imagery produced in the visual module has. Nonimagistic metaphors are comparisons that can be produced and understood within the language module. The modularity hypothesis, thus, insists that every structure of information must arise and be negotiable in one or another module (although it may be double coded). It gives us a clue to the mistake in Moran's argument.

A few examples are needed here. Moran offers, as an example of a metaphor that provides "no morsel for the mind's eye, ear, nose, or throat...Theseus's figurative saying (in *A Midsummer Night's Dream*) that the poet's pen 'gives to aery nothing / A local habitation and a name'" (p. 92). My own response, in fact, to the word *habitation* is to imagine a small cottage in the woods. The words *aery nothing* make me think of Shakespeare's Ariel, from *The Tempest,* probably because of the phonetic resemblance and the echo of the "aery charm" that Prospero abjures as he frees the sprite. I can barely justify these images, but neither could Moran deny that the lines in fact call them to my mind. I could propose another line from a Shakespeare sonnet that seems to me to be less imagistic: "Love is not love which alters when it alteration finds." But you perhaps will find an image for those lines.

It's not, however, just a matter of finding examples. The claim that there are metaphors that don't call up any image at all for anyone could not be defended because it would rely on a definition of literal meaning and a distinction between denotation and connotation that would itself be very difficult to argue. Classical definitions of the distinction would probably call phonological resemblance a connotation, but since we are arguing here about any sense data, not only vision, and since the connotative echo may call up an image, the distinction doesn't hold. If the air in "aery" presents nothing to the vision, what do I see when I look up at the sky? I doubt that Moran would want to argue that the scientific claim that air itself is not blue but invisible is appropriate here. Neither would Moran want to rely, I would guess, on any theory of word meaning that would support the claim that "habitation" is always and only an abstraction, even though the suffix *-tion* is generally used to indicate that. Neither would he want to argue that the word ***nothing*** makes the metaphor insensible, as we know from his example of "no man is an island," which we visualize in spite of the negative. In sum, current theories of word meaning cannot support the absolute distinction between metaphor and image.[1]

There is, however, a way to save Moran's otherwise attractive and functional argument about the force of a metaphor and at the same time achieve my goal of linking metaphor to the processing that takes place in the visual module. The way to do this, as I have already hinted, is to see the connection between image and metaphor as a gradient one: some metaphors are more and some are less strongly visual (or pictorial, or imagistic). Granting this gradience, we can then say that the force of the metaphor, as opposed to whether or not its assertion is convincing, is relative to the strength or salience of its imagery. A clearer and more striking image is harder to resist, harder not to "frame" or get a perspective on than a weaker, or less salient image. I cannot make much of aery nothing and the habitation, and even less of love finding alteration. (A tailor's shop? The alteration of a navigational course? Both seem only weakly and uninterestingly connectable to love though I might try to make even that unlikely connection if I were reading, say, a Wallace Stevens poem). Jackendoff's description of the visual module as the geometric/spatial module reinforces my feeling that a gradient of visual salience is involved. In David Marr's theory the understanding of "alteration" in the sense of a change of direction would indeed be processed in the visual module—much less, he asserts, than a fully delineated picture or image is needed to involve that module.

There are other aspects of Moran's model that need to be expanded and detailed here in order to make his understanding of metaphor more fully explanatory of the issue of change and innovation. First, his idea of the relationship between perspective, as he calls the visual aspect of metaphor, and the inferences from it to assertions must be rethought; what in particular needs to be emphasized is the power of the original visual framing device or perspective to produce new inferences. We need to understand here the difference between what Moran refers to as the "force" of the image, its irresistibility, even its identity with the act of grasping the metaphor, and the very great number of further images, inferences, and propositions that a forceful and original figure can generate. Moran is clearly aware of this power, although it is not the main focus of his essay. In his conclusion he reminds us that "neither an image nor the framing-effect of a metaphor is itself an assertion, and neither is by itself a proper object of belief or denial. But whole networks of beliefs are both involved in their composition and are part of what their audiences recognize and are expected to take away with them" (p. 112).

We have already seen in the earlier discussion of the inferences that can be produced from categorization judgments, and from the interrelation of inference and transformation, just how vast these networks are. Building on the recognition of the power of categorization and matching operations in cognition, Ellen Schauber and I (1986) described the necessary (but not sufficient) operation of any metaphor as a single transformation. A metaphor consists of at least one transformation, that is (as was seen in Gilbert's reading), the recognition of at least some degree of similarity within any module or between modules.[2] George Eliot's recognition (and later, her readers') that Eppie's gold curls are visually connected to Silas's gold coins, and that one calls up the other and can function in the place of the other, is a transformation. Moran's essay suggests the identification of what we called transformation and the production of framing figures or perspectives. His maker of metaphors conceives a transformation, that is, grasps a relationship and proposes it in a way that allows, even compels, the audience to consider the relationship.

Preference rules

Transformation, however, remains just another word for trope, collocation, or relationship, if it is not supported by an articulated notion of the two terms or representations being compared. The way to achieve this articulation and enrichment is to make use of the formalism of the preference rule: while a representation (e.g., an image, or concept, a word or a sound) may function grammatically as a single unit, the preference rule displays how it is not semantically singular, but is a set of separable conditions.[3] A match or transformation, then, is not made between single units, although language may lexicalize them as single words, but between two or more sets of conditions that are usually not internally coherent. A list of the semantic conditions of a word includes all the aspects of its meaning, even contradictory possibilities. A match between almost any two units will thus reveal similarities, differences, and conflicts. The contingencies of use (say, for example, the genre conditions of the discourse) contribute to a determination of which conditions are considered significant in the transformation.[4]

A preference model assumes that, since necessary and sufficient conditions to define words cannot finally be specified outside of the context of use, the best way to represent the semantic possibilities that constitute a speaker's knowing what a word means is as a structured but never complete or exclusive list of all the aspects of meaning that are distinguishably connected to the word. The richness of this semantic theory gives substance to Moran's claim that "whole networks of belief" are involved in a metaphor. More than "beliefs," of course, are related in a transformation or metaphor. Phonological resemblance or spatial or temporal similarities or contiguity could also account for the production of transformations. If metaphorical perspectives, then, display not only similarities but differences as well, and also distinguish necessary conditions from merely typical conditions, both the patterns of further transformation and the patterns of inference that can be produced from them are already many times more complicated than those that could be derived strictly on the basis of similarity.

The complexity of transformation and inference is then, first, a question of numbers: more conditions of meaning permit a greater number of possible matches. The semantic situation is further complicated and enriched by the fact that the different conditions of any unit don't have fixed weights but are, rather, weighted according to the semantic and pragmatic systems in play in any given interpretation: softness and pleasant scent, then maybe thorniness, are conventionally more heavily weighted conditions of roses than, say, the botanical category of their leaf structure, but the image of a rose can take its importance from its appearance out of season, or from Christian iconography, depending on the context. A specific context will, of course, highlight only some of these conditions, but the others remain as possibilities for further transformations.

The details of the preference model are not as important here as the impression even a superficial understanding of it provides of the complexity of the potential relationships between the transformations and inferences. Beyond the contribution it makes as a description of the crucial separation between the visual and the conceptual aspects of metaphor, then, Moran's analysis, expanded by the preference model, allows a glimpse of how the makers of an original metaphor generate the kind of innovations in literary systems that are the subject of this book: innovations, that is, that arise at least in part because of the internal instability of the human interpretive process.

Semantic instability has of course been the subject of much attention in literary theory, and there is no need to cover that territory again. In the preference model, instability and asymmetry are displayed as resulting from the conflicts and inconsistencies included in the lists of conditions that describe possible word meanings. Any judgment about which conditions are to be applied is threatened by other possibilities. Of crucial importance is the scope such instability allows an individual for innovative understanding and semantic exploration wherever closure can be delayed. From the instability of the metaphorical perspectives of matches follows the instability of the inferences that emerge from the image/perspective. Given the possibilities, then, for the combined associative and inferential generation of meaning that a single transformation can suggest, it is impossible to exaggerate the concurrent potential and instability that enters a discourse in the presence of figurative metaphor.

Schauber and I, by separating the volatile processes of transformation from the inferences that can be derived from them, intended to display the distinction between an open-ended generative process and the imposition of closure which we assumed would be imposed by already-in-place communal standards. Moran reverses our metaphor for metaphor: where our semantic model emphasizes the generative plenitude and freedom of transformation in the visual module and between the visual and conceptual modules, he cites the compulsion of the visual frames or perspectives produced. In our model, inferences were likely to be imposed by the rules of the prevailing cultural context. Moran, however, sees the inferences, not the images, as the open part of the metaphor which we are free to accept or reject. For him, the image actually forces a new perspective or a new point of view to be considered; it does not force an interpretation or close speculation on or inference from that new figuration. He underestimates, I would claim, the power of the conventional systems of significance, while we undoubtedly overlooked the resistance an individual can muster.

A significant defense of double coding thus emerges: both Moran and Schauber and Spolsky insist on recognition of the two-facedness of metaphor that arises from its access both to individuals' particular vision and to more public systems of cultural belief. The necessary presence of that doubleness, its very irreduceability, is demonstrated by the double reading the two theories together provide. Each wants to find a place for both freedom and constraint in the interpretive model, but each locates it differently.

The difference, of course, is just what is at issue here. Not only can minds apparently manage both possibilities, but there is an evolutionary advantage to preserving competition between modules. Interpretation is kept open to further transformation not in spite of, but precisely because of the force of a metaphorical perspective to shake up old certainties by allowing new matches to present themselves. And as well, there is a way to resist already-in-place conventional propositions and hierarchies. If we both feel the force and admit the provisionality of metaphorical vision, we can see it as a path from the contingent, perhaps accidental, maybe even freakish collocations of perception and serendipitous understanding to new inferences and revised beliefs. It encourages creativity by clearing a place in the language system for possibility (as opposed to probability) while maintaining contact with both personal and cultural systems of belief and value.

Here I approach a crucial stage in the argument of this book. If I have set forth some arguments that support the claim that separate mental processes produce noticeably separate results, I must still clarify the issue of where freedom and constraint of interpretation are located in the modular model. It is this question, then, that underlies my discussion in the rest of this chapter and will be taken up again in Chapter 7 after we have looked at some further examples of literary interpretation. Ultimately I will claim that the critical evidence and the theoretical argument allow the hypothesis that within each module, at least two distinct levels can be detected, one of which allows the generation of possibilities whose source is within the individual interpreter, and the other of which reins those possibilities according to intersubjective standards. I want now to question further and develop Moran's notion of perspective, and argue finally for the location of perspective in the visual module.

Moran says that what metaphor contributes, over and above assertion, is perspective. His recognition of perspective as a prompt for rereading supports my contention that the structures of the mind are themselves so constructed as to instigate, not only react to, innovation. He fails, however, to make the crucial link between perspective and the individual situatedness of the maker of the metaphor. He gives some hints that he suspects a connection: when he discusses the advantages of "somehow letting a certain thing be known or inferred by your audience, instead of explicitly saying it" (p. 101), he is emphasizing not only the separability of the image and the assertion of a metaphor, but specifically the separation of the assertion from the speaker's own investment in it. Just as the speaker can suggest something through a metaphor without being prepared to assert it, so too may the reader, while acceding to the vision, refuse to grant whatever assertion may or may not be inferred from it. And the maker of a metaphor *qua* hearer might be proposing something he or she is not yet prepared to stand behind or to assert, but wants nevertheless to open for exploration. Moran admits that it is hard

> to give an account of the cognitive function of the framing-effect in the context of the composition of the metaphor in thought. For this we would need a better understanding of such things as the figures one may find both uncashable and inescapable in one's thinking, and the situations of provisionally writing beyond oneself, or beyond one's present understanding of what one has written. For the turn to metaphor is not just slippage; it is also a calculated and conditional surrender to a quite particular verbal constellation. (p. 111)

One might expect Moran to speculate that the "cognitive function of the framing effect" is just the production of that metaphorical creativity itself, but instead he makes use of an older unmotivated and distracting claim that it is the speaker's "initiating beliefs" (p. 109) that produce the perspective and back up the assertions the metaphor makes. Instead of capitalizing on the crucial self-centeredness of his term *per-*

spective, he locates its origin in the realm of a speaker or poet's rational, propositional, conscious commitments that are normally shareable, communal, and expressible in language. But if this were the whole story then, as he himself wonders, what would the maker of a metaphor stand to gain from the metaphor? And why should he or she be denied the benefit that Moran allows its hearers, namely, the benefit of being able to explore and expand the endless suggestions of the metaphor?

It is surely more useful, and even more consistent with the rest of Moran's argument, to consider the source of the metaphor to be in and not prior to the perspective it suggests. There is even an argument to be made here for considering it to be identical with the framing process, that is, with the nonassertive part of the metaphor, in the visual module. Carl Hausman gets this right, I think, in his assertion that "a metaphorical expression functions so that it creates its significance, thus providing new insight, through designating a unique, extralinguistic and extraconceptual referent that had no place in the intelligible world before the metaphor was articulated" (1989:94).

I would want to argue this from my general commitment to the priority of situatedness to beliefs. If everyone is somewhere, and where you are determines how you will frame similarities and differences, then the metaphor maker's assertion of belief is similar to the hearer's consent to that assertion: both come after the experience of the metaphoric perspective. Although we want to credit the former with some prior ground for making the metaphor, we do not, I think, want to assert that creativity arises from reference to already-in-place beliefs. We must take into account the possibilities for reorganization resulting from the double vision of the more and the less self-centered perception. Talmy Givón (1984) describes the process of reframing the self in regard to the context as an important source of creativity:

> The process of *objectifying the 'I'* has always been an essential component in the adaptive neuro-biological arsenal of consciousness, allowing individuation, planning, and the exertion of will in action and communication. In the struggle for survival, the 'I' remains *outside* the frame, manipulating what is inside to its advantage. The very same 'I' may, however, choose to include itself *within* the frame, allowing self-reflection, re-contextualizing itself as *part of the whole* (1984:186).

Fodor (1983) cites philosophers of science (see Ortony 1979, passim) who suggest that hypothesis formation begins with a kind of analogical thinking. It is a mysterious process depending on an improbable transformation. The unforeseen but enabling analogy represents the *if* of a hypothesis. It precedes the *then* which are the derived inferences. Alternatively, the Freudian tradition of understanding dreams as self-serving (wish-fulfillment) visions could be invoked here. The dreams are images that frame desire, not belief.

Identifying the source of creative metaphor in the perspective of the speaker sits well with Moran's view that metaphor functions as if it were an image. An image is always seen, at least at first, from a single perspective. It is always partial, limited by the position of the viewer, but allows inference to what is occluded by the perspective. Pictorial perspective, in fact, is a fine metaphor for the self-centeredness of the phenomena of all perception. From where I sit, says Shakespeare, it looks like "Love's not Time's fool, though rosy lips and cheeks / Within his bending sickle's compass come" (Sonnet 116). An original metaphor is always a speech act framed by the performative that acknowledges its limited perspective. This would not apply to dead metaphors, of course, which are meaningful precisely because they are common, not private property.[5] Dead metaphors are, in this view, metaphors that have been preserved because they have proved themselves successful bridges between visual representation and linguistic/conceptual representation. Their incorporation into language, that is, into the memories of speakers of the language where they are available for reference, is a testimony to their success, to their continued usefulness in the ongoing struggle against the biological limitations of the mind.

In Chapter 7 I will explore more fully the cognitive theories of vision that adumbrate the benefits of what Moran calls the "surrender" to metaphoric vision, and at that time I will also explore the recent theoretical thinking on the possibilities and benefits of "provisionally writing beyond oneself." Moran's words suggest the explorations that have occupied feminists interested in the interchange between the individual and the culturally negotiable. Not only Gilbert's own transformations, but the ones I suggested as well, for example, demonstrate that vision can always be re-visioned. Being personal perspectives, transformations are not only "uncashable" but also always deniable, while culturally authoritative assertions, already cast in the form of public truths, are thereby more oppressive and less open to reformulation. At the same time, images demand attention while assertions allow, even invite, denial.

The modularity thesis suggests that neither the personal nor the communal view need be excluded. Multiple coding assures the interplay of modular readings without any biologically preset hierarchical relationship between them. Not only is there always the potential for conflict between the outputs of different modules, but as the next chapter will hypothesize, there is even room for intramodule competition between levels of representation within a module. If, in any given interpretive context one or the other is functionally preferable, the other possibility is always around as a challenge to whichever is temporarily installed as dominant. The instabilities, again, are built into the interpreting mind, not only into the changing world in which it dwells.

Advantages and risks of multiple coding

It should now be clear that the inevitable "disfiguring power of figuration" (1978b:25), which so worried de Man, has its advantages as well in the production of innovation. Jackendoff hypothesizes about the positive aspects of having modular memories rather than one single modality-neutral storage center. Certain kinds of knowledge are best represented in visual structure, while others may be more efficiently represented in conceptual structure (1987:200). The visual memory, for example, is the fitting place to understand colors, the comparative shapes of ducks, geese, and swans, as well as the faces of people one knows. The distinction between *depreciate* and *deprecate* can presumably be more easily stored as conceptual knowledge. Although one may be more convenient than another for long- or short-term storage, the possibility of translation is assumed. But translation may be costly in processing time, and may involve many steps. Because, as we have seen, translation can always only be partial, having *both* representations available is better than having either one.

One specific source of the awkwardness of translation between visual and conceptual structure may be understood from Jackendoff's claim that there is no distinction in the long-term visual memory between type concepts and specific tokens. More precisely, there are no visual type concepts at all, only the experience of specific tokens (1987:198). If you want to demonstrate this to yourself, try to picture a dog. You will picture a specific dog, either one you know, or some middling-size dog without any exotic characteristics. There is no way you can summon a single image that pictures both a thin short-haired chihuahua and a large shaggy sheep dog, although the single word/concept *dog* does cover both. Like *dog*, the meanings of many words are types, which can be used for many different tokens. This incommensurability shows that language cannot directly or easily represent the specificity of visual awareness.

The modularity hypothesis has, thus, accounted in cognitive terms for Keats's lament that the fancy cannot cheat so well as she is famed to do. Language cannot easily say everything that is seen or, apparently, everything that is felt or understood, even when resorting to inventive (innovative, creative) language behavior. To find expressive figurative language for the otherwise uncashable, inexpressible, or (a smaller claim) heretofore unexpressed, is indeed a special talent.

If, as Jackendoff assumes, the distinction between spatial and inferential structures of information is maintained in the central processor, then what we call thinking may be a dynamic in which chains of transformation and inference compensate for the typish bias of language and the tokenish bias of images. Carl Hausman's view of original metaphor suggests that he sees the creativity of the accomplishment precisely in its intermodularity, by means of which "noncognitive conditions cooperate with cognitive meanings" (1989:57).

If an abstraction can with any success be recast in some kind of conjunction with an image, feeling, color, or other linguistic experience, the interpretive powers of other modules can be turned on it. It is now, as it were, being looked at, felt, etc. Spatial transformations that do not belong to the abstract representation are invoked—even, if Moran is right, irresistibly invoked. Similarly, re-representing visual, emotional, or other concrete experience in abstract language is difficult and reductive but permits inference that might not have emerged had the translation not taken place.

Vera John-Steiner, in her chronicle of creativity, finds that scientists frequently report themselves to be heavily dependent on metaphor and visual thinking for problem-solving, even though their images will eventually have to be translated back into verbal or mathematical abstractions (1985:84ff.).[6] Jackendoff's modularity thesis (not Fodor's, however) thus lends support to the philosophers of science (e.g., Boyd 1979) and language and the literary theorists (e.g., Hausman 1989) who have argued that figurative language is productive of new knowledge.

The dialectic of alternating representations is potentially enormously fruitful and is, I would think, what most theorists of metaphor are thinking of when they speak of the open-endedness of figurative language. Because of the many ways images or concepts can be segmented and new conditions of different units matched, each new transformation or inference is itself capable of being re-represented in a great number of unpredictable directions, opening a geometry of possibilities. Since it would be reasonable to expect different kinds of creativity, that is, different kinds of novel structures to result from transformations and inferences applied to visual and to conceptual structures, we could conclude that while it may be more *convenient* to have one or the other kind of structure, it is more *productive* of new knowledge to have both, and even more, to be adept at converting one to another.[7]

Although the chains of inference or transformation I have been hypothesizing could also be sustained among undifferentiated structures of information in a generalized central processor, a good amount of the productivity I have described would be lost if the distinctiveness of representations, and thus the power of re-representation, was lost. It is, of course, the inability of the process to achieve a complete mapping between visual and linguistic structures, that is, the possibility of translation together with the impossibility of complete commensurability, which drives the process and which describes its open-endedness. Satisfaction will never be reached by the natural resolution or completion of the process; it must finally be decreed according to an external standard. Both visual and conceptual modules, then, offer freedom and closure. We can see that it is the combination of the open-endedness of the processes of transformation and inference, and the dialectic of re-representation between the visual and conceptual structures that is the source of the creativity of figurative language.

Jackendoff's description of why language is inadequate to express what can be envisioned is certainly consistent with the intuitions and with the arguments of literary scholars and philosophers over many centuries.[8] It explains why the richest or best linguistic products such as poetry are possible, but unusual because improbable and costly. In a modular theory, then, the distinction between figurative and abstract language is more useful than between metaphorical and literal language. If, furthermore, there is a processing distinction between reference to memory on the one hand and the constructive processes of inference and transformation on the other, then the separation of meaning as probable or improbable reflects that distinction.[9] It explains why the comprehension (not to mention the production) of poetry is so difficult for so many speakers of the language, while at the same time allowing an explanation of why it is nevertheless possible to train people to be able to read and even write poems. From this point of view, the ability to read and understand and write poems is an ability for which we all have the capability, although it is a capability that hasn't been exercised, in part because it is expensive in processing terms.[10]

The modularity hypothesis, with its assertion of intermodular cooperation and competition, lends support to a parallel project, mentioned earlier, and that is the project most recently undertaken by Wendy Steiner (1982) and W. J. T. Mitchell (1985), among others, to repair the damage done to aesthetic theory by the classical insistence on an irreconcilable distinction between literature and the plastic arts.

From a semiotic perspective, Steiner concludes that the relationships between the arts, as in all sign systems, are vastly more complex than had been appreciated: "A poet intent on a speaking picture or a painter intent on a mute poem has a vast array of technical properties to play with, any one of which, turned from its normal spatiality or temporality, may provoke the interartistic analogy" (p. 50). The processing discussion here has shown her assessment of complexity to be well warranted. The distinctions that have been insisted upon (according to Mitchell, since the Biblical prohibition against the fashioning of idols) have not emerged ex nihilo, but have a basis in the kinds of processing brains can manage. The interrelation between the arts represents no abuse of natural boundaries but is grounded in the mind's own ability to re-represent, to translate productively from one mode to another.

Steiner also catches the inexactness of the translation—or better, the resistance of any two modes to fall together: "It is only in extreme cases, e.g., concrete poetry, that the precise correspondence of a verbal text to the spatial-temporal norms of visual art is even conceivable" (p. 50). Every comparison of a specific painting with a specific poem, she claims, "helps us to understand the process of correlation and disjunction through which systems of sign vehicles and meanings are constantly realigned in the ordered flux of sign-functioning" (p. 69). The modularity hypothesis suggests schematically the biological reasons for both the correlation and the disjunction, but difficult as it undoubtedly is to chart these partial matches, it is not hard to find places where the activity of correspondence is valued. Henry James's ideal art connoisseur Mr. Verver, in *The Golden Bowl*, is thus praised: "Nymphs and nuns were certainly separate types, but Mr. Verver, when he really amused himself, let consistency go. The play of vision was at all events so rooted in him that he could receive impressions of sense even while positively thinking" (p. 154).

6 Immobile and Immortal in the Monument of Literary History

> Give me my robe. Put on my crown; I have
> Immortal longings in me.
>
> —Cleopatra, in *Antony and Cleopatra*

What are Cleopatra's immortal longings? They are directed toward mortality: she wants to die. Through death, she expects to achieve transcendence—permanence in another mode of existence. One last change will defeat change and, as so many Renaissance texts claimed, defeat death through death. The recent self-consciousness of historiography (for which we might take Hayden White's 1973 study *Metahistory* as an important representation) has described the traditional project of writing history, including the writing of literary history, as another project driven by immortal longings and aspiring to transcendence. Literary historians have traditionally labored to fix the texts they value in a unifying and continuous narrative. But it did not take long, once they recognized the ease with which they could be seen to impose rather than discover order in the flow of time, for historians to ask (as if in embarrassed recoil from their earlier narcissism) how they might gauge their own powers of distortion and whether they could or should resist them. Dominick La Capra notes (over a decade later) that "the difficulty is to develop an exchange with the "other" that is both sensitive to transferential displacement and open to the challenge of the other's "voice" (1985:72–73).

La Capra's call for an exchange between the present and the past is taken from a critique of the most fashionable of current historical studies which differentiate themselves variously as cultural history, new history, or annales history. What these projects have in common, however, is more important here than the distinctions among them.

Represented by several new and attractive journals, the project has generated great interest, but is hard to say if its literary historical form is living up to the epistemological goals that had been conceived for it. Despite twenty years of historiographic self-analysis, it is still far from clear on what grounds individual texts can be understood as bound to each other and to their historical surroundings—how commonalities between texts and events from the same time period or continuities between different periods are identified and why they are valued. In this chapter and the next I will examine the attempts of some critics to establish continuity between their own lives and texts from earlier periods, and between successive frames of literary history in my attempt to describe the interplay between the historical and the cognitive sources of change.

The writings of some English and American medievalists provide a particularly clear example of the way scholars in the 1960s reacted to students' demands for relevance (La Capra's "exchange") in undergraduate studies. But well before we get to the 1960s we find in England, at the start of the present century, an only thinly veiled ambivalence about the continuity or lack of continuity between a medieval text and its modern audiences. I had, perhaps, expected more self-assurance from the villains of current theoretical debate. Here are the opening sentences of R. K. Root's *The Poetry of Chaucer*, written in 1906 as a caution to readers. He reveals, by his very assertiveness, his worry that others may seek just that continuity he denies:

> It is five hundred years and more since Geoffrey Chaucer was "nayled in his cheste" and laid in what is now known as the Poet's corner of Westminster Abbey....If we are to enter into the spirit of his poetry, we must forget for the time being the present-day world, and all that has happened in five hundred years, and live again in a day long dead. (p. 1)

By the 1960s the submerged confusion, given only indirect expression in Root's text, about whether or how a reader might live in the past had been brought into the open by the greater critical focus on the reader. If understanding is either partially or largely formed by the reader's experience and expectation, as both cognitive and philosophical theories claim, then any narrative of the past (like any narrative of the present) will at best be the truth told slant. Readers in the 1960s, especially student readers (and who else reads Chaucer?) were wont to raise the issue: even on the assumption that twentieth-century readers could make themselves into fourteenth-century readers, the question of why they would want to do so remains. Twenty years ago and more the most frequently articulated but usually unargued answer to the question of why students in the twentieth century should continue to read old texts was that truth and beauty are perennially true and beautiful, and therefore perennially valuable.

This is what Charles Muscatine, a medievalist at the University of California at Berkeley, claimed when he gave the 1969 Ward-Phillips Lectures at The University of Notre Dame. Early in his first lecture, however, Muscatine admitted that this is not an entirely satisfactory answer: there are only a handful of texts, he noted, about which it is self-evidently true. He was led, thus, to make explicit the argument for the necessity of a knowledge of history by means of which we will be able to perceive the beauty of old texts. The argument goes like this: a knowledge of the historical context of past literature will remove the veil that is between the old texts and their twentieth-century readers, allowing the latecomers to see the beauty and truth not otherwise apparent in the old texts, and thus to see the permanent value of the texts. It will also allow us to examine the past as a display of possibilities for the future.

The contradiction, however, has not disappeared: if the beauty or truth of a text cannot be appreciated without enough "background" history to allow modern readers to infer those meanings contemporary audiences would have attributed to the authors of the texts, then ideas of truth and beauty are apparently *not* perennially true. Root, then, was more nearly correct than Muscatine, at least in that he didn't claim the permanence of standards of art or the relevance of the old texts.

One solution to the problem of finding continuities, then, would be to accept that it cannot be done and to settle for an inevitably distorted understanding of the past. Literary historians have, perhaps understandably, never rushed to embrace this solution since it would put them out of business. Another solution was to claim that an imaginative recreation of Chaucerian England isn't really so difficult to produce, because it wasn't, after all, so different from the reader's present.

This argument was made as far back as 1915 when G. L. Kittredge first published *Chaucer and His Poetry* (in its fourteenth reprint in 1967). Kittredge was more encouraging to his student audiences than Root was, explaining why reading Chaucer should be a pleasure rather than a problem:

> Chaucer lived in the middle ages...but he is the most modern of English poets....This is not a paradox; it is the sober, unrhetorical statement of a truism. For he knew life and loved it, and his specialty was mankind as it was, and is. Besides, his age was vastly like our own....It was...a singularly "modern" time....All the problems which vex the world today, either sprang into existence or made themselves especially troublesome in the sixty years of Chaucer's life. For there is a scarcely a political or social catchword of the present (even "feminism")...which does not fit the fourteenth century. (pp. 1–2)

To prove his point, Kittredge listed a number of concerns he understood to be shared by his own age and the late fourteenth century. His insistence on the modernity of Chaucer's world and thus, by analogy, the similarity of his students' untrained reading of Chaucer's poetry to the understanding fourteenth-century audiences would have evolved, minimized the difference between past readers and present. It also exaggerated the universality of the perceptions and values readers have claimed to recognize in the *Canterbury Tales.* The idealization of the reader, or the homogenization of the category of reader, then, solved one problem, but, as has lately been realized in feminist and Marxist literary theory, introduced others.

D. W. Robertson, Jr., to his credit, saw the danger of eliding the differences between medieval writers and modern readers. To his discredit, he failed either to recognize or to acknowledge the interested source of his insight, namely his own ambivalent fit within the reigning establishment of American medievalists. Until the English Institute of 1950, at which Robertson presented his contentious, even inflammatory paper entitled "Historical Criticism," most Chaucer scholarship had been following Kittredge's example, namely, providing its reading public with matches between what passed as an objective picture of the fourteenth-century historical background (assumed to be the values of

Geoffrey Chaucer as well) and the values of the twentieth-century literary community.

Robertson provided an explicit Christian substance to the generalization about difference that Root's rule expressed. In 1950 he was a youngish assistant professor at Princeton who had closer acquaintance with and stronger personal ties than many to the intellectual sources of medieval Catholicism. As Muscatine would do twenty years later, he bemoaned the state of criticism in which "the literary critic has tended to avoid historical materials altogether." His programmatic speech to the Institute defined and argued for a particular kind of historical criticism: "By 'Historical Criticism' I understand that kind of literary analysis which seeks to reconstruct the intellectual attitudes and the cultural ideals of a period in order to reach a fuller understanding of its literature." In the sentence that follows, Robertson asserts just what those cultural ideals were:

> First of all, medieval literature was produced in a world dominated intellectually by the church. Too frequently, modern historians have tended to deplore this fact rather than to make a sincere effort to understand it. Neither the church nor the doctrine it sought to teach was exactly like anything existing in the world today. (p. 4)

Robertson then continues in this tone to chastise critics for failing to notice that the only thing that made any difference to medieval tellers of tales was the distinction between *caritas* or love of God, and *cupiditas* or selfishness (i.e., love of whatever is not God). The critics' attention should be to these values, not to mere "transient aesthetic satisfaction" (p. 31). With tongue in cheek, he offered his gargantuan oversimplification of medieval thought and art as a gift to scholars: "Whatever it may mean to the historian, the dominance of the church in the Middle Ages considerably simplifies the task of the historical critic" (p. 4). All a critic had to do was identify this one theme in all of the artistic production of the time, and the job was done.

Robertson continued to irritate, if not enrage, the scholarly community by doing just what he recommended. His own work provided not only analyses of the obviously religious texts such as *Piers Plowman* (1951, with B. Huppé), but also turned out "exegetical" analyses of Chaucer's fabliaux (1962), arguing, for example, that they weren't secular or modern or tolerant, as they had been made out to be by critics like Kittredge, but were all allegories in which charity was praised and cupidity condemned. The many critics who found his analyses unsatisfying also found them difficult to fault: they indeed could be made according to the rules of interpretation already in place in the community of medievalists.

The problem with the theory, we see with hindsight, was that it was too powerful. If the opposition between *caritas* and *cupiditas* could not be found to be referred to explicitly in the text, then it could always be found at one of the four allegorical levels familiar to medieval scholars. That is to say, if it wasn't there, it was also there, and simply needed to be produced through inference and transformation. The argument put many senior scholars on the defensive, searching for ways to argue against Robertson's oversimplification without seeming to be ahistorical themselves.

The battle over exegetical criticism continued among medievalists for at least thirty years. Robertson didn't "win." His challenge, however, forced others to concede some points and to articulate theretofore tacit but widely agreed-upon standards. E. Talbot Donaldson's 1960 paper, for example, was a detailed rebuttal of three exegetical interpretations and a defense of a critic's right to an "aesthetic reading," namely a reading grounded in the values of the present interpreter. A reader looking for what "must be there," namely the allegorical meaning, is very likely, Donaldson protests, to "miss what is there...[to] miss a meaning arising from the poem that is better than anything that exegesis is able to impose upon it" (p. 2). Donaldson thus makes it plain that he believes his own competent reading (note he makes no argument for authorial intention) is the meaning "arising from the poem."

Donald Howard (1966) also undertook to respond to Robertson's challenge. He sketched a position that was eventually accepted as a reasonable *via media*, starting with the admission that "one can hardly deny that Christianity, being important to medieval life, was important to medieval literature. We cannot, then, read a medieval poem without some historical grasp of the dominantly Christian conditions under which the medieval poet wrote" (p. 22–23). The conclusion that all writers expected their audiences to read Christian doctrine into their poetry, Howard argued, is discredited by the common clerical admonishments of secular authors. Furthermore, "the fact that poets like Boccaccio and Chaucer retracted their secular works hardly indicates that they expected them to be read as Christian allegories" (p. 25). Howard also notices something important about Robertson's oversimple view of the medieval world, namely that it has been created to satisfy Robertson's own twentieth-century needs: "Robertson himself presents a wholly romanticized view of the period as one of universal serenity in which men felt no emotional conflicts. In doing so...he expresses everywhere a contempt for the present" (p. 30). Howard then asserts his own interest through the claim that Robertson is inexcusably blind to what seems to Howard to be a historical situation that must be accounted for: "the undeniable rise of secular thought and feeling beginning about the twelfth century" (p. 36).

The important point for us is to note that, regardless of whether the secular is "undeniable," it was undeniably interesting to Howard. He may well be correct to describe the central preoccupation of medieval culture as the struggle between the perfection demanded by the Christian ideal and the recognition of man's innate imperfection. But what he is also demonstrating is that his own view of history, including, as it does, a belief in the organic growth of secularism from the late medieval period into the modern world, is an important condition of significance determining what he himself will find interesting in medieval literature. Just as Donaldson's New Critical bias was evident in his attack, so Howard's can be seen in his affection for unresolvable complexity: "The difficulty of reading oneself back into a former age is something more than to uncover a dominant notion; it is rather to confront the area of struggle, to reconstruct the correspondences and oppositions among which an idea or institution existed and among which poets wrote (p. 33).

The interested reductiveness of Robertson's position as well as the critical arguments against it together make clear that an abstracted, objective, historical sensitivity was only one of the requirements of a medievalist as that community defined itself at the time. Interpretations acceptable to mainstream scholars, including Robertson, though he would not have admitted it, in fact followed two necessary rules. The first is the historical rule, an object-centered rule describing the historian's responsibility to the past, and the second the aesthetic rule, a viewer-centered rule describing the relationship of an interpretation to present values. The historical rule can be written as a gradient necessary condition:

GNC: An acceptable interpretation must not conflict with any of the necessary conditions of the rule of the genre in question for the period in question.

All literary historians have traditionally considered the historical rule to be a necessary rule. It requires the critical interpreter to posit at least one functional inference about the meaning of the genre of a text in its original context since this, at least in part, would establish the meaning of a text to its contemporaries. The rule commits the Chaucerian to attempt to decide, for example, whether *The Wife of Bath's Tale* was intended as a romance, and therefore expresses a benign view of the way things eventually work out for the best, or whether it was (and is, therefore) the lecture of a failed teacher whose commitment to the world of experience has betrayed her.[1] It similarly dictates that an interpretation of a fourteenth-century short poem that begins "O Maiden Mary Moder Milde" cannot claim that the poet is addressing his own mother whose name happened to be Mary. The historical rule is a gradient one because more or less historical accuracy is expected depending on what is known about the period, and therefore on what can be said about the various genres. It assumes, however, that the details needed for the inferences are more or less recoverable and that the process of making the inferences can proceed unproblematically.

An entailment of the historical rule is a heavily weighted gradient typicality condition that describes a preference for the interpretation that seems most likely to accord with the author's intention:

GTC: The author of the text believes (asserts, agrees with) the representations made by the necessary conditions of the genre used.

This functional condition is itself a version of John Searle's sincerity condition (1969:60–65). It distinguishes a parody from a sincere expression of the meaning conventionally associated with the form. It also requires (and assumes) unhindered inference into the past.

Historical scholars traditionally judge their (and each other's) success or failure in this recovery by a preference condition according to which those interpretations are preferred which reinforce patterns of structures and functions already familiar from the received interpretations of texts composed in the same historical time and place. The two major theoretical difficulties with this requirement are, first, that current interpretive processes and needs themselves produce the illusion of period consistency over a set of texts. Second, the consistency is produced at such a high level of generalization that the distinctiveness between genres and between texts of a genre disappears. Robertson's historical criticism followed the historical rule but was criticized on the second of these counts.

That scholars were able to object to Robertson's work, to identify what they considered its failures, is itself significant. It was a viewer-centered rule, which I will call the aesthetic rule, that provided the check. The aesthetic rule labels some interpretations unacceptable by putting up a second communal standard against the first.

This is the aesthetic rule, written as two necessary conditions (a well-formedness condition and a gradient necessary condition):

> WFC: An interpretation must identify features which distinguish highly valued texts, (i.e., texts considered to be works of genius), from the masses of texts considered mediocre because entirely stereotypical and thus undistinguishable one from another.
>
> GNC: Prefer that interpretation which distinguishes the text from its contemporaries by conditions which are also valued in the context of the interpreter.

For example, conditions of significance in large segments of the literary community being what they were in the 1960s, it was preferable to argue that the characterization of the Wife of Bath shows Chaucer to have been sensitive to and to have had a healthy appreciation of female sexuality than to suggest that the Wife of Bath's grotesque sexual appetite is intended to teach us that selfishness is ugly and sex sinful.

The crucial difference between the historical and the aesthetic rules is that the aesthetic rule does not require inferences about meaning that present epistemological difficulties. It is the second necessary condition of the aesthetic rule which insures that potential conflict between intended meaning (the historical functional conditions) and current interpretation will never arise to present a problem, since it posits what is cognitively most likely to happen, namely, that conditions valued in the context of the interpretation will be selected and patterned. Highly valued texts, thus, can be identified as such within a community without justifying the evaluation. Also, if the distinguishing features of those texts are structural features (say, complex versifying), the problem of conflicting world views need never arise. Meaning must be recoverable, but not all the possible inferences from it need be explored.

The aesthetic rule does, however, like the historical rule, presuppose the permanent recognizability or knowability of valued structures or forms: it assumes at least aesthetic (though not historical) transcendence. Note that the aesthetic rule applies to texts that are already in the canon, that are already considered to be distinguished, valuable texts. Thus Robertson's interpretive strategy, according to which he admits to concerning himself with only the first rule, might have been acceptable among his contemporaries had he restricted his application of it to noncanonical texts such as macaronic sermons on virtue. Instead he culled texts from the *Patrologia Latina* which had no value as literature in a literary community that wasn't very interested in history, and used them to reinterpret canonical literary texts in such a way as to demote the literary texts to the status of hitherto ignored sermons. Howard had noticed, however, and had suggested by labeling him a romantic, that while Robertson was denying to others the pleasure of finding what they wanted in a text, he was himself doing just that.

As time passed, critics without the catholic interests of Robertson and his associates eventually admitted that he had pointed to a gap. They acknowledged the error of having overlooked sources that could have enabled them better to meet the requirements of their own first historical rule. Since this rule is a gradient rule, being called on to upgrade it, while perhaps embarrassing, isn't damaging to the system as a whole, and so it was grudgingly allowed.

Robertson's call for the rejection of the general application of the aesthetic rule was itself rejected, however, as it had to be if literary history were to be preserved as distinct from literary criticism. A necessary rule cannot be ignored without destroying the system. Its rejection would have put the literary historical establishment out of business by denying the value of learning about old texts and, as well, denying the distinctiveness of their canon, their special texts. What could not be agreed to was the absorption of the valued texts, which could through the application of the aesthetic rule be made true and beautiful to at least some twentieth-century readers, into the category of didactic texts that could no longer teach or delight.[2]

We can see from a collection of essays published in 1984 called *Chaucer and Scriptural Tradition*, that Robertson's challenge to the rules of literary history had been met: its necessary rules had been defended, and the lesson he wanted to teach had indeed had an influence on gradient rules. Robertson himself was invited to contribute the lead essay in the volume. In the Introduction, however, editor David L. Jeffrey, while deferential to the importance of Robertson's corrective, refers to the "intimidation" scholars had felt in the face of "the superposition of a substantial library of patristic scholia and scholastic commentary between Chaucer and his Scripture texts" (p. xiii). He then casts the justification for the volume as a suggestion that a useful distinction might be made between more and less easily accessible sources of church doctrine: instead of the *Patrologia Latina,* "it may be the text of the Bible which should first be examined" (p. xiii).

Thus Jeffrey offers a compromise proposal about which nonliterary texts might be used to help scholars fulfill their commitment to the historical rule, and also declares his unshakable attachment to the aesthetic rule as well:

> We recognize that what makes Chaucer different (and from some points of view more attractive) than, let us say, Gower or Lydgate, is not that he employed a significantly different typology, lexicography, or even symbology: what sets him apart as a poet is the high drama of his dialectical method, and, above all perhaps, the radically new land of doubts and second guesses into which he thrusts the reader with respect to this question of the authority and the meaning of texts—even his own texts. (p. xiv)

The critical issues are expressed in the language of the late 1970s: the "radically" new, the questioning of authority, and the self-reflexivity of the text. Again, as with Kittredge and Muscatine, Chaucer is better because he is like us. Jeffrey ends his Introduction explicitly attributing to Chaucer his 1984 concerns by claiming that the application of the historical rule confirms the output of the application of the aesthetic rule:

> Chaucer is not interested in scriptural tradition merely as a repository of typologies, nor in using it merely to signal a kind of fideistic self-accrediting. He is interested in the largest questions of interpretation, in the reliability of text and textual tradition, and in the recovery of truth from the written word. (p. xvi)

In fact, it seems to be the other way around. It is the aesthetic rule that will inevitably bring the output of the historical rule into line with contemporary aesthetic norms.

Because this conventional weighting of the rules assures their cooperation, agreement is very broad on the need for both rules. Another recent critic, the neo-Marxist reader of Chaucer David Aers, insists that historical criticism requires both. He quotes Frank Lentricchia (1980) to make his point:

> Any adequate reading of medieval texts must hold to both critical moments.... That is, our reading needs to be informed by a serious attempt to reconstruct the text's moment of production, its own contexts of discourse and social practices within and for which it achieved meaning.... While understanding this essential historical attempt we must simultaneously acknowledge... "the unavoidable given of all cognitive processes—that knowledge, however we may define it, is received through a situated human consciousness, that has spatio-temporal location, idiosyncratic colourations, and philosophical and sociopolitical prejudices." (1986:7)

That Robertson himself had in fact followed both rules reinforces my earlier claim that both the rules are necessary rules of historical criticism. The aesthetic rule is the more heavily weighted of the two: there would be no reason to pursue distant contexts if they had not given some hint of their interest to present ones. Robertson's challenge to his community, however, was made possible precisely by the relationship of the two rules to each other. Robertson, as Howard noticed, did not entirely share the academic community's values. His clash with the dominantly liberal, and generally more skeptical, scholarly community had in fact demonstrated that their claim that understanding the past allows us to appreciate it is far from the whole story, failing, as it does, to acknowledge the heavier weighting of the aesthetic rule. It is, rather, an interest in some aspects of the past connected to some personal need that leads a scholar to try to begin to understand the old texts, but that need or interest is located in the present.

Muscatine, for example, hadn't noticed the aesthetic rule when, almost twenty years after Robertson, he claimed that to know the historical context was to love the literature. But Robertson had already called the bluff on that claim. His argument for the relevance of patristic standards of truth and beauty and the scholarly reaction to his claims had already exhibited the possibility that, if a text were understood entirely in historical terms, it would be found false and ugly.

It is ironic that Muscatine should lament, in his first lecture in 1969, that his ahistorical New Critical education left him badly prepared to understand history, because if such learning were possible, surely he should have learned something of the alterity of the medieval period from Robertson. Muscatine claims that "it is as history that we value medieval culture, seeing in it partly ourselves, partly what we no longer are, partly what we might be. As humanists we cannot escape being historians" (p. 3). Medieval life, he claims to believe, is distant enough to require special education and yet, when unveiled through the stratagems of historical study, will reveal itself close enough to be relevant as a display of possibilities for the world of today. The student of literature and history, then, can expect not only to reenter, imaginatively, a past world and understand what was valued in that world, but will have gained as well a speculum through which to observe the present world.

The difference between the two worlds, so Muscatine's claim goes, provides alternatives and therefore choices for the modern searcher after values. This is, of course, a classical claim for studying "the ancients"[3] and would, as Muscatine knew, also appeal to the students in his audience who claimed to be seeking after relevance. His rule is, thus, a gradient necessary condition:

GNC: Prefer the interpretation which reveals patterns from the past that can be understood as options for the future.

But when he gets down to the historical study he advises, Muscatine does not talk as Root or Robertson did about alterity, but as Kittredge did about the modernity of the fourteenth century. His description of the late fourteenth century in fact includes no examples of differences between that century and his own, but only similarities, and so it is hard to see how the comparison he claims to seek could ever be made from his own historical scholarship. His discussion emphasizes disruptions such as the Peasant's Revolt and the weaknesses in the church, suggesting that Chaucer lived during a period of crisis not entirely different from that of the 1960s. Then, through close readings of individual texts, he argues that Chaucer's ironic style was a fitting response to a world in which public morality and traditional Christian values were largely out of joint. Listen to the 1960s language:

> Chaucer's crowning ironic stance...emerges from a lifetime of feeling and of coming to grips with the alternative value systems that his culture offered. He tried, he tested, he experimented, he compromised, and even had moments of pessimism and failure....Apart from his perception and sympathy with life, Chaucer's great virtue is morale. It is a morale that is based, not on a doctrinaire conservatism, but on a felt acquaintance with all the alternatives. (p. 144)

Having acknowledged the limitations of his historical education, he produces a thumbnail interpretation of the fourteenth century, demonstrating how easy it is to select relevant historical constructs and ignore others.[4]

But even if it is granted for a moment, as Muscatine supposes, that it were possible to recover a fair picture of intended meaning and contemporary valuations so that it could be known what medieval audiences considered true and beautiful, it still must be asked whether, if postmodern audiences were made familiar with these conditions, that familiarity would be the same as making them see literature and art of other periods as the original and intended audiences saw it. Would whatever had been self-evidently true and beautiful then be so now? The unacknowledged assumption here is that understanding guarantees sympathy. But on what grounds can we assume the continuity or permanence of standards? Surely it is more reasonable to assume that, even if I could see the world as they saw it, I would still appreciate medieval literature only where its values coincidentally matched mine, or where its standards could be made to match mine.

The weighting of the aesthetic rule, essentially a viewer-centered rule, over the historical (object-centered) rule assures that the potential conflict between the two within an individual scholar's work will almost never arise. If it arose in 1950 between scholars, it was because Robertson's rules were similar enough to those of the community of medievalists to assure him an audience, but different in an important way as well. Personal differences such as the ones that separated Robertson from other medievalists are crucial determinants of interpretations. Times have changed since Alison of Bath felt she had to apologize for reading her own experience as authoritative. Communication within the community, however, depends on a shared set of necessary and typicality conditions of interpretation. The community is vigilant in protecting its necessary rules, but the variety and piquancy of a community's scholarly production come from the variety among the scholars on typicality conditions. As the community of scholars grows more heterogeneous, the set of typicality conditions expands. We are not surprised that, as Chaucer himself knew, diverse folk, diversely will they say.

Resistance to change: The conservatism of the experienced reader

In their dependence on the historical rule, both Robertson and Muscatine were relying on the discoverability of the conditions of historical genres. Muscatine thought that historical criticism faced a problem in building bridges between the historical culture and current requirements. But as his own successful performance showed, that was not the problem. For critics who have the competence to choose their references and guide their transformations and inferences until they reach a satisfying and coherent pattern or interpretation, such bridges will eventually be found. Both Robertson and Muscatine picked their history to match their twentieth-century requirements. Patterns are constructed and then made to look as if they were found. On the evidence of these historians, we would have to agree with Harold Bloom that literary critics "in their secret hearts love continuities" (1973:78).

Accepting this view, however, creates a new problem. If competent readers will always find the pathways to satisfaction and coherence, then there should be no such thing as critical failure.[5] Indeed, the larger community of medievalists insured the continuity of their canon and their ways of making history by rejecting Robertson's rejection of one of their rules. They insisted that both the historical and the aesthetic rule were needed, and rejected as well Robertson's demand for a reevaluation of the canon.[6]

As it happens, however, medieval scholarship itself offers a useful example of exactly the kind of critical failure to perceive or create continuity which, according to Harold Bloom and Stanley Fish, should be impossible. We might conclude, if the argument for the theoretically infinite plasticity of critical inventiveness has been convincing, that we are simply faced with incompetence. The other possibility is, and it is this possibility that is our theoretical interest here, that aspects of the interaction of the processes and structures of information within the various mental modules themselves offer resistance to some of the proposals of the ingenious reader. The following example illustrates the interplay of viewer-centered and object-centered understanding and suggests that the distinction between literary history and literary interpretation may be described by whether one or both perspectives are in play.

The link between the Middle Ages and the Renaissance

The specific literary crux I want to explore here begins with a commonplace of literary history for almost a century now, itself a corollary to the traditional periodization problem of demarcating the English Middle Ages from the English Renaissance. I am interested in the epistemological problems raised by the claim—related to but distinct from the claim that Chaucer was a "modern"—that Chaucer was a poet ahead of his time. His powerful poetic vision and innovations are said, for example, by George Saintsbury in his 1898 book *A Short History of English Literature*, to have been appreciated by his immediate successors, but not successfully imitated or developed. His achievement, as the story is usually told, is not felt as an influence on English literature until after about 150 years of more or less mediocre literary production, until the period usually called the early Renaissance:

> [Poetry] had, after Chaucer, fallen off...*in a manner which has still rather to be accepted than accounted for* (p. 242, emphasis mine).... Chaucer had gathered up all the stuff and all the methods of medieval work in English verse, had added much of his own, and had left poetry in a stage of relative perfection. But the succession failed. Even men who were of more than man's estate at the time of his death, like Lydgate and Hoccleve, could not manage what he left them. (p. 308)

Nor do the next ninety years of literary historical scholarship provide the necessary account. In 1985 Cambridge University Press published A.C. Spearing's *Medieval to Renaissance in English Poetry*, which makes another attempt to deal with the same question. Like Muscatine, Spearing had always followed both the historical and the aesthetic rule in his historical criticism of medieval literature (see, for example, Spearing 1972). He was now tempted to bring to bear one of the most powerful of current American theories of literary influence, namely that of Harold Bloom on the question of transition. While it is fair, I think, to say that Spearing is not engaged by the crises of faith with which Bloom and his sources, particularly Nietzsche, contend, yet he is open-minded enough to be willing to look for a long-sought answer in Bloom's new model.

The failure of the attempt lies in the ultimate incompatibility of conventional literary historical scholarship with Bloom's self-advertised and thorough rejection of that scholarship. Although he had sought it, Spearing himself finally rejects Bloom's way of providing a continuity because it is destructive of a continuity more valuable to him, that is, the continuity of his views of literary history. His exploration of what Bloom's theory of influence might do for medieval literary history gives us a chance to observe the operation of factors that limit the revision of literary history by working to conserve already-in-place critical systems. We can see what forces might produce "error"—failure to perceive or to invent continuities. A less capable traditional literary history would present failures of a kind that would confuse the issue of resistance. A literary historian who hadn't attempted to meet in some way the challenge of contemporary theoretical thinking couldn't display for us, as Spearing's study does, the conflicts and resistance the clash of conditions of significance produces.

Spearing's dignity conditions and alterity conditions

In order to argue that Chaucer was at least in some sense, although not chronologically, a Renaissance poet, the first thing Spearing does is to set out his categorizations, that is, his understanding of the differences between the conditions that describe the Middle Ages and the conditions that describe the Renaissance. Among the conditions that describe the European Renaissance are a cluster of conditions that specifically describe poets and poetry. He has inferred from the prose writings of Petrarch and Boccaccio and from the Italian and English poetic texts that these beliefs were held by the Renaissance poets themselves:[7]

Conditions of Poetry:

GNC 1: Poetry is intrinsically beautiful.
GNC 2: Beautiful poetry is of lasting value.
TC 1: Poems are, typically, signed with the author's signature because, as Boccaccio says, "the songs of the poets, like the names of the composer, are almost immortal," and as Petrarch says, poetry gained for the poet "immortality for his name." (1985:6–7)

Conditions of Poets:

GNC 1: The poet is engaged in an exalted vocation.
GTC 1: The poet may even be divinely inspired.[8]

For obvious reasons, I call these conditions of poetry *dignity conditions.* From these rules of poetry and poets, other conditions can be inferred as consequences, among them, the growing presumption of the poets that they could and should give advice to rulers, that they thus deserved to be included within the sphere of advisers surrounding kings, because the reading of poetry, Spearing adduces from Boccaccio, is "a learned moral discipline comparable to the interpretation of scripture" (WFC) (1985:7). Furthermore, texts are worthy of preservation in writing, and should be available as written texts (TC). These last conditions depend, of course, on the growing availability of printed texts, and the growth of literacy.

The English sources apparently, do not provide the same kind of explicit self-promotion that Spearing found in the Italian, yet he is not without resources: he infers the existence of these beliefs about the seriousness of the enterprise of literature from structural innovations he observes in Chaucer's poetry. One set of such structural conditions are the innovations of diction that mark the so-called aureate or high style, and the care Spearing finds Chaucer to have taken to make his syntax elaborate yet clear and expressive. These, along with coherence of paragraphing and "rationality of structure" or simplification of stories replaced the medieval polyphonic weaving of plots and, he infers, attest to the new seriousness with which poets regarded their work.

Note that Spearing is here trying to build the kind of bridges Muscatine hoped could be justified. In order to strengthen his claim that the dignity of poetry can be inferred from Chaucerian rhetorical innovation, Spearing makes use of a metaphorical transformation of apostrophe, according to which the presence of apostrophe is taken to indicate the presence of poetic inspiration. Apostrophe is one of the rhetorical tropes Chaucer adopts from Dante's high style and which, according to Spearing, is not frequently used in medieval poetry before Dante and Chaucer. The transformation according to which meaning is attributed to the trope is provided by Jonathan Culler, who has convinced Spearing that apostrophe is to be understood as "a crucial indicator of the claim to poetic inspiration" (1985:25). Spearing quotes Culler: "One who successfully invokes nature is thus one to whom nature might, in its turn, speak. He makes himself poet, visionary. Thus invocation is a figure of vocation" (Spearing, p. 25).

These various structural innovations were reproduced almost entirely successfully by Chaucer's immediate successors. But if the presence of these specific structural conditions led to the assumption of the dignity conditions, and it is the dignity conditions from which Spearing infers the "Renaissance" status of Chaucer's poetic achievement, then how can he resist the inference that Lydgate is also a Renaissance poet? Spearing's answer seems to be that, although many of these dignity conditions and the structural conditions from which they are inferred are necessary conditions of Renaissance poetry, they are not sufficient conditions. Poems Spearing does not consider to be "Renaissance" poetry also meet them.

In order for a poem to be securely categorized as "Renaissance" it must, as well, meet another set of conditions, which as a group might be called *alterity conditions.* Spearing has adapted these conditions from Peter Burke, who discusses them as "the sense of anachronism, or sense of historical perspective, or sense of change" (1969:1) and considers them an essential feature of the Renaissance sense of history. Spearing understands these also to be necessary conditions of Renaissance poetry; he finds them in Chaucer's poetry, but not in the poetry of Chaucer's fifteenth-century admirers. He does not see them appear again until Spenser. Taken together, the alterity conditions describe an attitude toward the pagan, classical past which Spearing claims appeared for the first time in the Renaissance and reappeared in later neoclassical periods as well. They can be described by three gradient necessary conditions, inferred by Spearing from Chaucer's poetry:

GNC 1: The Renaissance poet demonstrates "a recognition of the difference, the alterity, of the culture of classical Rome, as something which possessed its own autonomy but which had not been authentically transmitted through the intervening centuries." (p. 11)

GNC 2: The Renaissance poet demonstrates "a sense of the possibility of bringing this culture back to life by means of skillful imitation...not merely mechanical but an imaginative re-creation of the classical past." (p. 11)

GNC 3: The Renaissance poet demonstrates "a sense of reunion with the past, a new recognition of the universality of a high culture which had been supposed dead." (p. 11, but see also p. 55)

Just as the dignity conditions were inferred from some structural innovations in the poetry, these conditions were inferred by Spearing from other structural changes he observed. The first and third are, as well, the core of Western attitudes toward history that have prevailed until recently, according to Spearing. He is impressed, for example, by what he considers a (relative) realism in Chaucer's poetry, that is, by the absence, by and large, of the fantasy, magic, and wonders that fill medieval romance. Spearing also infers a new sense of the difference between the past and the present in what he considers to be a relatively realistic, detailed, and carefully constructed pagan past in comparison to the Arthurian never-never land. For example, even though Chaucer is interested in the philosophical similarities and differences between Christianity and pagan belief and often uses his poetry to explore those relationships, still he "is careful never to let his pagan characters refer to specifically Christian doctrines" (p. 41).

With these categorizations and inferences in place, Spearing now makes an important transformation and draws a crucial inference from it. He sees a match between this new sense of history exemplified in Chaucer's relation to the pagan past and the recognition that literature itself has a history. At this point, the alterity conditions and the dignity conditions reinforce each other to describe the sense of the importance of a national literary tradition in which a poet might work, and to which new poetry, if it was good enough, would be added. By his references, transformations, and inferences, Spearing thus has painted a picture of a self-conscious and dignified poetic tradition with a father figure, Chaucer. It is at this point that Spearing connects his search for an answer to Saintsbury's question with Bloom's concern for powerful poetic fathers, as described in *The Anxiety of Influence* (1973).[9]

The Bloom connection

Perhaps it was the analogy between the negativity attached to the story of the transmission after Chaucer in the traditional version of literary history and Bloom's view of the negative relationship between understanding and innovation that suggested the match to Spearing. He sees at least two Bloomian arguments as relevant to his own problems understanding the relationship between Chaucer and his successors. The first is that poets who come later, who follow, are related to poets who precede them by a ratio of misunderstanding or misreading, rather than by understanding. Claiming that "poetic history is indistinguishable from poetic influence" (1973:5), Bloom argues, based upon Nietzsche's complaint against the killing weight of history and a Freudian understanding of the Oedipal tensions between fathers and sons, that a poet is always latterly, belated, later than a great poet (a powerful precursor) whose poetry he must actively misread. "The strong imagination comes to its painful birth through savagery and misrepresentation" (1973:86). If Bloom is right, Spearing seems to say, the successor poet is bound to seem as though he has failed to understand the achievement of the powerful achievers who came before.

Bloom's second claim is that the conflict between a strong precursor poet and his ephebe/disciple is necessary to clear creative space for the younger poet: as in the Freudian view of the Oedipal relationship between father and son the younger must mis-take the father, that is, must interpret the father as mistaken in order to feel free enough to be truly adult, fertile, creative.

Spearing begins then, to collect evidence about various aspects of the father's appearance, performance, and influence in Chaucer's poetry. According to Spearing, Chaucer nearly always presents his fictional fathers unfavorably, "either as absent or cruel" (1985:103).[10] He never shows, in fact he denies, that good qualities can be inherited from fathers, although bad ones can. Chaucer's own relationship to his literary forebearers is also relevant. Spearing sees him as "unwilling to concede authority"...to Boccaccio, for example, whose *Teseida* was the direct source of Chaucer's *Troilus and Creseide,* and who was "of the right generation really to have been Chaucer's father, and who was truly his poetic father as writer of vernacular narratives which aimed at an imaginative reconstruction of pagan antiquity" (p. 103). The well-known modesty of Chaucer's persona as a narrator in most of his poetry (the dreamer who knows nothing of love, the historian who cannot go beyond his sources, the pilgrim who just repeats what he hears) produces another relevant inference: Spearing sees the modest persona as evidence that Chaucer is "unwilling to assume paternal authority" (p. 103) for his own poetry. The evidence leads Spearing to proclaim

> an acute paradox. [Chaucer] is the first English poet to exist as an "author," the first to be known by name as the father of a body of

> work; and yet throughout his career he seems to be striving towards the culmination achieved in *The Canterbury Tales*, the relinquishment of his own fatherhood, the transformation of his work into a text. (pp. 105–106)[11]

Spearing thus claims that Chaucer's refusal to play fully the patriarchal, authorial, and authoritarian role caused "widespread anxiety among his poetic descendants about the impossibility of the task they were undertaking" (p. 107). One of Spearing's main examples (surely Saintsbury would agree) of the failure of the generation of Chaucer's poetical sons is the case of Lydgate. He argues that Lydgate misunderstood Chaucer's innovations and thus, even while consciously attempting to follow in Chaucer's footsteps and often succeeding technically, misses the point. Although, for example, he copied Chaucer's aureate style, he had little sense of its appropriate use, and never mixed it with a plain style as Chaucer did to great effect.

Lydgate's poetry, furthermore, is not marked by Chaucer's sense of history, by the alterity conditions. Without them, the dignity conditions, which *are* found in Lydgate's poetry, seem somehow pointless. What had to be invented, according to Spearing, was how to make use of a poetic father figure; there never had been one, and "it was doubtless impossible for Lydgate, never a thinker of great resource, to envisage any form of use other than what he calls counterfeiting his master's style" (p. 108). Spearing now attempts to argue a subtle distinction: Lydgate, he claims, wanted to be Chaucer, not to learn from him at a distance. Lydgate's poem *The Siege of Thebes* was intended as an addition to the collection of the unfinished *Canterbury Tales.* Lydgate indeed explicitly tells his readers that with his tale he is joining the host's tale-telling competition, thus there is little doubt that he saw himself as completing his master's unfinished business. Spearing calls this an act of "misreading or misprision" in the Bloomian sense. He refers in this instance to Bloom's use of the term *tessera* to name the relationship between an earlier and a later poet in which the later poet sees himself as completing an incomplete, a "truncated" earlier poem.

If Spearing's argument had been convincing up to this point, it is here, when he casts Lydgate into the role of ephebe, that Spearing's failure to appropriate Bloom's insights to the solution of his problem becomes apparent. First of all, the kind of psychological struggle with a father that Bloom envisions would not have to be resourcefully "invented," it would surely be inevitable, were Lydgate the ephebe, the son. Lydgate, however, is not the kind of strong poet, a "major aesthetic consciousness," that Bloom's theory deals with in an interesting way, and Spearing himself recognizes this (p. 109).

Bloom's theory of misreading, furthermore, makes a claim about the necessity of rejection and repression, aggression and sublimation in the relationship between poets, but Spearing admits that Chaucer's followers (not only Lydgate) show no signs of anything but reverence for their poetic father. Thus, according to his own historical analysis, Spearing has no grounds for identifying Chaucer's successors as misreaders. In case we needed any further evidence that Bloom's view of the struggle constituting poetic history is incompatible with Spearing's understanding of Chaucer, it can be found in Spearing's suggestion that perhaps it was Chaucer's own benevolence, tolerance, and understanding of relativity that made it difficult for his "sons" to rebel (p. 109).

John Skelton's poetry, one hundred years later, made use of Chaucer's breakthroughs in progressive ways. In it, according to Spearing, "the anxiety of Chaucerian influence is overcome" (p. 243). Although these arguments have a Freudian coloring, they are not Bloomian. No strong figure in Bloom's theory, precursor or ephebe, could *qua* poet, have anything to do with tolerance. Nor would Skelton be classed as a powerful reader of Chaucer in Bloom's sense.

In sum, Spearing was attracted by what may have initially seemed to be a promising analogy between varieties of the negative, but it did not, in the event, prove successful in producing sufficient new references, inferences, and transformations to solve his problem of why Chaucer has always seemed out of his time. Even though Bloom seemed to offer a solution to a problem and seemed, thus, to hold out the possibility of providing a continuity where one hadn't previously been available, Bloom's theory doesn't seem to have done any better than Saintsbury did in identifying the kinds of continuities Spearing had hoped to find. Bloom's continuities are of an entirely different kind than those Saintsbury and Spearing sought.

A reading more consistent with Bloom's theory might have considered Chaucer himself in the role of misreader, since it is Chaucer,

Spearing claims, who looks at the work of his medieval fathers and tutors (e.g., Boccaccio), whose own tales were the sources of *Troilus and Creseide* and *The Knight's Tale*, saying, as it were, "you've got it all wrong—you've misread the classical past, but I understand it correctly." Spearing actually argues this indirectly by separating out a group of Chaucer's poems which he calls "classical romances" (p. 38) as the poems in which Chaucer most clearly illustrates his recognition of relativity, of the distance between the fourteenth century and the classical pagan past. In these poems, Spearing could have claimed, Chaucer rewrites the older stories of his Italian father "correctly." Chaucer's fifteenth-century admirers were, as Spearing himself describes them, but bumblers. Spearing concedes in his Epilogue that until Spenser, for whom Chaucer the Father's language is genuinely obsolete and the alterity conditions are met, there isn't another strong misreader.

Had he made this argument, however interesting as an exemplar of Bloom's theory of influence it might be, it would not have advanced Spearing's primary purpose of explaining the gap between Chaucer and English Renaissance poetry. In the next chapter I will suggest why it was inevitable that Spearing, while he may have been willing to consult an American theorist where it seemed helpful to his project, eventually found that his commitment to an old problem of historical recreation weighed heavier in the end, causing him to abandon Bloom's conditions before he abandoned his own goal. Bloom's view, in spite of his claims, is heavily weighted against considering historical context and, if historical at all, only in the theoretically uninteresting sense of recognizing chronological priority. Critical flexibility, we learn from Spearing, has its limits.

7 Writing Literary History

Neoclassicism, Modularity, and the New Histories

> He makes me angry
> ...harping on what I am,
> Not what he knew I was.
>
> —Antony, in
> *Antony and Cleopatra*

To accede to Harold Bloom's vision of the poetic chain of misprision would be to give up the possibility of literary history as a separate activity from interpretation. Spearing, as we have seen, was not willing to dispense with the alterity conditions of his discipline, that is, the historical rule which assumes the possibility of hearing the voice of the other with at least some measure of ideological innocence.

If Spearing had questioned either the propriety or the possibility of meeting its terms, he would presumably have abandoned the search for continuities and differences between medieval and Renaissance poetry, since the search depends on the existence of categories which are themselves a product of the presuppositions of alterity that prompt it. But Bloom's theory is irrelevant to the conventional conception of periodization, which depends on identifying the common features of texts produced within a given time frame. Bloom isn't interested in the question of whether past meaning is in any way accessible to the ordinary reader. His focus is the exceptional reader for whom respect for the alterity conditions would be submission from the start; it would be a self-defeating act leading to paralysis of the creative powers. It is, in fact, a necessary condition of the description of strong readers that they do not allow a historical, that is, a past contextual understanding to dominate or limit their readings. What they "misunderstand" is precisely the necessity of observing it. Instead (as Bloom learns from Nietzsche's essay "On the Advantage and Disadvantage of History for Life"), they read an old text anew with less regard for the alterity of its existence bound to a remote time or place than for its usefulness (i.e., meaning) in the present.

The collocation of Spearing's respect for the alterity and knowability of the past with Bloom's romantic exultation of present creativity and the egocentricity on which it depends allows an interesting and productive analogy to emerge. The alterity conditions Spearing postulated as conditions of Renaissance poetry and the historical rule to which literary historians have traditionally appealed share at least one crucial functional condition: both express a conviction that, while the past is different, it is accessible, and that access to it is valuable. The dignity conditions, for their part, share two necessary functional conditions with the aesthetic rule: both insist on the primacy of the values within the context of the interpreter, and both assume that the standards of beauty are permanent. All four, furthermore, share an important condition: both the historical/alterity conditions and the aesthetic/dignity conditions assert the permanent recognition or knowability, through change, of whatever is valued: one can value only what can be known.

Spearing's own tradition of literary history claims to weight the aesthetic condition less heavily than the historical: remember that he was willing to ignore the differences between Gower, Lydgate, Skelton, and Chaucer in order to permit a description of a pattern of continuity between the fourteenth and the sixteenth centuries. The force of Robertson's argument had been to recommend dispensing entirely with the aesthetic rule in the interpretation of English medieval texts. Bloom, for his part, has almost no use for the historical rule while reading Romantic poetry. Spearing seems to have been caught in the middle: his interest in Bloom's thought suggests that he recognized at least some aspects of the limits of his own view of literary history, specifically, its being unable to explain where a poet of great strength fits into a stream of generalizations that are intended to cover the great and the middling together. His commitment to literary history, however, his belief that its goals are reasonable and achievable in spite of its having disappointed him on this issue, forced him to resist Bloom's vision.

It would seem, then, that literary historians are neoclassicists insofar as they assume that a patch of distant time can be understood on its own terms as different from and as a model for one's own. So Root and Robertson claimed, and believed they had themselves achieved. Kittredge and Muscatine wanted it both ways, claiming that it was "out there" and that we could grasp it, but then failing to notice that their grasp had turned it into something that wasn't so different from "our" situation after all. There seems to be no way for a critic or a historian to avoid the third term that must be introduced between culture then and now, and that term refers of course to the current needs of the interpreter for revision of the now, sometimes called ideology. Even where the glorious past is revered, this reverence is inevitably accomplished through the never entirely transparent eyeball of the poet as representative human being. Poets may ignore one or the other, but historians cannot.

Viewer-centered and object-centered understanding

According to the modularity hypothesis, both the classical historicist perspective, in which some kind of objectivity is attainable, and the romantic or self-centered perspective have cognitive and physiological analogues; understanding makes use of both viewer-centered and object-centered representation. According to David Marr (1982), from whose work the distinction comes, the visual system produces several distinguishable kinds of representation. Of particular interest to us is the distinction he makes between two levels of visual representation, the "2½D sketch" and the "3D" model. Jackendoff describes the first as representing

> the geometry of the surfaces visible to the observer—including their contours, depth, and orientation—so that it is more than a flat, 2-dimensional image (a "picture in the head"). But since it represents only visible surfaces, not volumes, it is less than a full 3-dimensional representation—hence its curious name. (1987:172)

The important aspect of the 2½D sketch for us is that it is viewer-centered. That is, the information it provides is constructed with reference to the viewer's position at the moment of construction. It represents only surfaces, not objects, and is probably not dependent upon memory. The construction of the 3D model, on the other hand, is surely aided by information already in the visual memory, even in making decisions about what constitutes an object. At this level, objects are represented as occupying volume in space. But most important, the 3D model

> is *object-centered* rather than viewer-centered: it makes explicit the shape and size constancy of objects, regardless of the viewer's position. It is therefore the level most appropriate for encoding an object's shape in long-term memory, so that it may be recognized on subsequent occasions....(The viewer is unlikely to see it from exactly the same position again.)...
>
> What is particularly interesting about the 3D structure of an object is that it is *hierarchical*: it represents the 3-dimensional structure of objects not just in terms of holistic shape (i.e., it is not a "statue in the head"), but rather in terms of a hierarchical decomposition of the object into parts and parts of parts. (p. 174)

Hierarchical decomposition means that in the 3D model, for example, the finger is understood to be a part of the hand, the hand of the arm, the arm of the body. The visual equivalent of chains of inferences about relationships are thus part of this model. If you see a part of a body (or of a familiar object) you assume not only the existence of the rest. You infer, as well, many characteristics of its physical disposition in relation to the part you've seen: if you see a limp, bloody hand in a movie frame, you infer a horizontal body. Jackendoff explains that

> this, then, is what Marr means by saying the description is object centered: through recursive elaboration, the position of the parts of an object are specified ultimately with respect to the main axes of the object as a whole and can therefore be specified without mention of the viewer's position. Of course, in integrating the object as a whole into the scene, its position with respect to the viewer must be specified. But this can be determined entirely by specifying the position of the object's main axis, and the position of the parts will fall into place automatically. (p. 175)

In the visual system, the viewer-centered representation and object-centered representation are both necessary to full visual competence. It is crucial that the construction of a higher-level model does not substitute for or supersede lower-level representation. The double coding possibilities here permit adaptability as does double coding between the conceptual and visual modes. Either one or the other is, at a given moment, able to provide the appropriate representation for a given function.[1] Notice that the opposite of viewer-centered representation in this description, namely object-centered representation, need not be any more "true" or "real" than the viewer-centered model. It is, if anything, less "real" since its three dimensionality is not present to the retina, but must be inferred. Its "objectivity" means only that it is understood in relationship to itself; it postulates object continuity. It constructs the hierarchical relationships encoded in the model so that the existence and spatial orientation of a whole object can be inferred from the perception of a part.

While this 3D model is the highest level of visual understanding, visual awareness ("awareness" is what we are aware of seeing, as separate from what we know by inference from what we see), according to Jackendoff, is projected from the 2½ D level. Visual awareness is, thus, viewer-centered. Even though you know (infer) a whole body exists when you see someone standing behind a podium, for example, your visual awareness is not of the whole body. Conceptual structure, however, the highest linguistic level, has its richest and most direct connections with the 3D model, so that we have the possibility of thinking and talking about objects as either viewer- or object-centered. You have no trouble inferring (imagining) the disposition of the occluded parts of what you see, and then no trouble talking about them as if you saw them.

I want to expand, for a moment, on the importance of the claim that the 3D model, even though we talk about it as a higher or more integrated level, does not function as a corrective to or substitute for the 2½ D model, but as an alternative, useful for different purposes, as this point will soon be crucial to the central argument of this book. The 2½ D sketch assembles and represents incoming perceptual information for immediate use, but does not store it. In order to move among objects, viewer-centered information is needed. If, however, all the information that passed in front of one's eyes were stored, the memory would very soon be full of out-of-date information. "Before resorting to almost any real storage, one must convert to something like the 3D model representation which is much more stable than the viewer-centered appearance of an object in a fleeting world" (Marr 1982:352). Where one representation fails to be relevant or functional the other can be summoned. Furthermore, either model provides some sort of resistance to the too easy acceptance of the other simply by virtue of its presence or possibility. The resistance or corrective comes not from the object-centered model but from the differences between the two versions.

This hypothesis about the processing of visual information is suggestive as an analogue to the pair of rules I have charted in the competence of literary historians. Under some conditions of significance, literary historians are interested in scrupulously excluding anything that might be understood as viewer-centered bias from their accounts of history—whether or not they can succeed in so doing. Under another set of conditions of what a historian might achieve, it is assumed that such bias either cannot or should not be excluded from historical interpretation. What I have been uncovering among medievalists, and what will be seen in this chapter from a further look at some current rewriting of medieval literary history, is the inevitability of the presence in all historical accounts of both viewer-centered and object-centered perspectives in more or less permanent tension. Attempts to exclude one or another seem bound to fail; the differences between old and new historians show up as different weightings of the two perspectives. This is significantly parallel to the double perspective in the visual system.

It is important to note that viewer-centered and object-centered perspectives do not overlap with nontechnical use of the terms *subjectivity* and *objectivity* in literary theoretical discussion because both types of vision, as understood here, serve the individual. The object-centered model is not objective either in being unstructured by or irrelevant to the individual. Nor is it objective in the sense of being unambiguous, because it is far from being monolithic. It presents a hierarchy of relationships between distinguishable parts of an object, but what unit will be considered an object is left open and is apparently responsive to the need of the moment. Thus we are free to infer several 3D views of an object or of a text, relating it to a number of expanding contexts. Different schools of criticism, then, would define themselves as taking up these distinguishable perspectives, all of them in different proportions both object- and viewer-centered.

That the two representations within the visual system are different and yet both necessary, that they apparently cooperate to provide information for different needs, suggests that any discussion which forces a choice between viewer-centered and object-centered history distorts the functions of each and the relationship of one to the other. The existence of these two levels suggests that, if the visual system can deal with objects which are in some crucial aspects independent of the observer by making the visual equivalent of verbal inferences, there may be reason to believe the brain has similar flexibility in other modules as well and can respect the alterity of new possibilities presented to it.

Speaker-centered vs. public language

The visual system, then, we might say, is built so as to keep a balance between public and private vision. The argument I want to make now is that a generalization of this visual possibility into the broader sphere of conceptual structure, or vision-as-knowing, while still highly hypothetical, is not "merely" a metaphor. I would not want to justify the exploration (strip-mining might be a better image) of the territory of cognitive science for just another metaphor of understanding. The analogy is, rather, presented here as a hypothesis about brain function and, more specifically, about the existence of a previously unspecified level of language structure. I find three distinguishable kinds of evidence that allow a wild surmise of its existence.

First, as we have already noted, Marr's evidence for the existence of an object-centered level of visual representation is the ability to recognize a familiar object when seen from a different perspective, even from a perspective never seen before. Evidence that this may be a generalized characteristic of the way nonvisual knowledge is stored in memory comes from the work of R. C. Anderson and J. P. Pichert (1978), who have studied people's ability to recall verbally presented information (stories) in a context different from the one in which it was originally encountered. Anderson and Pichert hypothesize that schemata, that is, patterns based on past experience of collocation and hierarchical relationships, mediate both the process of storage and the process of retrieval from memory. Schemata are not necessarily conscious (though they can be). It is assumed, however, that many schemata are shared among members of a culture and thus represent the mind's generalizations away from the specific detail of a single experience. This is, of course, how Marr characterizes the organization of visual memory. Anderson and Pichert's results suggest, furthermore, that details of a verbal experience that may not have been incorporable into the prevailing schema are still retrievable from memory. Verbal/conceptual memory might, in this view, be largely schematized, and schematizing would facilitate retrieval, but nonschematizable information is also apparently stored. This would be paralleled in the visual system by our experience of very specific memories (Wordsworth's daffodils?), which may be stored apart from and for reasons other than their value as objectivizations (i.e., schemata) useful for re-recognition.

Second, another parallel between the visual and the linguistic systems which argues for the reasonableness of the claim that large amounts of mental processing might well distinguish object- from viewer-centered representation is the asymmetricality of the two perspectives, relative to individual needs. As was earlier noted in the discussion of the visual system, both object- and viewer-centered representations serve the viewer, though in different ways. It is no news to readers of literary criticism that the situation is the same in the constructed understanding of a text. It was, I believe, Stanley Fish (1976) who first pointed out to literary audiences that even what counts as an object is defined within the context as whatever is an appropriate unit for attention. The object can then be related to a theoretically infinite number of other "objects," from musical styles to ideologies to other people. Each ratio will allow the emergence of an interpretation, but entail a characteristic exclusivity of attention. It is, of course, the viewers who are able to construct/recognize these units and these relationships, and who will choose among or revise them according to the relevant conditions of satisfaction.

This asymmetrical relationship between viewer-centered and object-centered understanding is expressed by Terry Eagleton in his description of the relationship of individual interestedness and objectivity in discourse:

> In order for the concept of "interested discourse" to have meaning, it is not necessary to posit some mythically disinterested discourse; it is merely necessary to claim that some forms of discourse are more objective that others....I am not arguing, it should be noted, that some forms of discourse are more objective than others because they are more *disinterested.* The delusive bond between objectivity and disinterestedness, part of our Arnoldian heritage, needs to be broken. Anyone who is not "interested" will never "see the object as it really is," if only because he or she, superbly untainted by all whiff of interest, would see no point in looking in the first place. The most simple argument from the relation of knowledge and interest is that if we were not somehow interested we would not bother to find anything out in the first place, not even the kinds of knowledge crucial to our biological survival. (1985:117)

Eagleton's appeal to biology is prescient. As we have seen, it is within our biological capability and in our interest to make use of two different perspectives. In vision, the 2½ D representation is the level of visual awareness. It is what we see, and need to see to avoid bumping into objects. We never see with 3D vision, although we think with it; it is an inferred representation, you will remember, which is equivalent to as full a visual understanding of the world outside and independent of one's body as is available. The postulation of a rule at a higher level than both these two rules, namely that all interpretation serves the individual, allows us to retain the distinction between what is more and what is less interested at the lower level.

This would allow, for example, Nina Auerbach's grounding of early feminist criticism in the critic's own experience to be brought into line with the account of interpretation given here. Originating in subjectivity, this feminist criticism chose to linger there because of the value placed on the individual perspective. Rather than rushing to conceal its "interested" origins, it dawdled, deferring universalizing generalizations as long as possible.

Third, my last argument for the existence of and significance of double coding throughout the interpretive system derives from the recent and as yet inconclusive struggles of feminist scholars with the assumption that, even if thought and feeling linger in an imaginary viewer-centered stage, this kind of thinking or knowing must sooner or later be abandoned for the sake of wider communication. Finally, it is widely assumed, only the 3D possibility of language allows the individual experience to be shared. I would be surprised to hear of a feminist theorist who has not thought about how or even whether the valued individuality of the female subject can be preserved in its transformation from its bodily, primarily nonverbal awareness into conceptualization and expression in language. "Language," in these speculations, is generally assumed to be univocal, hierarchical, object-centered, public, and capable of expressing only those propositions that derive from what is usually thought of as rationality.[2] Here is Hélène Cixous's famous attack on that kind of language, from her 1976 essay "The Laugh of the Medusa":

> Nearly the entire history of writing is confounded with the history of reason, of which it is at once the effect, the support, and one of the privileged alibis. It has been one with the phallocentric tradition. It is indeed that same self-admiring, self-stimulating, self-congratulatory phallocentrism. (p. 283)

Feminist scholars have proposed, however, that there is another kind of language representation, although it is not easy to describe. Call it, for the moment, as Cixous has, *écriture féminine:*

> It is impossible to *define* a feminine practice of writing, and this is an impossibility that will remain, for this practice can never be theorized, enclosed, coded—which doesn't mean that it doesn't exist. But it will always surpass the discourse that regulates the phallocentric system; it does and will take place in areas other than those subordinated to philosophico-theoretical domination. It will be conceived of only by subjects who are breakers of automatisms, by peripheral figures that no authority can ever subjugate. (p. 287)

I propose we begin to think of this language as the equivalent of 2½D vision. Indeed, the evidence from vision encourages attempts to describe and name it. As for now, though, definitions of the as yet undiscovered are difficult. We have some claims about what it will not be, and some guesses about what it will do. It will be more attuned to the body than to abstractions, less bound by the hierarchical logic of syntax and more expressive of physical experience and private emotions:

> A woman's body, with its thousand and one thresholds of ardor—once, by smashing yokes and censors, she lets it articulate the profusion of meanings that run through it in every direction—will make the old single-grooved mother tongue reverberate with more than one language.... Her language does not contain, it carries; it does not hold back, it makes possible. When id is ambiguously uttered—the wonder of being several—she doesn't defend herself against these unknown women whom she's surprised at becoming, but derives pleasure from this gift of alterability. I am spacious, singing flesh, on which is grafted no one knows which I, more or less human, but alive because of transformation. (Cixous 1976:289–293)

Julia Kristeva talks about this new language in terms that connect it to postmodernist art and to political dissidence. In it, a writer

> experiments with the limits of identity, producing texts where the law does not exist outside language. A playful language therefore gives rise to a law that is overturned, violated and pluralized, a law upheld only to allow a polyvalent, polylogical sense of play that sets the being of the law ablaze in a peaceful, relaxing void. As for desire, it is stripped down to its basic structure: rhythm, the conjunction of body and music, which is precisely what is put into play when the linguistic *I* takes hold of this law. (1986b:295)

There is no shortage of skeptics to point out the difficulties of the project of excavation or invention which these women have initiated.[3] What is being written about this elusive, underdetermined level of language is metaphorical in the sense that all path-breaking scientific language must be metaphorical.[4] Figuration is not only inevitable but desirable at this early stage of theorizing when the goal is to describe a level of language specifically suited to the representation of those kinds of truths that are valued before, and also because they are not yet fully negotiable in the public sphere.

If in Western culture this level of language has been unrecognized and unused, it is not going to be easy to locate it and get it into working order. The task is probably made additionally difficult by our having to coordinate the rehabilitation through the medium of 3D language which, at least for the time being, "speaks us." There are even now, however, genres in which this language, or something near it, can emerge—in poetry, and in fiction. The literary evidence of the existence of this level would offer an explanation for the quite proper reluctance of Cixous and Kristeva to assert that *écriture féminine* is essentially gendered, that is, linked to sex chromosomes. Both women acknowledge that men and women can write in this mode. Cixous, for example, cites Colette, Marguerite Duras, and Jean Genet as exemplars. Kristeva speculates about the appropriateness of literature to this enterprise:

> Is it because, faced with social norms, literature reveals a certain knowledge and sometimes the truth itself about an otherwise repressed, nocturnal, secret, and unconscious universe? Because it thus redoubles the social contract by exposing the unsaid, the uncanny? And because it makes a game, a space of fantasy and pleasure, out of the abstract and frustrating order of social signs, the words of everyday communication?...This identification with the potency of the imaginary...bears witness to women's desire to lift the weight of what is sacrificial in the social contract from their shoulders, to nourish our societies with a more flexible and free discourse, one able to name what has thus far never been an object of circulation in the community: the enigmas of the body, the dreams, secret joys, shames, hatreds of the second sex. (1986a:207)

Kristeva acknowledges here that since women more than men have felt the burden of "the sacrificial logic of separation and syntactical sequence at the foundation of language and the social code" (1986a:199), it isn't surprising that they are carrying out the most active research and experimentation, from which, eventually, both men and women will benefit. She describes this work as

> attempts, in the wake of contemporary art, to break the code, to shatter language, to find a specific discourse closer to the body and emotions, to the unnameable repressed by the social contract. I am not speaking here of a "woman's language," whose (at least syntactical) existence is highly problematical and whose apparent lexical specificity is perhaps more the product of a social marginality than of a sexual-symbolic difference. (1986a:200)

The outcome of this new work, according to Kristeva, is "of epochal significance:" (1986a:200)

> Through the efforts of thought in language, or precisely through the excesses of the languages whose very multitude is the only sign of

> life, one can attempt to bring about multiple sublations of the unnameable, the unrepresentable, the void. This is the real cutting edge of dissidence. (1986b:300)

The first steps of feminist scholars to identify this emergent level of language structure have already been taken. From their explorations, as well as from the analogy offered by the experimental results on language processing and the evidence from vision, we are beginning to explore the entailments of the hypothesis that the ability to take advantage of parallel kinds of knowledge without collapsing them may be a general characteristic of human thinking. What would this hypothesis have to contribute to the discussion of the relationship between literary texts and their historical contexts? I see it as offering support for my earlier claim that there are two kinds of knowledge about literature—one described by alterity conditions and the other by aesthetic conditions—and that they compete for dominance without canceling each other out. The dignity conditions of poetry and the aesthetic rule both are viewer-centered in that they derive from the consciousness of the viewer self-perceived within the context of interpretation. The alterity conditions and the historical rule are text- or object-centered. A higher-level viewer-centered rule insures that both serve the individual who needs, variously, both viewer- and object-centered representations.

This formulation allows us to acknowledge the fundamental interestedness of human cognition without having to collapse the lower-level rules and lose the distinction they describe. The double possibility is what allowed the eventual emergence of a temporary equilibrium in the arguments among medievalists in the 1950s and 1960s. Robertson may have had 2½ D reasons for poring over the *Patrologia Latina*, and yet presented his interpretations as object-centered, that is, as primarily representing a relationship between the text and its context. His crusade, resisted for a while by many medievalists, in the end can be seen to have been accepted as a corrective for an earlier 2½ D kind of historicism represented by Kittredge's "Chaucer-our-contemporary" approach. Muscatine, defending his 2½ D position, claimed a different version of the object-centered validation from the one Robertson claimed. He claimed instead to present a relationship between the values in the text as understood from the context and the values of his own, and his students', world. In the 1990s we are not surprised that these positions, different as they may have seemed at the time, and still do from some points of view, are all examples of the way viewer-centered perspectives can trigger studies that finally satisfy the alterity conditions of object-centered rules as well.

A crucial claim of early feminist criticism, represented here in Judith Fetterley's reading, can now be seen as having proclaimed that what male readers had been presenting as object-centered analyses were, in fact, 2½ D visions arising from and satisfying male needs to the exclusion of women's needs. Fetterley's own work demonstrates that resistance comes from the "I." Harold Bloom and Sandra Gilbert, each in their own way, make strong claims for the benefit to the reading community of a personal, even distorting 2½ D sketch as the heart of interesting writing. 2½ D vision is, for them, not a stage to pass beyond, it is the central value of their writing.

Interaction of the object-centered and the viewer-centered

Aside from the addition of a level of structure to the model of mental activity we are postulating as supporting interpretation, the above hypothesis crucially reweights the 2½ D and 3D levels in both language and vision so that, instead of the 2½ D being a step to be passed through and beyond, it is valued for the particular kind of knowledge it can provide. The relationship between any of the pairs of possibilities (visual/linguistic, viewer- or object-centered), then, could be said to be a cooperative one: each level will handle what it can do best. Or it might be a competitive relationship, as Minsky (1986) assumes it to be, and as seems to have been the case in the literary historical criticism we have been examining.

Postulating a competitive relation between alternatives as a source of new knowledge, Ernst Gombrich enlisted the support of Karl Popper,[5] the historian of science, who has described the dialectics of mind as that between hypothesis formation and testing. In his discussion with John Eccles (Popper and Eccles) Popper argues that we have various ways of knowing, and have to find out which one is best suited to a specific situation: "I think that the integration of the different senses and their mutual cooperation is very largely a matter of the mutual checking and mutual criticism, as it were, of one set of interpretations by another" (1983:435).

If this hypothesis is anywhere near the mark, it installs the making of mistakes into a theory of interpretation in the way Bloom installs misreading into a theory of creativity. Multiple coding, on the view being argued here, makes mistakes inevitable, productive of change, but primarily productive of a functional richness of interpretive possibilities. In the 1956 Mellon lectures, Gombrich spoke about "the sacred discontent" that arises as the result of the perception that the expected and the actual don't match:

> The hallmark...of the postmedieval artist is not facility, which he avoids, but constant alertness. Its symptom is the...many sketches which precede the finished work and, for all the skill of hand and eye that marks the master, a constant readiness to learn, to make and match and remake till the portrayal ceases to be a secondhand formula and reflects the unique and unrepeatable experience the artist wishes to seize and hold.
>
> It is this constant search, this sacred discontent, which constitutes the leaven of the Western mind since the Renaissance and pervades our art no less than our science. (1969:173)

Gombrich's formulation, with its emphasis on the need to find the solution that fits the particular person's perception at a particular moment, describes better than Popper's notion of refutation the way in which the conflicts between multiple representations serve individual contingency without triumphalism. Popper (1963) would toss out refuted hypotheses, but at this point the history of science and the history of poetry and art diverge. Bloom would not stop reading Wordsworth because Wallace Stevens "revised" Wordsworth's vision, nor would Gombrich banish medieval art from the galleries because its perspective was inaccurate. Perhaps we should conclude, then, that the insistence of readers on maintaining their own perspective in interpretation should not ultimately be a barrier to understanding and communication. One should be able to understand an issue from different perspectives without having to dismiss one or the other as wrong.

In the model of interpretation, then, I would include the following hierarchy of rules. Initially, biological self-interest determines those objects that will be noticed from among a field of possibilities. As has already been mentioned, the evolutionary argument assumes that the survival of the species is a testimony to its having evolved to recognize its own interest speedily and reliably. It is at a higher level of integration between perception and understanding that objects offer resistance—exist in 3D versions. It is at this level that learning from experience, and thus change, is possible.

There should also, here, be some possibility of learning from the experiences of others. The path of least resistance, however, is simply to misread. Muscatine provided one example of how much easier it is to misread, to head for the familiar and either reinterpret or ignore the rest. Feminist critics, too, while displaying the possibility of "second language learning," that is, identifying with male narrators and heroes, have complained about the pain of reading against the grain, and have generally preferred not to.

Feminist criticism is now widely credited with making clear how heavily personal experience weighs in the aesthetic rule—in the determination of what is interesting and important, in the determination of what counts as a fact. Auerbach echoes the Wife of Bath as she declares, "My own work and that of the women I admire give their allegiance to the messiness of experience" (1985:229). She emphasizes that the feminist experience has been diverse, "rooted in the mixed and changing conditions of the history that is our lives" (p. 230). She rejects detachment but also skepticism. The despair about what can be known of the world and history is replaced by an unargued, explicitly quasi-religious faith in the covenant inscribed in the flesh:

> Lives are our medium of exchange. Books are inseparable from the private experiences that authorized them, while these experiences take on the semipublic and shared quality of our books. Finally, this conjunction is the only gospel we trust. (p. 231)

Leaving space for the other

In order to understand what it would mean, in cognitive terms, to leave a space for the other to define him- or herself as different, we need to go back to cognitive home base: the making of categorization judgments, and thence to the inferences that arise from them. You will remember that any categorization is a matter of deciding to give the same name to two things that are not entirely identical. The question is: "Is *A* an instance of *B*?" And the answer is always yes ***and*** no. *A* is like *B* in some ways and different in others. Let's go over the steps of that judgment slowly. On the assumption that I understand (represent) both *A* and *B* as sets of conditions (necessary, typical, gradient, and nongradient), I then categorize each by making a preference judgment about each from the set of conditions and the relative weights of those conditions.

For example, I have promised to buy a birthday cake for Aaron on my way home from work. In the bakery, I see the usual set of white and pink iced confections, but I also notice the cheesecakes in another case. Shall I buy one? It certainly isn't what his mother had in mind when she asked me to buy a birthday cake. Could that cheesecake count as a birthday cake? You'd never find the recipe for it under Birthday Cakes in a cookbook; it hasn't got icing or roses, but we could write on it with chocolate syrup and put candles on it, and it is Aaron's birthday, and his favorite cake is cheesecake.

The first thing to notice here is that the ambiguity of the categorization judgment slows down the process. But slowing down a categorization is a privilege at the higher levels of cultural discussion, with survival (conditionally) assured; no enemy is lurking to eat me while I decide whether a cheesecake counts as a birthday cake. As an interpreter, I am using a cognitive process evolved to enhance survival in an extended, opportunistic way; cultural behavior is hitching a ride on already-in-place cognitive processes. Survival into the cultural spheres allows the luxury of considering alternatives without jumping to a categorizing conclusion.

The next interesting aspect of this categorization decision is that I am taking into account Aaron's personal preferences. In fact, his known preference for cheesecake would be heavily weighted in my decision. The weighting here is partially a result of my set of conditions for categorizing birthday celebrations as opposed to other celebrations on which sharing a ceremonial cake might be appropriate: on birthdays we expect to indulge the personal preferences of the celebrant. I add this detail here to show how deeply and inescapably any one categorization judgment is embedded in other categorization judgments.

So the first step was to introduce delay—same process, just slow it down. But it's the second step that is an astounding cultural innovation: before you decide how to weight the similarities and differences, *you listen to the other's evaluation* of them. Can you imagine a mouse asking the tiger if he was hungry? If he preferred rabbit meat to mouse meat? But when our basic needs are met and we're up to discussing birthday cake, our inherited categorizing equipment allows us to include someone else's weightings in our own categorization preference judgments. We have evolved, we might say, or learned, thus, to grant others the space for self-definition. And we might even extend this lesson from individuals to groups. We might just be prepared to ask others how they see themselves before reaching categorization judgments.[6]

This is just what has been happening in a recently ideologically aware America. Reevaluations of all kinds of categorizations are underway. Readers who are adept at making recategorizations are also learning to slow down the process and listen to others, and thus to include, in new categorizations, the weightings of others. The interest in academic diachronic recategorization (new histories) follows hard upon the social synchronic recategorizations that have been happening since the 1960s, as distinct cultural groups negotiate to redivide and share the cultural space of American life. The same social forces that prompted the recategorization and revaluation of different groups of Americans split autobiography into Eastern American, Western American, and European autobiography. It has also prompted literary historians to listen again to history speaking or, more precisely, to try to listen to different voices speaking from history. The ability to hear and take another's voice into account is now a highly valued skill. And it isn't so easy to do.

If you remember back to the discussion of Gerald Edelman's Neural Darwinism, he explains how neuronal populations can adapt to new environmental demands. According to his theory, it is predictable that cultural changes will arise in academic circles, or in what Morse Peckham called high culture. For one thing, this is one level of current social organization at which elemental survival is usually not an issue.

Furthermore, part of the self-definition of high culture has always involved valuing creativity and change. Learning to slow down the making of judgments and thereby to remain open to information from a variety of sources is explicitly valued in the classical sources from which the West inherits its system of higher education.

Here is one of those places that brain theory seems actually to be able to explain things we have intuitively known but haven't even tried to incorporate into an epistemological theory. The cartoon of the self-made rich man who snorts at contemporary paintings in a gallery and says, "I don't know about art, but I know what I like, and this ain't it," makes Edelman's point for him. He hasn't been educated to wait until he learns conditions of judgment and their weightings from the current arbiters of avant-guard culture. He doesn't delay his judgment to take into account the newest revisions of the code. This is not to say he is not "enculturated"—of course he is, and couldn't not be, but his social status has changed, placing him in a class for which he is not educated. Specifically, he hasn't been taught from childhood the value of slowing down certain kinds of categorizations. And when you have a set of categorizations (when you have learned to hate all the people your relatives hate), it is easier to keep doing it the old way. In addition to *South Pacific*, there is a substantial amount of literature—*Gone With the Wind* comes to mind—that notices that the ability to adapt to new conditions has survival value in times of abrupt and threatening change.

New historical criticism

Many of the new historical and cultural critics reveal a parallel between their attempts to listen to the voices of others who share their current historical context and their listening to the voices of the past by vigorous and colorful personifications of those voices. The critical metaphor has changed: a text was once a passive object, often a reflecting mirror located on the wall of social space. It is now an active, thinking participant. In a paradigmatic Stephen Greenblatt essay, for example, a Shakespeare play is seen to be "brooding upon" or "haunted by" (1985:114) an issue. The theater "elicits complicity" (p. 115), "appropriates," and "acknowledges" (p. 121). As if to reinforce this, these cultural critics are explicitly less interested in events than in the ways the events are spoken of, in whatever can be recovered of the voices of other people in other places and other times.

Myra Jehlen, in a programmatic introduction ("Beyond Transcendence") to a collection of new historicist essays, cites the attempt to understand various subjectivities as a founding motive of the new historical project. In the wake of the poststructuralist critique of the humanist's "representative man," she grounds new historicism in the following gradient necessary condition on interpretation:

> GNC: Prefer that interpretation which demonstrates a "recognition that the political categories of race, gender, and class enter into the formal making of...literature." (1986:1)

Jehlen's condition makes a vast difference in the thematics of the new cultural history. Much of the excitement the new essays generate surely comes from the entrance onto the stage of a whole new set of characters and their concerns. In addition to kings, clergymen, fair maidens, and old hags, they seek to understand jugglers, millers, peasants and cowboys, women and children, the black, the brown, and the red-skinned, too. This preference rule, of course, opens up the canon to include the literary and the nonliterary writings of the new cast of characters, so that in addition to new people and their interests we have a flood of new texts to read as well.

This project is dependent on new categorization achieved, as discussed above, by slowing down and listening, and it requires, furthermore, an account of the interaction of the alterity/historical condition with the dignity/aesthetic condition of writing literary history. As this was the conclusion arrived at on the basis of all the old literary historical work described in the last chapter, it is not itself new, though its neo-Marxist articulation is, and so is the awareness of the ways in which these forces pull the reader in opposite directions. Deconstructive critics such as Paul de Man (1971) described the conflict in metaphysical terms of despair: the two pulls would make both literary history and literary criticism impossible. But if we have learned anything from the cognitive evidence it is that in spite of their apparent contradiction when considered abstractly, a functional understanding of the situation of the interpreter suggests that both the viewer-centered and the object-centered perspectives are necessary. Furthermore, the tension between the two is itself productive.

Without making any such cognitive claims, and often vulnerable for seeming not to notice the existence of a problem, new historians avoid the Slough of Despond as if they were taking Popper's advice (1976) to remember that, though communication is difficult, it is not impossible. Furthermore, political acumen has led some of them to suspect that the deconstructive *mise-en-abîme* is too nearly an evasion of responsibility. But while they do introduce new terms into the discussion, and consciously seek new evidence, the processes of interpretation are not new.

The conflict between rules, as Sacvan Bercovitch sees it, works itself out in the new historians' essays in a "dialogic mode of analysis....They engage the conflicts at issue, rather than seeking either to resolve them or to rest in irreconcilability" (1986:ix). The gradient necessary condition here requires that the interpreter:

GNC: Prefer "to ground textual analysis in history;...to make history a central category of aesthetic criticism." (1986:viii–ix)

I take this to mean that the new historical critics aim to make the two rules play off against each other, instead of allowing one to dominate the other, forcing resolution. Howard Felperin (1987), commenting on the work of one of the most active and interesting practitioners of new historicism, Stephen Greenblatt, denies that the balance can be maintained. Unless it wants to admit to J. Hillis Miller's charges (1987) that it has learned none of the lessons of poststructuralism, new historicism must recognize itself as inevitably a conventionalism rather than a realism. What that means is that the aesthetic rule is inescapably more heavily weighted than its historical rule—so heavily weighted as to make clear the difficulty if not the impossibility of observing the historical rule. The point is, although 2½D vision does not actually usurp 3D vision, we would be in an infinite regression if the aesthetic condition is in fact satisfied by resorting to an old kind of history reading new data: what satisfies the new historicist's search for satisfaction and coherence is to assume the knowability and thus the usability of the historical material about the life situations of the politically powerless classes—at least as material for the production of patterns and inferences when collocated with literary texts.

Thus Felperin notes that while new historicists like Greenblatt are aware of the danger,

> such knowledge does not prevent them from going about their business of interpretation as if they did not, and from staking their own claim to interpretive privilege, albeit covertly, in the process. "I do not shrink from these impurities," Greenblatt writes, "but I have tried to compensate for the indeterminacy and incompleteness they generate by constantly returning to particular lives and particular situations, to the material necessities and social pressures that men and women daily confronted, and to a small number of resonant texts." (p. 266)

In spite of the effort to fudge the issue (how much better is it to have fewer problematic texts than more?), there is ultimately no way of escaping the need for privileged historical facts in any historical project. Which facts are privileged, however, has not only changed, but has changed by allowing the voice of the other to be heard. Thus, Felperin complains that, in spite of their denials, the rule of new historical criticism consists of this gradient necessary condition:

GNC: Whatever information is gathered from historical sources is treated as univocal fact and is available for grounding an interpretation of a more open and polysemous text.

Felperin's critique would be right except that the newly valued "facts" are not all equally facts. Some are more clearly voices, and their status is newly significant not because they are any more or less secure than the facts we've agreed are all relative, but because we value them as expressions of self-definition, and as such we are prepared to withhold judgment. That they emerge onto the stage of interpretation at all is a result of an agreement to let them speak, no matter what their status as facts. That's what I do when I agree to buy the cheesecake for Aaron: I don't decide that in some essential way cheesecake is birthday cake; I decide that in this particular case the best judgment is to buy the cheesecake. It is not a matter of fact, and certainly not of permanent recategorization. It is a matter of letting Aaron have his say, of suspending my views to leave space for his.

Lee Patterson, for example, for his essay on Chaucer's *Miller's Tale* (1987a), gathered as much information as he could about millers and their social status in a study of the resistance to social change in the late fourteenth century. Although fully aware of the epistemological situation in which postmodern historians find themselves, Patterson nevertheless asserts the necessity of assuming a "category of the historically real" (1987b:63). He wants to listen to what can be learned about medieval millers even as he recognizes that he cannot assume the univocality of his sources any more than he assumes that Chaucer's text is free of political swerve. Of course it would be much better to have a real fourteenth-century miller to swear back at you when you misinterpret him, but we're not going to get that. So our choice is to keep listening to the same kinds of people we've been listening to for a few hundred years, or to try to let some new ones be heard. A distinction can be made here, though it will be slippery, I've no doubt, between assuming the veracity of data or facts and trying to read in such as way as to hear what other people have to say. There is something to be said for the ethical value of bending over backwards to hear another person, even if we grant the inevitability of distortion, and even while we retain a healthy skepticism about historical data of the less personal kind.

The skepticism of poststructuralism toward data or facts does seems to have forestalled, in other cultural criticism, the traditional combing of the historical record such as Patterson has performed. Greenblatt, for example, normally offers anecdotal evidence, unsupported by the wide research into sources traditional historians would have produced as evidence that any particular incident was in fact typical at a given time and place. The implicit rule I read in Greenblatt's claim to prefer dealing with a few small particulars is that, given the difficulties of reconstructing past times and the assumed inevitability of the reader's bias, anecdotes are as serviceable as any other evidence that might be brought forth.

Further, given the increased indeterminacy introduced with each additional text, a social science-like survey or "coverage" of a set of documents—far from providing additional security to the interpretation—would further distance it. But beyond this gesture toward Nietzsche, neither Greenblatt nor Patterson is prepared to dispense entirely with some set of valued or authoritative historical facts on which to ground his new readings.

If Greenblatt has decided to use fewer rather than more of the problematic facts, Patterson collects all the data he can. Furthermore, when his research on whether millers were rich or poor, or were the enemies or the champions of the peasants, does not present him with the clear picture he had sought, he does not throw the evidence out of his essay, as an honest old historian also would not. He feels bound to report that "the particular role that millers played in the struggle for peasant independence remains enigmatic" (1987: 467). His aesthetic rule, however, allows him to continue interpreting: he can bring other evidence of what he understands people to have felt and present this evidence as even better than evidence of whatever the facts might have been. "Most important, however, is *the fact* (emphasis mine) that the peasants themselves seem to have seen the figure of the miller as capable of embodying both their grievances and their desire for an almost apocalyptic reckoning" (p. 468). This evidence, of course, is far from unambiguous itself, by any standards. Nevertheless, when we have in place a distinction between evidence, however compromised, of a person's self-definition and the evidence of material data also always already compromised, we have good reason to be more tolerant of the former. We develop our object-centered judgments by allowing others their own viewer-centered views.

In both styles of new historical scholarship—Patterson's with its introduction of as much of the old kind of information as can be had about newly interesting subjects, and Greenblatt's, centered on the presentation of an exotic anecdote or two—the historian has raided some previously hidden textual treasure trove (sometimes documents that for their simplicity and lack of connection with the higher social classes have been heretofore ignored by historians) to provide the reader of literary texts with new voices and images. These in turn suggest new categories, inferences, and transformations, from which new patterns and thus new readings are produced. The striking appearance of novelty in the new histories, I would claim, comes entirely from this kind of revision rather than from a new understanding of the relationship of primary data to interpretation.

The making of the inferences is, as always, guided by conditions of significance in the context of the interpreter, called, now, ideology. According to Jehlen, ideology is a "category of knowledge" which can "mediate terms—'subjectivity' and 'external reality'—that are otherwise irreconcilable. This amounts to a reversal of the earlier conception [of ideology as distortion]: Instead of obscuring reality, ideology now is just what in fact reveals it" (1986:8). This produces the following gradient necessary condition:

GNC: Interpretation must reveal the ideology which informed the text's creation.

Since, as Jehlen describes it, ideology is "the term that mediates the finite entities of text and context, and also of individual author and cultural history; that is a term that demarcates the limits of individualism and the imagination" (p. 10), then the job of a new historian is to reveal the culture's ideology at work mediating between the author as a producer of texts and his culture. Jehlen's rule, here, is not substantially different from Bercovitch's rule. If ideology is a mediator between culture and the individual, then the analysis of the interaction will perforce reveal the dynamic or dialogic as Bercovitch requires.

This is a tall order, demanding no less of today's literary historian than a lucid enough insight into cultural meaning of a past period to be able to understand how an author related to it, and how the literary text embodies or transforms it. It is also, however, an old order. It is a restatement of the historical rule requiring a critic to form an interpretation such that it doesn't conflict with the functional genre conditions (i.e., the expression of meaning) of the period in question.

One more necessary condition sets even higher goals. The project of the new historians is distinguished from the old by their commitment to an understanding of interpretation as cultural work or praxis—a belief that their effort as historians actually engages with prevailing ideologies and thus can have a positive influence in the social sphere. Jerome McGann explains the failures of the old school as a result of its self-conception "in a recollective frame....Thus 'referentiality'...tended to be construed as bearing upon persons and events which lay behind us, in a completed form of pastness...." He thus proposes this condition for the new histories:

> GNC: "Any present deployment of historical criticism will have to renovate the original program....The picture which the historical critic makes is one which includes a future as well as a present and a past." (1985:10)

Jehlen also assumes that "the central purpose of ideology [is] to connect ideas to social action and that ideology represents not just meaning, but the realization of meaning in the world" (1986:14). Bercovitch expresses this same heavily weighted typicality condition of new historicism, namely the commitment to change the future, as a consequence of his belief that "language has the capacity to break free of social restrictions and through its own dynamics to undermine the power structures it seems to reflect....[Since] aesthetic structures shape the way we understand history, so that tropes and narrative devices may be said to use historians to enforce certain views of the past" (1986:viii), it is the task of literary historians, Bercovitch says, to produce interpretations

> GNC: "not just to show how art transcends culture, but also to identify and explore the ideological limits of their time, and then to bring these to bear upon literary analysis in such a way as to make use of the categories of culture, rather than being used by them." (p. viii)

Listening to others

Patterson's essay presents an elegant and original proposal about meaning in Chaucer's *Canterbury Tales.* His achievements and failures say much about the difficulty of meeting Bercovitch's necessary condition. Quoting R. K. Root and E. T. Donaldson, he begins his essay by inserting his own scholarship into the traditional debate about Chaucer's relationship to his cultural and political surroundings. Most modern readers of Chaucer testify that, even six hundred years later, they can identify with him and his concerns, they can understand his reactions. What, Patterson asks, induces readers to feel that they are in the presence of a "transhistorical consciousness" (1987a:458)?

Muscatine located the source of Chaucer's "uncanny ability to present himself as...historically undetermined" (Patterson's words, p. 458) in the pervasive irony of the poetry which had its roots in the social crises of the late fourteenth century. Patterson takes up the suggestion, developed by a series of scholars after Muscatine, that it was Chaucer's own ambiguous social position that gave him the kind of freedom that allows an ironic or detached overview. He counters their claims, however, with different historical evidence leading to a different conclusion about Chaucer's social position.

Earlier scholars, he claims, studying conventional historical records that are mostly silent about the underclasses of society, ignored the revolutionary turbulence of the rural population which was beginning to get its hands on some of the surplus value of its own labor, and was hankering for more. Considering the peasantry as an inert mass rather than as a reagent in the social chemistry of the period led them, he claims, to overestimate the clash between the courtly aristocracy and the urban bourgeoisie. His own research, following Jehlen's first preference condition suggesting he look at different historical sources, convinces him that these last two were, in fact, more likely to have been aligned against an increasingly belligerent peasantry than set against each other. The real threat to social stability, he argues, came not from the new mercantile class in the cities but from the lower classes in the countryside; it was directed against the court, the church, and the merchant bourgeoisie alike.

This inferred realignment is installed in the essay and privileged as historical fact in accordance with Felperin's condition. It allows Patterson to make new inferences about individual tales, and most important, to propose a new explanation for Chaucer's arrangement of *The Canterbury Tales*—their sequence and its meaning being a long-debated and never convincingly interpreted critical problem in Chaucer studies. The order of the tales, Patterson argues, reveals Chaucer's sympathy with the claims of the underclasses for a share in the power and prosperity of their world but, as well, his fear of that power. In Patterson's proposed ordering, the *Tales* present a sympathetic portrait of peasant values but follow it with a "containment" of the threat of peasant self-assertiveness. Finally, the apolitical Parson is called in; his sermon puts everyone in his eternally right place.

Patterson begins by referring to the widely held view that Chaucer's positioning of the first two tales—*The Knight's Tale* followed by *The Miller's Tale*—accomplishes an undercutting of the courtly values of the first tale by parodying them in the second:

> It is my argument that the *Canterbury Tales* stages Chaucer's rejection of the cultic values of the courtly world in explicitly political terms with the Miller's *quiting* of the Knight. But this embrace of peasant self-confidence is immediately registered as threatening, and the subsequent development of the Tales serves to contain this threat—a containment that is accomplished first by the Wife of Bath, with her privileging of a socially undetermined (and politically inert) subjectivity, and then in the complementary tales of the Friar and the Summoner, in which peasant self-assertiveness is both dissipated into internecine squabbling among ecclesiastical agents and appropriated, at the end of the Summoner's Tale, by seigneural authority. (p. 465)

At the heart of his argument is a reading of *The Miller's Tale* in which Chaucer's sympathy with natural law over class domination is revealed. The victims of the joke are parodic representatives of the court and the church. If the church had long taught the natural rightness of class distinctions, then the Miller presents the other side of the argument, much like the one presented in the well-known rhyme associated with the Peasant's Revolt of 1381: Whan Adam delved and Eve span / Who was then a gentleman?

> In place of the Knight's paranoid insistence on the continual need for supervision and constraint, the Miller describes...a world that shatters all efforts at confinement but that nonetheless contains its own principle of equilibrium in a sense of natural fitness and decorum. In locating at the thematic center of his Tale a benign, virtually prelapsarian *lex naturalis*, the Miller is thus reversing the terms of antipeasant defamation. Far from being fallen and degraded, nature here serves as a beneficent and supportive principle; far from being in need of compensation by the lex positiva created by men, the *lex naturalis* is seen as providing an unerring standard....Nature provides a self-evident norm of fairness, an originary and still authoritative principle of equality. (p. 474)

The generous but subversive lesson taught here is soon suppressed, Patterson continues, by the order of the Tales that follow: "As soon as the claims of the peasant class consciousness are put forward they are countered" (p. 482). Patterson argues against a large proportion of earlier criticism that, in spite of the signs of Chaucer's "turning away from the dominant ideology" (p. 464), ultimately he "places his poetry in the service of the dominant merchant patriciate from which he himself originally derived" (p. 483).

Patterson details the ways in which one tale requites another until, by the end,

> the true forces of social change abroad in Chaucer's historical world are...definitively disarmed, and we retreat into a world of aesthetic appreciation, in which peasant energy, however potentially threatening, is reduced to a playful manipulation of the images of the official culture that leaves the realities firmly in place. (pp. 486–487)

Patterson's literary history is most clearly new in its exploration of previously unnoticed sources of cultural meaning in its study of one group of peasants, the millers, and in its attempt to fit the peasant class into an understanding of the social dynamic of the period. Many other aspects of his argument show this sensitivity to the realities of the power structure as opposed to earlier understanding of it, based on more partial sources, both contemporary and modern. We saw this kind of innovation in the essays studied in Chapters 2 and 4, which change the literary system by introducing the new categories of race, gender, and class. The new historical dedication to opening up the categories of readers and of classes of people to be considered as audiences and as powerful markers on the chess board of social existence subsequently opens new spaces for inference and patterning, as Patterson's essay reveals.

Patterson's essay also meets the necessary condition of new historical study as described by Jehlen in that it understands its main project as the explication of the ideology that informs the text. Patterson, in an early parenthesis, tells us exactly what he means by ideology: "Not simply a crude false consciousness but rather an organized system of beliefs, meanings, and values by which people endow their world with significance and thereby make it accessible to practical activity" (p. 458).

Making the world accessible to practical activity is what Jehlen called "mediation between subjective and external reality." Ideology is the medium that relates the individual to the collective so that each can influence the other. Ideology, it is further claimed, channels the flow of power and control within a society, such that articulating the structures of ideology is a way of tapping into that flow of power and perhaps then, being able to change its direction.

Has Patterson, then, produced an analysis that answers to the necessary condition Bercovitch claimed for a new historicism—has he achieved "a dialogic mode of analysis" in which social forces "engage" aesthetic form and vice versa? Certainly Patterson has made an effort to listen to voices from the past that had been effectively silenced by the focus of earlier criticism. How successful he was is difficult to know. He has also made a respectable argument that social conditions (granting him that they were as he infers them to be) influenced the aesthetic form of *The Canterbury Tales.* That the literary text had any influence on the social world would be much more difficult to argue. Even if we were to grant that the literary presentation of subversion and subsequent containment serves a ludic purpose in the social world, the claim that a text had "contained" or forestalled change and reinforced the power structure in which its author had a stake would be virtually impossible to demonstrate.

What could possibly count as evidence that a text restrained the subversion it itself suggested? That there was no such subversion? Indeed, for a good while after, if we may credit conventional history, the urban bourgeoisie continued to dominate the rural peasants. But of course, eventually, there was subversion; there was change. I cannot imagine how one would go about even arguing, much less demonstrating, the relationship to any specific text of the social changes that came about in the centuries subsequent to the text.

We would have to conclude then, even if we accept all of Patterson's arguments, that while his own dialogue with the past has amplified previously unheard voices, the dialogics between Chaucer's text and its social context have not been revealed to be any less one-way than those described by traditional historical argumentation. In spite of his use of the verb *stages* ("*The Canterbury Tales* stages Chaucer's rejection...") instead of the traditional *reflects,* Patterson has not gone beyond a demonstration, very much in the mold of Robertson and

Muscatine, that the rhetorical pattern of Chaucer's poetry is homologous with its creator's relationship to his social world.

Might Patterson have met McGann's condition that criticism engage to change the future by his own critical text? Like Sandra Gilbert, he seems, in the end, to have been used by old categories. Both read their texts as ultimately reinforcing old hierarchies—flirting with protest or revolution, but ultimately rejecting them. Gilbert, however, pessimistically claimed the inevitability of women's failure to escape their fathers. Patterson at least refrains from arguing the inevitability of Chaucer's conservatism, though it is in some ways odd to find him rejecting the opinion of generations of Chaucer scholars who saw the poet as a prophet, indeed as a midwife to the new world of the Renaissance. Greenblatt, as well, in the epilogue to *Renaissance Self-Fashioning,* acknowledges with regret that he found, instead of evidence of self-fashioning, evidence that individuals had little freedom to change the ideology in which they lived, or to influence the social praxis around them.

The new historical project of first abandoning the unifying myth of a transcendental man for an appreciation of the multiplicity of interacting social categories and, second, of committing themselves to use ideology to make a difference in the world has thus been only partially accomplished; critics are listening to different voices. Fetterley hoped consciousness was power, but at least some of the new pluralists find determinism where there might have been subversion and change. We have seen in the essays on *Hamlet*, and here again, that it is virtually impossible to stand behind a claim that a text has had an influence in the building of ideology, nor is it easy to write a critical text that would have an influence on the context of the critic.

Yet the danger of solipsism seems to have been reduced. The literary argument about whether Chicano critics read what feminist critics write joins the broader cognitive problem about how understanding and learning of something new takes place. What begins to emerge here is a way of explaining the widely shared intuition that, in spite of pandemic and often tragic misunderstanding between people, it seems occasionally to be the case that some people can at least partially understand some other people. The recategorization rule that permits this will surely be strengthened as we practice it and teach students to value it. The separations of the modularity hypothesis and the translation processes they suggest have provided a starting place for a fuller exploration of the issue.

The modular mind itself, then, is the cognitive equivalent of "ideology." It mediates between the individual's specific life experience as recorded in memory, and the world as it impinges on the individual. However, its processes, and here is the hope for the commonality amid diversity on which mutual understanding depends, are not all equally subject to ideological swerve. Some are wired to understand more objectively than others. It is the combination, as we have already seen, of the entirely modular processors, uninfluenced by experience and therefore open to novelty, acting alongside at least two separable higher-level processes that *are* subject to the influence of experience, and thus ideology (but differently subject to it) that permits learning and thus permits such intercourse as exists between minds and the world and between minds and other minds.

8 The Dynamic of Freedom and Compulsion

> There's sap in't yet.
>
> —Antony, in *Antony and Cleopatra*

> My desolation does begin to make
> A better life.
>
> —Cleopatra, in *Antony and Cleopatra*

> Happy is your grace,
> That can translate the stubbornness
> of fortune
> Into so quiet and so sweet a style.
>
> —Amiens, in *As You Like It*

The echoes of *Antony and Cleopatra* that haunt this study were meant to add a whiff of Shakespeare's authority to my claim that the creativity of change emerges from multiplicity and flexibility. As the play does, so I hope this study will invite speculation about the entanglements of constraint with freedom. In the tragedy, fatalism overwhelms immortal longings: Enobarbus reads Antony's assertion of hope ("there's sap in't yet") as he plans one last campaign to retain his place in the Roman triumvirate as pathetic self-delusion. He thinks that Antony cannot avoid his fate, seeing his faith in himself as "a diminution in our captain's brain"—a futile attempt to "outstare the lightning" (III.xiii). Much of the evidence here supports the attribution of Antony's tragedy to his brain. He was able, if only momentarily, to raise some resistance to the expectations of others but was, at the last, consumed by them. Only death provides escape from living within a culture. The better life Cleopatra sees emerging from her desolation is a life after death.

The desolations of American life in the 1960s and 1970s are marked in many of the essays I have discussed in this book. I began this study assuming that I would find the contribution of the genetic inheritance to interpretation to weigh on the side of determinism, as an ally of cultural compulsion and against human illusions of freedom. I began convinced that it was naive to assume that a literary critique could act in the world, but the modularity hypothesis (whatever the status of the specific competing claims made by its various adherents), as modelled by preference rules, has allowed the rudiments of a more complex picture to emerge. Biology does, apparently, allow us to make a better life; and, furthermore, if we are going to make a better life, we are going to do it in certain biologically determined ways. I add thus, at the head of this chapter, Amiens's appreciation of Duke Senior in the forest and venture to claim, as an interpretation of the evidence I have gathered here, that stubbornness of fortune can, now and then, be translated into quiet and sweetness.

The model of the modular mind, with its hypothesis of gaps between modules and also between levels of processing within modules, has allowed the display of a system of perception and thought that both produces and at the same time works at compensating for instability. Not only can we see how the semantic structure of a category (a type) or an individual text (a token) is bound to produce the permanent supplementarity of meaning that destabilizes all naming, as the poststructuralists argued, but we can also see that the gaps in the interpretive system, far from being accidental, are necessary and innate aspects of our genetically inherited epistemological equipment. While no amount of bridging will succeed in permanently closing the gaps, large stretches of mental life are devoted to finding temporarily satisfactory connections.

Structures of information from different modules that are only partially comparable or even contradictory need to be brought into at least approximate registration; furthermore, there are at least two levels within each module (the number *two,* admittedly, is a placeholder for an unknown number of levels) that have different functions and produce competing representations. Continual negotiation between them is necessary to the stability of the organism, although the competition itself permanently threatens that stability. Change has always just occurred, and is just about to occur in a dynamic of change and stability that can be read as either comic or tragic.

The optimist might begin by emphasizing that modular processes, built to deal with information that has not been encountered before, provide the crucial entry for novelty. Unrestrained by the drag of memory to which they have no access, they respond quickly and automatically. Free of the influence of already-established patterns that may even refuse to recognize the importance of new data, modular processes react without prejudice and are thus paradigmatically "open-minded." They don't think or abstract or generalize. They are entirely self-centered in that they can respond only to what is presented to the intake mechanisms of the body (eyes, skin, etc.). They produce masses of messages, according to which the body can appropriately reorient itself in relation to its constantly changing environment. The relationship of one message to another is purely chronological and value-free. Ultimately, "thought" occurs. Many threads are woven together; past experience is brought to bear, double coded information can be translated, possibilities visualized, logical inferences and deductions produced. Nelson Goodman calls this "world making"; psychologists, such as Jean Piaget and more recently Jerome Bruner, call this "accommodation" and "construction," respectively, stressing the actively adaptive power of the individual. Our mental structure, fortunately, as they see it, allows us to learn to cope in a threatening and complex world.[1]

Pessimists, however, might sense something self-defeating about our powerful ability to accommodate, especially where high culture is concerned. They ask whether we might not accommodate too quickly, thus failing to leave room for the strangeness of the other—especially since it is this very strangeness that we found so attractive in the first place.[2] If our modular processes cannot resist seeing, feeling, hearing sounds, etc., then the body is virtually victimized by outside stimuli. Those little bits of modular information, on this view, don't stand much of a chance of resisting the already-in-place paradigms. Surely in the central processes where memory governs, it could be said that prejudice reigns. Old paradigms or schemata insure that new data will be read in old ways, or may even refuse to recognize new data if they cannot be brought into relationship with an already-in-place schema.[3]

The questions of how much freedom individuals can wrest from their environments and who benefits thereby remain deeply problematic, and I certainly cannot claim to have answered them here. I will be happy simply to have indicated their complexity. Much recent critical discussion has emphasized the politically repressive effects of the received cultural paradigms or discourses while ignoring the parallel need of communities for secure communication. It is demagogic, however, not to acknowledge that the need to reduce the risk of miscommunication is often compelling. It is not prima facie idiocy for communities to develop a jargon, that is, a set of stipulated definitions to which all members of the community consent. It is an advantage, for example, within the community of neurologists, for all members to agree on what the *corpus callosum* is. If we all can see the benefits of a smoothly functioning society, however, we can also see the individual loss that occurs when *smooth* becomes *smother*. The trick, of course, is in knowing how to retain flexibility and freedom where that is an advantage, while consenting to be governed elsewhere. How far can we agree to a social contract without being overtaken by repression?

I would claim that the evidence surveyed here supports the proposition that dominant cultural paradigms are not the only forces of structuration in human life. They are engaged in a constant struggle to maintain a society's political existence and its communicative systems, as against the resistance mounted by the needs of individuals to recategorize, reorganize, repair, reform, remake, and reenvision in potentially antisocial directions.

The inevitability of contradiction

The examples of interpretation we have examined here demonstrate that new interpretations don't make "progress," as it were, not even toward greater internal consistency, let alone toward some kind of settled and correct understanding. We have seen how an innovative reader, prompted by dissatisfaction with an unstable and unsatisfying interpretation or by an external change of a personal or a political kind, adds a new rule or revises a rule in his or her literary system. The reader who has added a rule, however, makes no attempt at the housecleaning that would judge the compatibility of the new and the old. Thus, we saw Cox proposing a new category, but it was left to Krupat to call attention to an inconsistency between the new rule and an old one about which books would be considered canonical. Krupat also challenged the first half of Cox's well-formedness rule, according to which "the author, writing the story of his or her life, is revealed to be a self-made person." But Krupat, in turn, is himself similarly inconsistent, ignoring, for example, women's diaries. Fetterley changed the reliable narrator rule but left the conventions of realism in place although they were also taught to her by untrustworthy interpreters. Girard's reading of *Hamlet* argued that Shakespeare had given us enough clues to sanction a rejection of the genre, but failed to consider the implications of not having a genre by which to read. Gilbert reweighted imaginative transformation as a form of argument, but repeated the very error she identified as George Eliot's in her own acceptance of the Freudian myth. Spearing accepted Bloom's aesthetic rule without noticing its inevitable conflict with his historical rule. The new historians embrace Jehlen's rule about race, class, and gender, without noticing how it conflicts with the conventional or communal base of mutual understanding they, as poststructuralists, assume.

The new rule or changed rule, of course, receives the attention always demanded by the new. Ray Jackendoff suggests that attention is expensive in the sense that it uses a lot of the resources of short-term memory. With a new rule occupying the center of attention, the interpreter of course benefits from the habituation that allows the old rules to continue some interpretive business as usual. One casualty, therefore, of the limited amount of short-term memory and the lack of attention that can be given to the old rules of the system is going to be the consistency of the system as a whole. As P. N. Johnson-Laird (1986) would predict (on the assumption that there is not an innate logical processor in the mind), it is difficult for the reader, even given a processing time of weeks or months, to envision all the possible interactions of all the old rules with the new one. The result is that a new system is never likely to be entirely internally consistent.

For the same reasons as the innovator does, readers may miss the inconsistencies. They also will need to pay most attention to the innovation and may not envision all its possible interactions with the other rules at work in the interpretation. This will be true for all readers to some degree, in spite of the special care some readers—editors, for example—may take. Wayne Booth (1979), in his plea for toleration between critical schools, concludes that while critical systems may be incommensurate, it should not be too much to expect internal consistency. My evidence, however, is that he is wrong: innovation may virtually entail inconsistency because of the nature of human brain structure and capacity.

Paul de Man argued for what seemed to him the inevitable appearance of discrepancy in all innovative literary criticism and suggested that it is "a constitutive characteristic of literary language in general" (1971:ix). Speaking of the New Critics, for example (though he makes clear that all literary critics are in the same situation), he portrays them as

> curiously doomed to say something quite different from what they meant to say....A penetrating but difficult insight into the nature of literary language ensues. It seems, however, that this insight could only be gained because the critics were in the grip of [a] peculiar blindness. (pp. 105–106)

He attempts to explain the necessary presence of contradiction in a new system in several more or less inappropriate ways. First, he claims it to be the inevitable result of "the impossibility of making the actual expression coincide with what has to be expressed, of making the actual sign coincide with what it signifies" (p. 11). However, this particular kind of "impossibility," that is, the potential gap between a preexisting system of conventional, probable meanings and any specific intended meaning does not even imply, much less entail, paradox or contradiction. It is perfectly possible for a speaker to intend exactly what the conventional meaning of the language is most likely to communicate; the permanent possibility of irony or hypocrisy being only that—a permanent possibility, but not a necessity or even, depending on the genre, a probability. The gap between the signifier and the signified, furthermore, cannot account for what de Man has, more by his rhetoric than by argument, declared a metaphysical paradox. It is more likely to produce imprecision and ambiguity.

Another problem with de Man's argument is that he insists on retaining a category of literary language, including both literary texts and certain kinds of criticism of those texts, as separate from non-literary language. In response, as it were, to Edmund Husserl's demand that philosophy be a critique, de Man proposes a transformation between ***philosophical knowledge*** and ***literary language*** on the grounds that both make "crisis-determined statements" (p. 16) which take their insights from their self-reflexivity, or self-conscious self-criticism, yet also reveal blind spots. What de Man seems to be struggling toward here is a recognition that the gap between the signifier and signified will be particularly problematic when the intention of the speaker, or of the reader for that matter, is to express a new and as yet unconventionalized meaning, *faut de mieux*, through the inherited conventional language. The problem is specifically novelty, which is a typical but not sufficient condition of the category of the literary.

De Man's argument proceeds mostly by transformation rather than by logical inference and suffers from its very high level of abstraction. The intrasubjective problem of using an inherited cultural code to express individual meaning is assimilated to the problem of the intersubjective communication of such unconventionalized meaning. There is no fundamental difference, in de Man's account, between literature and the criticism of it, and thus literary criticism is as crisis-ridden as Husserl's philosophical critique. The elegant abstractions like "poetry is the foreknowledge of criticism" (p. 31) are presumably the authoritarian (unargued) pronouncements which Lentriccia (1980:184, 300) resents and condemns as sentimental, traditional, and confused.

I am sympathetic with Lentriccia's objection to feeling bullied by rhetoric, but at the same time I believe that de Man's claim for the interconnection of blindness and insight has been as widely convincing as it has been because it is largely correct, even though it is overstated and badly argued. His examples were genuine, even though the reasons he was able to adduce for his insight were wrong. What de Man was noticing in critic after critic was the way a powerful and innovative rule seems to require the lion's share of attention from both the critical innovator and its first audiences. Inconsistencies seem inevitable between the new rules and the old rules (still followed habitually), which had in an earlier context been tried and found true.

Thus in the example of the New Critics, their innovative rule (according to de Man) was

GNC: Prefer the interpretation which discovers "a plurality of significations that can be radically opposed to each other." (p. 28)

The New Critics simultaneously valued (again according to de Man) an understanding of the organic unity of a text. This principle, however, was not a new one, but itself an inherited part of an earlier system of romantic criticism:

GNC: Prefer the interpretation "revealing a continuity affiliated with the coherence of the natural world." (p. 28)

That there is not, however, an entailed relation between the insight and the blindness is demonstrated by the clarity with which de Man himself perceived the contradiction, and the ease with which his readers have grasped his insight. The thirty odd years between their original formulation by the New Critics and their rejection by de Man would not permit this insight if language or language processing actually could enforce a blindness. De Man does seem, however, to have perceived correctly that when an individual, or even, as with the New Critics, a group of individuals, gives birth to a significantly innovating rule, there will be a cooccurrent blindness to the inconsistencies of that innovation with already-installed rules.

If, as has been suggested, this blindness is a result of the amount of space available in short-term memory, it would allow an advance on de Man's claim, fitting concurrent innovation and blindness into a larger understanding of mental processes. It deprives them, however, of some of the mystery with which they were invested in de Man's oracular language. It also explains why contradictions will probably be detected sooner or later. Furthermore, the explanation provided here allows the separation and the separate assessment of the claim (a reasonable claim, according to the modularity hypothesis) that the introduction of powerful new rules into the system is likely, for reasons of biological design, to produce contradictions which may not immediately be noticed, from de Man's less defensible claim that a particular kind of blindness allows a particular kind of insight.

In order to argue, for example, that it is the "very premises on which the New Criticism was founded" (p. 32) that lead to its characteristic blindness, de Man retells the story of the development of that criticism rather selectively. He assumes a distinction between causes and principles and then chooses a near pair from among them so that the pattern that emerges is at least rhetorically more rather than less paradoxical. He picks out W. K. Wimsatt and Monroe Beardsley's 1946 "rejection of the principle of intentionality" (p. 32) as a founding premise, and then matches it against the belief in the integrity of literary form that must be based on a unifying intention. Another historian of critical schools, focussing perhaps on the centrality of the new critical attention to form and imagery as the founding premise of New Criticism, would make de Man's paradox disappear.[4]

It is more reasonable, in the light of the model I have been developing, to recognize the many places in the process of interpretation where misses and error are possible. When and if a relatively coherent interpretation emerges, it is a result of many preference judgments adjudicating between claims that often involve conflict and blindness, even irony and inevitability, but inconsistency is further demonstrated by its eventual recognition. Krupat's reaction to Cox, feminist criticisms' development beyond Fetterley's rule, and the ultimate integration of some of Robertson's particular historical concerns into medieval literary history all suggest that if a specific innovation is considered to be worth preserving by enough people for whatever reason, it is eventually integrated into the relevant literary subsystem. This is not a principle of benign optimism but a reflection of the combination of human limitation and the mechanisms for overcoming those limitations.

The generalization is true on the larger scale of entire interpretive paradigms, such as the New Criticism or American deconstructive criticism. Like de Man's essay, Gerald Graff's *Literature Against Itself* (1979) is a good example of a study that is able from the perspective of time to expose the implications of a set of rules. Stanley Fish's (1973) view of the contradictory implications of stylistics is another clear-sighted critique. Ellen Schauber and I (1986) describe how an interpretive rule proposed by the French poststructural philosophers was changed to fit in with the priorities and possibilities of literary criticism in America. The later critics are not more perspicacious than the innovators, but in addition to having the usual less than altruistic motives for criticism, they have simply had time to think.

It must also be noted that at the same time as one new rule is working its way through the system, other changes are asychronically being suggested and accepted or rejected and partially integrated or revised in partially overlapping sequences. Claudio Guillén (1971) suggests that Fernand Braudel's temporal model (1958), which recognizes several different simultaneous durations, might help describe ongoing literary change: some changes occur in the short term, some take longer, and some take so long as to be difficult to perceive. The conflicts between nonsimultaneous processes of change can prompt further change independent of external political change.

The complexity of changes a literary system can be challenged by and can respond to at any one time suggests that no reader will ever be in control of a unified and consistent system, such that another innovation could be said to disrupt it. For any one reader, or for a reading community as a whole, "the system" probably includes some halfway or almost entirely integrated rules that had been new at an earlier stage, as well as rules, including of course conditions of significance, in various stages of obsolescence. Genre rules, for example, may describe young, middle-aged, or mature genres. Mary Louise Pratt, discussing the relationship between the short story vis-à-vis the novel, notes that the short story is sometimes found "being used to introduce new regions or groups into an established national literature, or into an emerging national literature in the process of decolonialization" (1981:187). She cites examples of healthy traditions of short story writing preceding the later emergence of novels in the history of social and cultural self-consciousness. In a given literary history, then, the short story might be an old and well developed genre, perhaps past its prime, while the novel is young and developing.

Pratt's data about short stories in developing national literatures is interesting in relation to the evidence presented here that genre changes and reinterpretations (I am thinking particularly of Girard's and Cavell's rereading of Hamlet and Krupat's influence on the canon of American literature) are potential sites of influence from texts to cultural life. Now that we have identified several such interfaces, further work can continue investigating the power of various aspects of genre not just to express but to instigate change. As we saw in regard to *Hamlet,* tragedy is a particularly recalcitrant genre from which to draw new inferences, even for readers who are committed to revisionism. Yet some readers of *Hamlet* succeeded. Whether their new inferences are widely convincing is a separate issue.

The claim that must be made against de Man's tragic view here is that the local details of rule changes at the margins of modules or between levels within modules simply don't support his overarchingly large, abstract, and pessimistic claims. I would rather read the modularity arguments as supporting a comic vision: things can be repaired. It is time now to bring together a list of the kinds of change that have been identified in these studies and their location in the model in support of that benign vision.

A summary of the possibilities for change in the modular mind

First, the study of categorical instability exemplified by revisions in genre names (autobiography—American autobiography—Western American autobiography) provided an opening insight into the complexities of human systems of knowing. By exposing the perpetual presence of contradictory semantic conditions and, therefore, of other categorical possibilities, the display of the categorization process provided by the preference model exhibited how any categorization judgment is weaker or stronger, but never an absolute. Since any text is only more or less a member of a genre category, a genre assignment is only the best one can do under the circumstances, but is never absolutely right or wrong. The presence of the other possibilities puts pressure on any judgment, and more on a weaker one. Contextual pressures, the theory goes, resulted in the reweighting of conditions of the genre; differences that had not previously seemed as important as similarities now seemed so, and thus new distinctions were felt to be needed. The examples examined here were of categorization judgments made primarily within the conceptual or language module, although they took into account categorizations within other modules as well. Visual categorization, it is assumed, operates on the same principles, and exhibits the same instability.

Second, the interplay between categorization and the inferences that categorization judgments permit were seen, in the essays on *Ham-*

let, to be a potential source of change—here producing a changed inference as the necessary functional condition of a genre. The inferences from genre, that is, the conventional meaning expectations associated with genres, are powerfully conservative, but powerful readers, in this case Girard and Cavell, were able to have it their way.

Inferences that control categorization judgments were the subject of attention in Fetterley's resisting reading of Hemingway. Because inferences are not entailed but are dependent on earlier preference decisions, such as categorizations, and on decisions about which details are to be counted as significant, they share the insecurity of those categorizations and are thus also permanently open to revision. The reinferencing that underlies Fetterley's rereading arose internally as a consequence of her refusal to continue to ignore the promptings of her kinesthetic sense. Her understanding of the plot led her to the conclusion that both mother and child were killed off, as it were, to avoid complicating the hero's life and self-image. For Hemingway, she inferred, their deaths were necessary, even good. Yet her kinesthetic sense provided a conflicting reading of what is and is not desirable, and she reweighted the output of the different modules. She refused to subordinate bodily identification to the demands of plot structure and conventional definitions of the hero, even though there was limited cultural prompting and no academic reward for her reweighting.

Third, the example of Gilbert's analogical argument, presenting a different kind of evidence, opened another perspective on changes apparently instigated by competition between the representational possibilities of the different modules. Gilbert demonstrated the power of associative or analogical thinking and, as well, the power of established theoretical models to limit analogy. Her interpretation of Eliot's *Silas Marner* was produced from chains of transformations, many of which were based on visual or aural homologies, rather than on logical relationships. The analogical argument she presented was itself authorized by a change in the cultural weight granted to that style of argument as opposed to the more traditional preference for logical/deductive arguments exemplified by, say, Cox and Krupat.

Last, in the examples already mentioned, competition between modular processes produced readings that could be characterized as predominantly logical and conceptual, or predominantly transformational and visual, although it is clear that neither kind of processing could itself produce a reading—both (and others as well) are always needed. In the historical essays, furthermore, it was possible to see evidence of different kinds of processing from two levels within a single module and to see in their distinctive styles a preference for one or the other.

This distinction would seem to support the cognitive claim for double processing, that is, of understanding from an object-centered and from a viewer-centered point of view. As a corrective to historical relativists who argue that all understanding is inevitably biased by and toward the observer's point of view, the evidence from the visual system suggests that it is in fact in the observer's interest to have two different kinds of vision: 2½ D viewer-centered vision serves for short-term negotiation (not bumping into furniture), and 3D object -centered vision serves for longer term storage (e.g., recognizing the same thing when seen from another angle) and as input to the conceptual/language system. Literary historical criticism was seen to be more or less permanently swinging between these two poles, attempting an accommodation between a degree of faithfulness to the otherness of a historical past and the inevitable and weightier pressure of contemporary needs and values.

Furthermore, the distinction between levels of processing within a module suggested the possibility that the two levels of vision, the 2½ D and the 3D, had significant parallels in the linguistic/conceptual module and that these parallels were not mere metaphors of vision applied to language. I argued that the feminist search for a level of language expression that has been called *écriture féminine* is consistent with the surmise that there may be two distinguishable levels in the language module, the functions of which parallel the functions of the two levels within the visual module. If the 2½ D visual level is self-centered in terms of perspective and function, serving the immediate needs of the individual by providing sequences not worth storing, the equivalent in the language module might produce a stream of consciousness language that is minimally grammatically marked but richly representative of the flow of bodily and emotional experience.

If the 3D level of vision edits, abstracts, and generalizes, recasting sequences into stable forms that can be stored for use in future identification, the equivalent level in the language module might be the level of processing that turns word salad into publicly negotiable structures by recasting them in the syntax of the public language. Greater attention to the 2½D level, if the feminist theorists are right, might open the door to creativity by focusing on and thus allowing access to presocialized feelings and understanding that are then reweighted as newly valuable before being cleaned up for public display. There is so much still to be explored about this level that we can't say too much about its creativity. If it turns out to be indeed a level of knowledge that is as yet unstructured by public language, then it may be the site of what is particularly individual about that individual. Of course there is always the possibility that what is individual will be found to be not at all unique but just standard issue sensory life.

However, it is the translation of the structures of knowledge from this level to the 3D level that is widely considered to be the central task of and site of language creativity. Here, where 2½D structures from at least the language and the visual, but presumably from the other modules as well, feed into the central processor and ask for articulation in a public language, the high creativity of the artist finds its greatest challenge. The creativity we have examined here is at a somewhat less exalted level, but also consists of the production of negotiable versions of readers' understandings of literary texts.

Building culture into the survival of the species

At this point, with the mention of readers and their needs, I would like to recall Richard Dawkins' claim that ideas can enter into the flow of evolutionary change: ideas that enhance the survival potential of the species will be reproduced. Translated into the historical argument about change and adaption being mounted here, this suggests that we in fact change our literary interpretive methods to survive in a changing world: cultural pressures for change and a measure of biological security cooperate fortuitiously in high Western culture. Pressured to recognize the interests of living readers, as perhaps over the intentions of (dead) authors, critics actually begin to listen to those readers. We can afford to listen because our physical survival is not threatened in the way it was when we first grew or developed the brain mechanisms for rapid categorization. What we have been able to do, under the pressure of ideas, is adapt the categorization methods originally evolved to allow survival in the face of hostile animals for use in producing an enriched categorization which can, in turn, take the ideas of others into account in categorization judgments. In today's world, where the enemies of survival are not tigers but various forms of mechanized violence from freely available handguns to tactical nuclear weapons, knowing how to listen to others may well increase the species' chances of survival. By slowing down a brain process we have been using for years, by delaying processing so as to allow for seeing and hearing the claims of others not only for existence but also for self-definition, we are adapting to changed demands of the environment in just the way we are built to adapt.

Categorization changes, thus, basic to all further processing, lead from this point of view to a promising series of changes; recategorizations change the reading lists of university courses and the publication lists of publishers. Revisions of our literary historical narratives are caused by and contribute to reweighting of experimental or previously excluded modes of processing and previously silenced voices. When we finally sum it up, it seems obvious: we bend at the joints, we adapt in the ways we have evolved to adapt. But the systems of knowing are not fully described when we say they are responsive to change; they respond by being themselves in constant competition with each other to produce reinterpretations of an increasingly complex world that are more satisfactory because they are more complex.

Resisting reading

In the current literature of cultural interpretation, literary critics compete with art historians who compete with anthropologists, all eager to show ever more exotic examples of adaption, that is, of culture reinforcing its own structures. But we have known for a long time that children could get used to working in cotton mills twelve hours a day, or even that they could improvise a level of stability and self-preservation in concentration camps. It is crucial, now, that we turn our attention to further investigation of the hypothesis that minds can actually resist merely adapting to culture, can actually respond innovatively to their world and its texts in ways which may run counter to, or suggest alternatives to, reigning cultural patterns. In the face of the overwhelming and convincing evidence that interpretation does indeed change along with other cultural shifts, the fact that change is also internally driven must be recognized and studied.

In order to locate this possibility within the cognitive system, we have had to extend the modularity hypothesis to recognize the systematic power of gaps in mental structure as a stimulus for creative reorganization and the structural possibility of slowing down categorization sufficiently to take into account others' accounts of their own self-definition. We are still far from the goal of making Amiens' optimism work widely outside pastoral romance. All of the gaps within the human interpretive system that seem to invite innovative bridging need further exploration in both cognitive science and interpretive theory.

I have, here, focused on the power of the conceptual/linguistic module and the visual module together as they contribute to the production of literary texts and literary criticism. I feel acutely, however, the neglect of the kinesthetic aspects of understanding, mentioned only briefly here as an aspect of a reader's identification with character, but surely important as well to rhyme and meter in poetry. Furthermore, the production of poetic language could be studied as bringing together the structures of knowledge of the visual and the kinesthetic and the linguistic modules. The differences between painting and language will present other areas for exploration of instability at modular processing boundaries.

The goal is now to produce a finer-grained understanding of the balance between an innate ability to process information that relates a human body to its immediate environment and an equally innate ability to make meaning from the collocation of that personal experience within the surrounding culture. The challenge to cultural and historical criticisms here, that is, to their attempts to interpret the body in its various ideologically structured contexts, lies in the claim that a significant part of that context is the body itself, specifically the mind/brain in that body, and its structures and competencies.[5]

In conclusion, like the boy actor playing Rosalind who comes on stage as the Epilogue to *As You Like It*, offering to kiss all the men in the audience if they applaud the play, I beg leave to remind you that one of my claims for the hypothesis of the modular mind is that it provides a hypothesis to explain critical inconsistency, that is, the cooccurrence of conflicting rules in an interpretive system. Since the processing of new structures of information is costly in both time and brain space, the subconscious attention it requires makes it inevitable that there will not be sufficient attention immediately available to work out all the logical consequences of adding a new rule to an already functioning interpretive system. Contradictions will emerge slowly from the interactions within a community. I will be rewarded for my performance if this study encourages my readers to seek out and criticize its contradictions.

Notes

Introduction

1. The gaps that need to be bridged here are not entirely unlike those gaps in the literary text that Wolfgang Iser, working within a Gestalt psychology, postulated as activating the interpretive processes. I am happy to acknowledge how much I have learned from Iser's work but believe nevertheless that there is a significant difference between his claim that the gaps "arise out of contingency and inexperienceability" (1978:166) and, as I would rather have it, their arising out of *systemic* inexperienceability.

2. Neither these speculations, nor the necessary exploration of the connections between neurological structures and cognitive structures, nor the reductionism of theories about them can be my concern here. The theoretical assumptions about the connections may be pursued in Popper and Eccles (1977), Eccles (1984), Fodor (1979), Arbib and Hesse (1986), Churchland (1986), Edelman (1989), Jackendoff (1987), Dennett (1991). There is very little discussion in this book of the empirical evidence from neurology and psychology, which comes to me second hand and is cited in my sources. That I haven't done the laboratory research myself is not, however, to be taken as a concession that my use of it is any more metaphorical than its use in the reports of the primary research.

3. Left to their own devices, cognitive scientists studying verbal texts are likely to construct their own vastly oversimplified texts or use short excerpts from the popular press as examples for study. These samples exhibit, not surprisingly, exactly the structures they expect to find in (texts. Even students of metaphor can still be found discussing examples such as "Sally is a block of ice."

4. I find Arbib and Hesse (1986), Chapter 8, to be a clear explanation of

the difficulties of the notion of ideal (literal) language and also of how Wittgensteinian thought underlies both a theory of fuzzy categorization and the assumption that metaphoric processes are not supplemental to language but central to an adequate semantic theory. Philosophical, linguistic, and neurological arguments for the centrality of categorization can be found respectively in Quine (1969); Jackendoff (1983), Chapters 5 and 6; Jackendoff (1987), Chapter 8; Lakoff (1987); and Edelman (1989). Edelman even identifies perception with categorization: "Perception may be provisionally defined as the discrimination of an object or an event through one or more sensory modalities, separating them from the background or from other objects or events....Perception involves categorization, a process by which an individual may treat nonidentical objects or events as equivalent" (p. 26).

5. For a fully worked out example of how the preference model can display the complexity of the interaction of factors relevant to second language learning, see Bernard Spolsky (1989).

6. Psychoanalytic theory would presumably predict that internal conflict would produce cultural change even in a politically inert environment. Cognitive scientists have not been as sensitive as Freudians to the power of the conflicts within normal subjects. They seem to assume, in general, that normal brains work smoothly, and they generally associate difficulties and limitations with trauma and brain lesions. This is no doubt a limitation of their perspective.

7. Roger Seamon (1989) has correctly complained about the circularity of theorists' use of their own interpretations to demonstrate their theories.

8. See Spolsky (1991), which argues that the positions of both the continental pessimists and the American optimists reduce to the same overgeneralization about the power of language to express meaning.

Chapter 1

1. Chomsky argues this on what he calls the argument from the deficiency of the stimulus. The world of language into which a child enters with almost adult competence by the age of six or seven has not, even in the most fortunate of cases, presented him with sufficient data to construct the language rules he now controls. There has to be an innate language component in the mind which is preset to take its stimulus from the language behavior it does encounter and to set the parameters of its internal structures so as to produce language.

2. The details of the proposal are in Fodor (1983), pp. 36–37.

3. A crucial text in the innateness debate is the record of the Chomsky-Piaget debates (Piattelli-Palmarini 1980). The work of Bates (1979), for example, with very young children, and of Poizner, Klima, and Bellugi (1987) with the sign language of the deaf, has led them to conclude that what is innate is the capacity to symbolize, which Bates believes is a "relatively modality free" (p. 177) innate capacity. She argues that children could just as well learn a gestural language as a vocal one, if their culture required it. Poizner, Klima, and Bellugi (1987) also make the argument that the language capacity of the brain can be realized in more than one modality. See also, for some reports of a large amount of research denying strong modularity, Garfield (1987).

4. The notion of metaphor as a bridge or mediator is usefully discussed by Fernandez (1974) and Beck (1978). Neither has the modularity hypothesis to work with, but both assume something like it, at least as between visual and conceptual thought processes.

5. Argued, for example, in 1975b, Chapter 2, against Searle's claim (1982, a reprint of a 1972 article) that Chomsky doesn't take the function of communication seriously enough.

6. I have always liked Searle's characterization of Chomsky's view of man as "essentially a syntactic animal" (in Searle 1982:15). Even if it is a vastly overrestricted view of human potential, it does explain the uniqueness of syntax as part of what it is to be human. Hesse gives a short and perspicuous characterization of propositional logic: "Propositional logical relies upon enumeration of premised, univocal symbolization, and exclusively deductive connections." Hesse's next phrase is important: "And these cannot be...a good simulation of human thought" (1988:318).

7. See W. J. T. Mitchell (1986), especially Chapter 4 on space and time, and G. E. Lessing's *Laocoon: An Essay upon the Limits of Poetry and Painting* (1766).

8. We cannot experience this distinction introspectively because the operations of thinking are subconscious; our knowledge of the systems can only be known by inference. Most cognitive scientists, however, recognize the separation between two kinds of structures of information, giving the distinction different names: propositional vs. analog (Shepard and Cooper 1982), descriptive vs. depictive (Kosslyn 1980) or algebraic vs. geometric (Jackendoff 1987).

9. Sperber's study of symbolism, in many ways a perceptive and stimulat-

ing forerunner of modular hypotheses in his recognition that the processes of symbolism are not language bound, surprisingly expresses the prejudice that language-type thinking is more important than visual thought in his assumption that symbolic processes only come into play when "cognitive" ones fail (1975:121–122). His prejudice here is strong enough to keep him from seeing the evidence he himself presents: just twenty pages later he expresses the relationship between the two processes as circular (pp. 144–145). This, surely, is the more reasonable hypothesis.

10. PDP models are explicitly and in principle nonbinary, that is, they do not describe their processes as algorithmic functions, although there are places where these models also postulate something like brain computation. The theories of Fodor and Jackendoff assume that, ultimately, brain function must be expressed in a single, reductive and binary language of mind. I have written (Spolsky 1985) about the unreality of assuming neurological processes to be binary. Garfield (1987) and Churchland and Sejnowski (1988) also present arguments and empirical evidence against Fodor's strong modularity. Academic competition being what it is, the researchers involved tend to exaggerate their differences, but from the point of view of this study the differences are not as significant as their common assumption of modularity.

11. Patricia Churchland (1986) provides a good discussion of the issues involved in reducing a brain theory to a theory of mental life. Even as recently as 1986 it was quite reasonable to argue that it couldn't be done, but she has gathered (and refuted) the arguments in support of the proposition that it was never going to be possible to explain what it felt like to see blue in terms of neuron firings. The discussion has not entirely gone away, but Edelman's book certainly contributes to its weakening. I have had the opportunity to read an unpublished manuscript by James Paul Gee, *The Social Mind*, which speculates about the connections between brain structure and surrounding cultural expectations.

12. Dennett notes the connection, calling the human brain, at one point, "the Joycean machine" in contrast to the idealized computer-brain, the Turing machine. The confluence of brain theory and postmodernist thought brings me to mention here the caveat of Donald Spence, who notes that "theories of the mind are particularly vulnerable to three kinds of influence: the prevailing zeitgeist and current technology; the personal history of the theorist; and...the reigning narrative metaphor" (1990:344). He made these remarks in the course of complaining about the power of Freudian theories of mind, which despite their unfalsifiability have become binding on current crit-

ical thought. Since I am sympathetic to his position, I am sorry that I could not, given the scope and goals of my own work, go into detail about the empirical data supporting the theories I describe. They convince me, however, that the theories presented herein are not unfalsifiable, as the attacks on Fodor, for example, have proven to be.

13. See Oatley (1978) and Arbib (1987:344ff.).

Chapter 2

1. Spengemann notes that autobiography in America "has been repeatedly examined for evidence of the national *geist*" (1980:201) and cites studies before Cox's that highlight the role of autobiography in America. Cox is, however, the first to specify the conditions of an American subgenre.

2. Note that there is no partial way of meeting a well-formedness condition, such as Cox's requirements of self-made life and book, or of the author's intention to present a model life. However, the condition that one's autobiography make an imaginative gesture is a condition that can be met with more or less imaginative transformation. In contrast, then, to the well-formedness condition, which is discrete, the gradient necessary condition expresses a range over which the condition is considered fulfilled. The fact that the text includes details that are not imaginative does not compromise the judgment that this condition is satisfactorily met.

3. These TCs and GTCs are numbered in the order of the weighting Cox seems to give them. The absence of a more heavily weighted condition has a greater influence on the strength of the resulting judgment than does the absence of a less heavily weighted condition. But whether they admit gradience or not, the distinguishing feature of typicality conditions as opposed to necessary conditions is that the absence of any of these conditions does not scuttle the categorization. A typicality condition can be entirely unfulfilled and the text can still be satisfactorily categorized as a type of the token, as long as the necessary conditions and some subset of the typicality conditions are met.

4. This is on the face of it an absurd claim: who is egocentric if not Buffalo Bill Cody? But Krupat seems to be trying to make the more reasonable point that these Western heroes didn't claim to be unique; they wanted to be considered the best in exactly those roles all men were expected to fill.

5. See Schauber and Spolsky (1986).

6. Quine (1969) and Jackendoff (1983:149) discuss both the importance of the drive toward stability and the inevitability of instability in the revision of taxonomies.

Chapter 3

1. See Michael Walzer (1987) for an attempt to describe the kind of social critic who stands a chance of making a difference.

2. See Philip Edwards's Introduction to *Hamlet* (1985:37) for mention of others who have argued similar "contamination theories."

3. The reference is to the developmental theory of D. W. Winnicott (1968).

4. Richard Levin (1988) has argued that blaming the patriarchy is an overgeneralization that cannot support the arguments it is used to make.

5. She cites Leverenz's article, but doesn't build on it.

6. It must be noted here that Hawkes has misrepresented Greg, who was every bit as much a rationalist and a defender of "the rational Shakespeare" as Dover Wilson was. The quotation from Greg about "giving up on Shakespeare's rationality" is not, as Hawkes leads us to believe, Greg's conclusion, but is, in fact, the challenge, entered by Greg at the beginning of his article, which he takes up to prove that the play can, in fact, be interpreted very reasonably if the ghost's story is seen as a projection of Hamlet's own imagination. This distortion of Greg inevitably undermines our confidence in Hawkes's reading and invalidates his claim that Dover Wilson was challenged to answer Greg in defense of his own need for control. It does not, however, logically endanger the general argument for the existence of a relationship between a reader's political and critical activities.

7. For a view of how Girard saw his work in relation to its social context, see the interview with him in *Diacritics,* March 1978.

8. In parody, for example, the traditional structural conditions are preserved but others which suggest the possibility that the author is not committed to the traditional assertions of the genre are added. See Schauber and Spolsky (1979) and (1986).

9. See Spolsky (1991), for a discussion of the failure of Bloom's failure.

10. Todorov's recognition (1976) of the identity of a genre with a

speech act sees both as entirely conventional, overlooking the logical operations involved in making use of conventional types. E. D. Hirsch, Jr. (1967) recognizes that a genre determination is much more than taxonomic, but he did not specifically note its relation to inference and deduction.

11. A formal working out of the kinds of logical operations that categorization permits has been attempted by Sperber and Wilson (1986b:93ff.).

Chapter 4

1. "Life's Empty Pack: Notes toward a Literary Daughteronomy," *Critical Inquiry,* 11,3 (1985):355–384.

2. Later Gilbert and Gubar (1987) express some skepticism or perhaps disappointment with this project, as they summarize what they refer to as "a long, bifurcated tradition of feminist and masculinist fantasy" (p. 228) about the connection of language to biological gender. They conclude that, while these myths may be necessary as sources of identity and probably represent real fears about the power of the "mother" tongue, they do not demonstrate that women's introduction into the "symbolic contract" is inevitably compromised by their gender.

3. This point is, by now, uncontroversial. See Culler (1983) and Gilbert (1984).

4. Booth (1961:30–31) explains how we deal with narrators that an author has intentionally made unreliable, but admits that if a narrator is untrustworthy because of a novel's faulty construction it may indeed make the book unreadable, or not worth reading.

5. It subsequently was, of course, in all versions of suspicious or deconstructive reading.

6. See the discussion of essentialism in Fuss (1989).

7. See Gilbert (1979) and Auerbach (1985) for statements of it. A parallel interest in investigating the power of bodily understanding has been developed by George Lakoff and Mark Johnson (1980), Lakoff (1987), and Johnson (1987). I am largely in sympathy with this work but am puzzled by its untimely blindness to the gender differences between bodies in a period of flourishing feminist theory. It astonishes me that Johnson says, "Experiential basicness is a relative matter. Yet because our bodies are very much alike with respect to their physiological makeup, we would expect to find commonly

shared (if not universal) gestalt structures for many of our physical interactions within our environment" (p. 62).

8. A full discussion of psychoanalysis and feminism cannot be undertaken here, but see Greene and Kahn 1985, especially Chapters 4 and 5.

9. Mitchell states in her preface to *Psychoanalysis and Feminism* (1974) that although "the greater part of the feminist movement has identified Freud as the enemy...a rejection of...Freud's works is fatal for feminism" (p. xv).

10. The word ***transformation*** is always, in my experience of its use, an abstraction used as a place-filler for the as yet only partially specifiable processes that replace one structure with another or add one to those already in place. As Piaget (1970:11) notes, it is a way overcoming the limits of synchrony in the study of the learning activities of human minds. Learning itself, or change, as Piaget argues, is not a process strict synchronic method can handle. I use the word here because Gilbert uses it, and it seems appropriate to her procedure. I will suggest a somewhat more specific description of transformation later in this chapter.

11. How the match takes place in the brain is almost entirely mysterious, but presumably has something to do with the way storage is arranged in the long-term visual and linguistic memory. For the present argument, it is the structure of the output of the process that matters. This issue is discussed more fully in the next chapter.

12. "In classical analogical reasoning we are given a source system *(S)*, and initial comparison with a target system *(T)*, and the goal is to infer further unknown features of *T*" (p. 319).

Chapter 5

1. This is not to say that image and metaphor are coextensive, or that a metaphor is fully described by calling it an image. A full definition of metaphor is not relevant here. My argument needs only the claim that part of the description of metaphor must necessarily overlap with image.

2. This minimalist description of metaphor applies equally well to metonymy, for example, and, broadly speaking, to the range of figurative tropes. Its limitation as a definition of figuration is its extreme generality, but it serves the purpose here of showing how matching operations, with the inevitable mismatches that accompany every match are crucial destabilizers at the heart of even the simplest interpretive operations.

3. In Chapter 3, the kinds of American autobiography were described and distinguished by preference rules.

4. Compare, for example, a doctor telling you she can't see you before she sees her patients in the hospital and T. S. Eliot's comparison of the evening to "a patient etherized upon a table." Even though the same sense of "patient" is involved, and *mostly* the same conditions of meaning are present (sickness, hospitals), only in the context of a lyric poem might conditions of meaning relating to the suffering of Jesus (the passion) likely be evoked. The connection to the passion is itself generative, as that word is also described by a rich set of conditions, ad infinitum.

5. See Lakoff and Johnson (1980), Lakoff (1987), and Turner (1987).

6. See, for example, Petrie (1979), Kuhn (1970) and (1979), Black (1954–55), Boyd (1979), and Ortony (1975). See also Ricoeur (1973), Haynes (1975) correcting Ortony (1975), de Man (1978), and Oatley (1978).

7. See Paivio (1986) for a full argument for the dual coding hypothesis.

8. See, for example, Black (1972) and Ambrose (1972).

9. This confirms E. D. Hirsch's (1967) claim that literal meaning is really only most probable meaning. See also my 1988 article on the limits of literal meaning.

10. In a parallel argument, feminists have claimed that the social constraints on women's writing derive precisely from its being a route to challenge and change.

Chapter 6

1. See Schauber and Spolsky (1977).

2. It is not the disappearance of a category per se that is objectionable, but the disappearance of a valued category: in this case, secular, even coarse, medieval stories. At about the same time as Robertson was arguing that all medieval poems were sermons, Northrop Frye's archetypal criticism was dissolving the difference between literary texts and a great deal of popular or folk literature, letting in texts that had not previously been considered worthy of academic notice. Territoriality is at work here: the academic domain may be increased but not decreased.

3. See, for example, Charles Altieri's (1983) discussion of the canon. "The past that canons preserve," he claimed, "is...a permanent theater helping us shape and judge personal and social values...and the most plausible hope for the influence of literary study in the future lies in our ability to transmit the past as a set of challenges and models" (p. 40).

4. A. C. Spearing suggests quite the opposite interpretation of the century when it serves his purposes. Chaucer, Spearing argues, had freedom to criticize his society as openly as he did because of an underlying stability in the fourteenth century. This freedom disappeared in the fifteenth century when, for example, the Church was feeling more threatened by the Wycliffite heresy, according to Spearing, and thus Chaucer's successors had to be much more careful to veil criticism of the church and the government (1986:89, 90–91).

5. This is what some of Stanley Fish's work seems to teach (see, for example, Fish 1980).

6. Robertson himself edited an anthology, *The Literature of Medieval England*, which presented a competing canon, as it were, in 1970. The aim was to redirect the teaching of medieval literature early enough in the careers of future scholars to eventually have an impact on the canon of the community. It was a signal failure.

7. Spearing points out that poetry written before 1360 "may have possessed [these qualities] but didn't lay claim to [them]" (1985:5).

8. Spearing quotes Boccaccio: poets are not "mere story tellers, but rather...men of great learning endowed with a sort of divine intelligence and skill" (1985:6).

9. Bloom himself, as Spearing acknowledges, didn't think his theory applied to poetry before Shakespeare.

10. Tony Davenport (1986), reviewing the book, points out that Spearing has omitted consideration of two Chaucerian fathers who might challenge this generalization.

11. Spearing has taken the distinction between a "work" with an intending author, hovering father-like in the background, and a "text," which is free of that control and open to the interpretation of its readers from Roland Barthes (1977a and b).

Chapter 7

1. Holquist (1989) sees mutual confirmation of the multiplicity of human perspectives in Marr's work on vision and in various theoretical statements in Bahktin and in the writings of the Prague School linguists. Karčevskij, he rightly notes, emphasizes the generative asymmetry of the situation as preventing the accomplishment of stasis.

2. See Showalter (1981) for a summary of the ways women's language might be theorized as different from men's.

3. See, for example, Moi (1985), Jones (1985), and Gilbert and Gubar (1987).

4. See Boyd, Kuhn, and Pylyshyn (1979) and Hesse (1988a).

5. The discussion of Popper's position is clearest in his dialogue with the neurophysiologist John Eccles in the conclusion to their jointly authored book, *The Self and Its Brain* (1977).

6. I am reminded here of Juliet Michell's (1974) defense of Freud. He was the first person who wrote about female sexuality who had actually institutionalized the procedure of listening to what women had to say in order to understand them. Now that we are accustomed to the procedures of psychoanalysis we are perhaps not surprised, but Mitchell is right to point out how revolutionary it was. Later theorists have questioned how well Freud listened, but that is a different matter.

Chapter 8

1. See Goodman (1978), Piaget (1958), Gruber and Voneche (1977), and Bruner (1986).

2. See Culler (1975) and Hartman (1980).

3. See for example, John et al. (1973) for neurological misreading, and Arbib (1988), Arbib and Hesse (1986), and Oatley (1978) on cognitive schema theory.

4. See Davis and Schleifer (1989) for just this claim.

5. See Johnson (1987) and Lakoff (1987) for expansions of this argument.

References

Aers, David. 1986. *Chaucer.* Brighton: Harvester.

Altieri, Charles. 1983. "An Idea and Ideal of a Literary Canon," *Critical Inquiry*, 10, 1:37–60.

Ambrose, Alice. 1972. "The Problem of Linguistic Adequacy." In *Philosophical Analysis*, edited by Max Black. Ithaca, NY: Cornell University Press.

Anderson, R. C. and J. P. Pichert. 1978. "Recall of Previously Unrecallable Information Following a Shift in Perspective," *Journal of Verbal Learning and Verbal Behavior*, 17:1–12.

Arbib, Michael A. 1987. "Modularity and Interaction of Brain Regions Underlying Visuomotor Coordination," *Modularity in Knowledge Representation and Natural-Language Understanding*, edited by Jay L. Garfield. Cambridge, MA: MIT Press, pp. 333–63.

———. 1988. "Modularity, Schemas, and Neurons: A Critique of Fodor," *Computers, Brains and Minds,* edited by Peter Slezak and W. R. Albury. Dordrecht: Kluwer

Arbib, Michael A. and Mary Hesse. 1986. *The Construction of Reality.* Cambridge: Cambridge University Press.

Auerbach, Nina. 1985. "Engorging the Patriarchy." In *Historical Studies and Literary Criticism*, edited by Jerome J. McGann. Madison, WI: University of Wisconsin Press, pp. 229–39.

Bach, Kent and Robert M. Harnish. 1979. *Linguistic Communication and Speech Acts.* Cambridge, MA: MIT Press.

Barthes, Roland. 1977a. "The Death of the Author." In *Image-Music-*

Text, translated by Stephen Heath. New York: Hill and Wang. London.

———. 1977b. "From Work to Text." In *Image-Music-Text*, translated by Stephen Heath. New York: Hill and Wang.

Bates, Elizabeth. 1979. *The Emergence of Symbols: Cognition and Communication in Infancy*. New York: Academic Press.

Beck, Brenda E. F. 1978. "The Metaphor as a Mediator Between Semantic and Analogic Modes of Thought," *Current Anthropology*, 19, 1:83–97.

Belsey, Catherine. 1979. "The Case of Hamlet's Conscience," *Studies in Philology*, 76:127–48.

———. 1986. "The Romantic Construction of the Unconscious." In *Literature, Politics and Theory: Papers from the Essex Conference 1976–84*, edited by Francis Barker, Peter Hulme, Margaret Iversen, and Diana Loxley. London: Methuen, pp. 57–76.

Bercovitch, Sacvan, ed. 1986. *Reconstructing American Literary History*. Cambridge, MA: Harvard University Press.

Bevington, David, ed. 1990. *William Shakespeare: Antony and Cleopatra*. Cambridge: Cambridge University Press.

Black, Max. 1954–55. "Metaphor," *Proceedings of the Aristotelian Society*, N. S. 55:273–94.

———. 1972. *The Labyrinth of Language*. London: Pall Mall Press.

———. 1979. "More About Metaphor." In *Metaphor and Thought*, edited by Andrew Ortony. Cambridge: Cambridge University Press, pp. 19–43.

Bloom, Harold. 1973. *The Anxiety of Influence*. New York: Oxford University Press.

———, Paul de Man, Jacques Derrida, Geoffrey Hartman, J. Hillis Miller. 1979. *Deconstruction and Criticism*. New York: Continuum.

Bloomfield, Morton. 1972. "Allegory as Interpretation," *New Literary History*, 3:301–17.

Booth, Wayne C. 1961. *The Rhetoric of Fiction*. Chicago: The University of Chicago Press.

———. 1979. *Critical Understanding: The Powers and Limits of Pluralism.* Chicago: The University of Chicago Press.

Boyd, Richard. 1979. "Metaphor and Theory Change: What is 'Metaphor' a Metaphor for?" In *Metaphor and Thought*, edited by Andrew Ortony. Cambridge: Cambridge University Press, pp. 356–408.

Braudel, Fernand. 1958. "Histoire et Sciences sociales: La longue durée," *Annales E. S. C.*, XIII:725–53.

Brooks, Cleanth and Robert Penn Warren. 1976. *Understanding Poetry.* 4th ed. Holt, Rinehart and Winston: New York.

Brooks, Peter. 1984. *Reading for the Plot: Design and Intention in Narrative.* New York: Knopf.

———. 1987. "The Idea of a Psychoanalytic Literary Criticism," *Critical Inquiry*, 13, 2:334–48.

Bruner, Jerome. 1986. *Actual Minds, Possible Worlds.* Cambridge, MA: Harvard University Press.

Burge, Tyler. 1987. "Marr's Theory of Vision," In *Modularity in Knowledge Representation and Natural Language Understanding*, edited by Jay L. Garfield. Cambridge, MA: MIT Press, pp. 365–81.

Burke, Peter. 1969. *The Renaissance Sense of the Past.* London: Edward Arnold.

Cavell, Stanley. 1987. *Disowning Knowledge In Six Plays of Shakespeare.* Cambridge: Cambridge University Press.

Chomsky, Noam. 1975a. *The Logical Structure of Linguistic Theory.* New York: Praeger.

———. 1975b. *Reflections on Language.* New York: Pantheon.

———. 1986. *Knowledge of Language: Its Nature, Origin, and Use.* New York: Praeger.

Churchland, Patricia Smith. 1986. *Neurophilosophy: Toward a Unified Science of the Mind-Brain.* Cambridge, MA: MIT Press.

——— and Terrence J. Sejnowski. 1988. "Perspectives on Cognitive Neuroscience," *Science*, 242:741–45.

Cixous, Hélène. 1976. "The Laugh of the Medusa," translated by Keith

Cohen and Paula Cohen. 1983. Reprinted in *The Signs Reader: Women, Gender, and Scholarship,* edited by Elizabeth Abel and Emily K. Abel. Chicago: The University of Chicago Press, pp. 279–97.

Clampitt, Amy. 1984. *The Kingfisher.* London: Faber & Faber.

Clark, H. H. 1969. "Linguistic Process in Deductive Reasoning," *Psychological Review*, 76:387–404.

Cohen, L. J. and Avishai Margalit. 1972. "The Role of Inductive Reasoning in the Interpretation of Metaphor." In *Semantics of Natural Language,* edited by Donald Davidson and Gilbert Harman. Dordrecht, Holland: D. Reidel, pp. 722–40.

Cohen, Ted. 1975. "Figurative Speech and Figurative Acts," *Journal of Philosophy*, 71, 19:669–84.

Colomb, Gregory G. 1989. "Cultural Literacy and the Theory of Meaning: Or, What Educational Theorists Need to Know about How We Read," *New Literary History*, 20, 2:411–50.

Couser, G. Thomas. 1979. *American Autobiography: The Prophetic Mode.* Amherst, MA: University of Massachusetts Press.

Cox, James M. 1971. "Autobiography and America." In *Aspects of Narrative*, edited by J. Hillis Miller. New York: Cornell University Press, pp. 143–72. Also appeared in *Virginia Quarterly Review*, 47:252–77.

Craig, Hardin and David Bevington, eds. *The Complete Works of Shakespeare.* Revised Edition. Glenview, Il: Scott, Foresman.

Culler, Jonathan. 1975. *Structuralist Poetics: Structuralism, Linguistics, and the Study of Literature.* Ithaca, NY: Cornell University Press.

———. 1977. "Apostrophe," *Diacritics*, 7, iv:59–69.

———. 1983. *On Deconstruction.* Ithaca, NY: Cornell University Press.

Curry, Walter Clyde. 1926. *Chaucer and the Medieval Sciences.* London: Oxford University Press.

Davenport, Tony. 1986. Review of A. C. Spearing, *Medieval to Renaissance in English Poetry. English*, 35, Summer.

Davidson, Donald. 1978. "What Metaphors Mean," *Critical Inquiry*, 5, 1:31–47.

Davis, Robert Con and Ronald Schleifer. 1989. *Contemporary Literary Criticism: Literary and Cultural Studies*, Second Edition. New York: Longmans.

Dawkins, Richard. 1989. *The Selfish Gene*. New Edition. Oxford: Oxford University Press.

De Man, Paul. 1971. *Blindness and Insight*. New York: Oxford University Press.

———. 1978a. *Allegories of Reading: Figural Language in Rousseau, Nietzsche, Rilke, and Proust*. New Haven, CT: Yale University Press.

———. 1978b. "The Epistemology of Metaphor," *Critical Inquiry*, 5, 1:13–30.

———. 1979. "Semiology and Rhetoric." In *Textual Strategies: Perspectives in Post-Structuralist Criticism*, edited by Josué Harari. Ithaca, NY: Cornell University Press.

Dennett, Daniel C. 1991. *Consciousness Explained*. Boston: Little Brown.

Derrida, Jacques. 1974. "White Mythology: Metaphor in the Text of Philosophy," *New Literary History*, 6, 1:5–74.

———. 1980. "The Law of Genre," *Critical Inquiry*, 7:55–81.

Donaldson, E. Talbot. 1960. "Patristic Exegesis in the Criticism of Medieval Literature: The Opposition." In *Critical Approaches to Medieval Literature: Selected Papers from the English Institute, 1958–9*, edited by Dorothy Bethurum. New York: Columbia University Press.

Dusinberre, William. 1980. *Henry Adams: The Myth of Failure*. Charlottesville, VA: University Press of Virginia.

Eagleton, Terry. 1984. *The Function of Criticism: From the Spectator to Post-Structuralism*. London: Verso.

———. 1985. "Ideology and Scholarship." In *Historical Studies and Literary Criticism*, edited by Jerome J. McGann. Madison, WI: University of Wisconsin Press.

Eakin, Paul John. 1985. *Fictions in Autobiography: Studies in the Art of Self-Invention*. Princeton, NJ: Princeton University Press.

Eccles, John C. 1984. *The Human Mystery*. London: Routledge and Kegan Paul.

Edelman, Gerald. 1989. *Neural Darwinism: The Theory of Neuronal Group Selection.* Oxford: Oxford University Press.

Eggers, Walter F., Jr. 1980. "The Idea of Literary Periods," *Comparative Literary Studies*, 17, 1:1–15.

Eliot, George. 1967. *Silas Marner.* Harmondsworth: Penguin.

Eliot, T. S. 1951. *"Hamlet," Selected Essays.* Third Edition. London: Faber and Faber, pp. 141–46.

Felperin, Howard. 1987. "Making It 'Neo': The New Historicism and Renaissance Literature," *Textual Practice*, 1, 3:262–77.

Fernandez, James W. 1974. "The Mission of Metaphor in Expressive Culture," *Current Anthropology,* 15:119–46.

Fetterley, Judith. 1978. *The Resisting Reader: A Feminist Approach to American Fiction.* Bloomington, IN: Indiana University Press.

———. 1984. "Who Killed Dick Diver? The Sexual Politics of *Tender is the Night*," *Mosaic*, 17, 1:111–28.

Fisch, Harold. 1986. "Biblical Realism in *Silas Marner*," in *Identity and Ethos: A Festschrift for Sol Litzin on the Occasion of His 85th Birthday*, ed. Mark H. Gelber. New York: Peter Lang.

Fish, Stanley. 1973. "What is Stylistics and Why Are They Saying Such Terrible Things About It?" In *Approaches to Poetics*, edited by Seymour Chatman. New York: Columbia University Press, pp. 109–52.

———. 1976. "Interpreting the *Variorum*," *Critical Inquiry*, 2, 3: 465–85.

———. 1980. *Is There A Text in This Class? The Authority of Interpretive Communities.* Cambridge, MA: Harvard University Press.

———. 1989. "Change." In *Doing What Comes Naturally: Change, Rhetoric, & the Practice of Theory in Literary and Legal Studies.* Durham, NC: Duke University Press.

Fisher, John H. 1973. Review of Charles Muscatine, *Poetry and Crisis in the Age of Chaucer* in *South Atlantic Quarterly*, 72.

Fodor, Jerry A. 1979. *The Language of Thought.* Cambridge, MA: Harvard University Press.

———. 1983. *The Modularity of Mind: An Essay on Faculty Psychology.* Cambridge, MA: MIT Press.

Fonagy, Ivan. 1971. "Double Coding in Speech," *Semiotica*, 3, 189–222.

———. 1965. "Form and Function of Poetic Language," *Diogenes*, 51, 72–110.

Freud, Sigmund. 1976. *The Interpretation of Dreams,* translated and edited by James Strachey. Harmondsworth: Pelican.

Frye, Northrop. 1957. *Anatomy of Criticism.* Princeton: Princeton University Press.

Fuss, Diana. 1989. *Essentially Speaking: Feminism, Nature and Difference.* New York: Routledge.

Gardner, Howard. 1985. *Frames of Mind: The Theory of Multiple Intelligences.* London: Paladin.

Garfield, Jay L., ed. 1987. *Modularity in Knowledge Representation and Natural-Language Understanding.* Cambridge, MA: MIT Press.

Gee, James Paul. n. d. *The Social Mind.* Unpublished ms.

Gilbert, Sandra M. 1979. "Life Studies, or, Speech After Long Silence: Feminist Critics Today," *College English*, 46:849–63.

———. 1984. "The Education of Henrietta Adams," *Profession 84.* New York: MLA, pp. 5–9.

———. 1985. "Life's Empty Pack: Notes Toward a Literary Daughteronomy," *Critical Inquiry*, 11, 3:355–84.

———. 1987. *No Man's Land: The Place of The Woman Writer in the Twentieth Century.* New Haven, CT: Yale University Press.

Gilbert, Sandra M. and Susan Gubar. 1979. *The Madwoman in the Attic: The Woman Writer and the Nineteenth-Century Imagination.* New Haven, CT: Yale University Press.

Girard, René. 1984. "Hamlet's Dull Revenge," *Stanford Literature Review*, 1, 2:159–200.

———. 1978. Interviewed by "*Diacritics*" in *Diacritics*, 8, 1: 31–54.

Givón, Talmy. 1984. "Deductive vs. Pragmatic Processing in Natural Language." In *Method and Tactics in Cognitive Science*, edited by Walter Kintsch, James R. Miller, Peter G. Polson. Hillsdale, NJ: Erlbaum, pp. 137–90.

Gombrich, Ernst H. 1969. *Art and Illusion: A Study in the Psychology of Pictorial Representation.* Princeton, NJ: Princeton University Press.

Goodman, Nelson. 1968. *Languages of Art: An Approach to a Theory of Symbols.* Indianapolis: Bobbs-Merrill.

———. 1978. *Ways of Worldmaking.* Indianapolis: Hackett.

Graff, Gerald. 1979. *Literature Against Itself.* Chicago: The University of Chicago Press.

Greenblatt, Stephen. 1980. *Renaissance Self-Fashioning.* Chicago: The University of Chicago Press.

———. 1985. "Shakespeare and the Exorcists." In *After Strange Texts: The Role of Theory in the Study of Literature*, edited by Gregory S. Jay and David L. Miller. Birmingham: University of Alabama Press, pp. 101–23.

Greene, Gayle and Coppélia Kahn, eds. 1985. *Making a Difference: Feminist Literary Criticism.* London: Methuen.

Greg, W. W. 1917. "Hamlet's Hallucination," *Modern Language Review* 12, 4:393–421.

Groves, Philip M. and Kurt Schlesinger. 1982. *Introduction to Biological Psychology.* 2nd ed. Dubuque, IA: Wm. C. Brown Co.

Gruber, Howard and Jacques Voneche, eds. 1977. *The Essential Piaget.* New York: Basic Books.

Guillén, Claudio. 1971. "Second Thoughts on Literary Periods." In *Literature as System: Essays Toward the Theory of Literary History.* Princeton: Princeton University Press, pp. 420–69.

Harris, R. J. 1976. "Comprehension of Metaphors: A Test of the Two-Stage Processing Model," *Bulletin of the Psychonomic Society*, 8:312–14.

Hartman, Geoffrey. 1980. "Understanding Criticism." In *Criticism in the Wilderness.* New Haven, CT: Yale University Press.

Hartshorne, Charles and Paul Weiss, eds. 1931. *Collected Papers of Charles Sanders Peirce.* Cambridge, MA: Harvard University Press.

Hausman, Carl R. 1989. *Metaphor and Art: Interactionism and Reference in the Verbal and Nonverbal Arts.* Cambridge: Cambridge University Press.

Haynes, Felicity. 1975. "Metaphor as Interactive," *Educational Theory*, 25:272–77.

Hawkes, Terence. 1985. *"Telmah".* In *Shakespeare and the Question of Theory*, ed. Patricia Parker and Geoffrey Hartman. New York: Methuen, pp. 310–32.

———. 1986. *"Telmah."* In *That Shakespeherian Rag: Essays on a Critical Process.* London: Methuen, pp. 92–119.

Hemingway, Ernest. 1953. *A Farewell to Arms.* New York: Scribner.

Herr, Michael. 1977. *Dispatches.* New York: Alfred Knopf.

Hesse, Mary. 1988a. "The Cognitive Claims of Metaphor," *Journal of Speculative Philosophy*, 2, 1:1–16.

———. 1988b. "Theories, Family Resemblances and Analogy." In *Analogical Reasoning*, edited by David H. Helman. Dordrecht: Kluwer.

Hirsch, E. D., Jr. 1967. *Validity in Interpretation.* New Haven: Yale University Press.

Holquist, Michael. 1989. "From Body-Talk to Biography: The Chronobiological Bases of Narrative," *Yale Journal of Criticism*, 3, 1:1–35.

Honeck, R. P and R. R. Hoffman, eds. 1980. *Cognition and Figurative Language.* Hillsdale, NJ: Erlbaum.

Horowitz, Mardi J., ed. *Psychodynamics and Cognition.* Chicago: The University of Chicago Press.

Howard, Donald R. 1966. *The Three Temptations: Medieval Man in Search of the World.* Princeton, NJ: Princeton University Press.

Iser, Wolfgang. 1978. *The Act of Reading: A Theory of Aesthetic Response.* Baltimore: The Johns Hopkins University Press.

Jackendoff, Ray. 1983. *Semantics and Cognition.* Cambridge, MA.: MIT Press.

———. 1987. *Consciousness and the Computational Mind.* Cambridge, MA: MIT Press.

Jacobs, Nicolas. 1974. Review of Charles Muscatine, *Poetry and Crisis in the Age of Chaucer, Essays in Criticism*, 24.

James, Henry. 1972. *The Golden Bowl.* Harmondsworth: Penguin.

Jeffrey, David Lyle, ed. 1984. *Chaucer and Scriptural Tradition.* Ottawa: University of Ottawa Press.

Jehlen, Myra. 1986. "Introduction: Beyond Transcendence." In *Ideology and Classic American Literature*, edited by Sacvan Bercovitch and Myra Jehlen. Cambridge: Cambridge University Press, pp. 1–18.

Jelinek, Estelle C. ed., 1980. *Women's Autobiography: Essays in Criticism*. Bloomington, IN: Indiana University Press.

John, E. R., Bartlett, F., Shimokochi, M., and Kleinman, D. 1973. "Neural Readout from Memory," *Journal of Neurophysiology*, 36:893–924.

Johnson, Mark, ed. 1981. *Philosophical Perspectives on Metaphor*. Minneapolis: University of Minnesota Press.

Johnson, Mark. 1987. *The Body in the Mind: The Bodily Basis of Meaning, Imagination, and Reason*. Chicago: The University of Chicago Press.

Johnson-Laird, P. N. 1983. *Mental Models: Towards a Cognitive Science of Language, Inference, and Consciousness*. Cambridge: Cambridge University Press.

———. 1986. "Reasoning Without Logic." In *Reasoning and Discourse Processes*, edited by Terry Myers, Keith Brown, and Brendan McGonigle. London: Academic Press, pp. 13–49.

John-Steiner, Vera. 1985. *Notebooks of the Mind: Explorations of Thinking*. Albuquerque: The University of New Mexico Press.

Jones, Ann Rosalind. 1985. "Writing the Body: Toward an Understanding of l'Ecriture féminine." In *The New Feminist Criticism: Essays on Women, Literature, and Theory*, edited by Elaine Showalter. New York: Pantheon.

Kandel, Eric R. 1979a. "Small Systems of Neurons," *Scientific American*, 241, 3:66–76.

———. 1979b. *Behavioral Biology of Aplysia: A Contribution to the Comparative Study of Opisthobranch Molluscs*. San Francisco: W. H. Freeman.

Kaplan, Sydney Janet. 1985. "Varieties of Feminist Criticism." In *Making a Difference: Feminist Literary Criticism*, edited by Gayle Greene and Coppélia Kahn. London: Methuen.

Karčevskij, Sergej. 1929. "Du dualisme asymétrique du signe linguistique," in *Travaux du Cercle Linguistique de Prague*. Prague.

Kittredge, George Lyman. 1915. *Chaucer and His Poetry*. Cambridge, MA: Harvard University Press.

Knapp, Steven and Walter Benn Michaels. 1982. "Against Theory," *Critical Inquiry*, 8, 4:723–42.

Knight, George Wilson. 1949. *The Wheel of Fire: Interpretations of Shakespeare with Three New Essays*. London: Methuen.

Kosslyn, S. 1980. *Image and Mind*. Cambridge, MA: Harvard University Press.

Kristeva, Julia. 1986a. "Women's Time." Translated by Alice Jardine and Harry Blake. In *The Kristeva Reader*, edited by Toril Moi. Oxford: Blackwell, pp. 187–213.

———. 1986b. "A New Type of Intellectual: The Dissident," translated. by Sean Hand. In *The Kristeva Reader*, edited by Toril Moi. Oxford: Blackwell, pp. 292–300.

Krupat, Arnold. 1981. "American Autobiography: The Western Tradition," *The Georgia Review*, 35, 2:307–17.

———. 1985. *For Those Who Come After: A Study of Native American Autobiography*. Berkeley, CA: University of California Press.

Kubler, George. 1962. *The Shape of Time*. New Haven, CT: Yale University Press.

Kuhn, Thomas. 1970. *The Structure of Scientific Revolutions*, 2nd ed. Chicago: The University of Chicago Press.

———. 1979. "Metaphor in Science." In *Metaphor and Thought*, edited by Andrew Ortony. Cambridge: Cambridge University Press, pp. 409–19.

La Capra, Dominick. 1985. *History and Criticism*. Ithaca, NY: Cornell University Press.

Lakatos, Imre. 1970. "Falsification and the Methodology of Scientific Research Programmes." In *Criticism and the Growth of Knowledge: Proceedings of the International Colloquium in the Philosophy of Science* (London, 1965), vol. 4, edited by Imre Lakatos and Alan Musgrave. Cambridge: Cambridge University Press.

Lakoff, George. 1987. *Women, Fire, and Dangerous Things: What Categories Reveal about the Mind*. Chicago: The University of Chicago Press.

Lakoff, George and Mark Johnson. 1980. *Metaphors We Live By*. Chicago: The University of Chicago Press.

Langbaum, Robert. 1957. *The Poetry of Experience: The Dramatic Monologue in Modern Literary Tradition.* London: Chatto and Windus.

Lentriccia, Frank. 1980. *After the New Criticism.* London: Methuen.

———. 1983. *Criticism and Social Change.* Chicago: The University of Chicago Press.

Lerdahl, Fred, and Ray Jackendoff. 1983. *A Generative Theory of Tonal Music.* Cambridge, MA: MIT Press.

Leverenz, David. 1980. "The Woman in Hamlet: An Interpersonal View." In *Representing Shakespeare: New Psychoanalytic Essays,* edited by Murray M. Schwartz and Coppélia Kahn. Baltimore: The Johns Hopkins University Press, pp. 110–28.

Levin, Richard. 1988. "Feminist Thematics and Shakespearean Tragedy," *Publications of the Modern Language Association,* 103:125–38.

Levinson, Stephen. 1983. *Pragmatics.* Cambridge: Cambridge University Press.

Lévi-Strauss, Claude. 1966. *The Savage Mind.* Chicago: The University of Chicago Press.

———. 1969. *The Raw and the Cooked.* New York: Harper Row.

Lewis, Robert W., Jr. 1970. "The Tough Romance." In *Twentieth Century Interpretations of A Farewell to Arms,* edited by Jay Gellens. Englewood Cliffs, NJ: Prentice-Hall.

Lewis, R. W. B. 1955. *The American Adam: Innocence, Tragedy, and Tradition in the Nineteenth Century.* Chicago: The University of Chicago Press.

Lodge, David. 1988. *Nice Work.* London: Secker and Warburg.

Marr, David. 1982. *Vision.* San Francisco: W. H. Freeman.

Marslen-Wilson, William and Lorraine Komisarjevsky Tyler. 1987. "Against Modularity." In *Modularity in Knowledge Representation and Natural Language Understanding,* edited by Jay L. Garfield. Cambridge, MA: MIT Press, pp. 37–62.

———, E. Levy, and L. K. Tyler. 1982. "Producing Interpretable Discourse: The Establishment and Maintenance of Reference." In *Speech Place and Action,* edited by R. J. Jarvella and W. Klein. New York: Wiley.

Martin, G. D. 1981. *The Architecture of Experience: A Discussion of Literature as the Context of the World.* Edinburgh: University of Edinburgh Press.

Marx, Leo. 1964. *The Machine in the Garden.* Oxford: Oxford University Press.

McClelland, James L., David Rumelhart and the PDP Research Group. 1986. *Parallel Distributed Processing: Explorations in the Microstructure of Cognition.* 2 vols. Cambridge, MA: MIT Press.

McGann, Jerome J. 1985. *Historical Studies and Literary Criticism.* Madison: The University of Wisconsin Press.

Meese, Elizabeth A. 1986. *Crossing the Double-Cross: The Practice of Feminist Criticism.* Chapel Hill: The University of North Carolina Press.

Mervis, Carolyn B. and Eleanor Rosch. 1981. "Categorization of Natural Objects," *Annual Review of Psychology*, 32, 89–115.

Meyer, Leonard B. 1983. "Innovation, Choice, and the History of Music," *Critical Inquiry*, 9, 3:517–44.

Miller, J. Hillis. 1987. "The Triumph of Theory, the Resistance to Reading, and the Question of the Material Base," *Publications of the Modern Language Association*, 102, 3:281–91.

Minsky, Marvin. 1986. *The Society of Mind.* New York: Simon and Schuster.

———. 1988. "Emotions and the Society of Mind." In *Emotions and Psychopathology*, edited by Manfred Clynes and Jaak Panksepp. New York: Plenum, pp. 171–79.

Mitchell, Juliet. 1974. *Psychoanalysis and Feminism.* Harmondsworth: Pelican.

Mitchell, Margaret. 1936. *Gone With the Wind.* New York: Macmillan.

Mitchell, W. J. T. 1986. *Iconology.* Chicago: The University of Chicago Press.

Moi, Toril. 1985. *Sexual/Textual Politics.* London: Routledge.

———, ed. 1986. *The Kristeva Reader.* Oxford: Blackwell.

Moore, Terence. 1986. "Reasoning and Inference in Logic and in Language." In *Reasoning and Discourse Processes,* edited by Terry Myers, Keith Brown, and Brendan McGonigle. London: Academic Press.

Moran, Richard. 1989. "Seeing and Believing: Metaphor, Image, and Force," *Critical Inquiry*, 16, 1:87–112.

Muscatine, Charles. 1972. *Poetry and Crisis in the Age of Chaucer*. Notre Dame, IN: University of Notre Dame Press.

Myers, Terry, Keith Brown, and Brendan McGonigle, eds. 1986. *Reasoning and Discourse Processes*. London: Academic Press.

Neill, Michael. 1983. "Remembrance and Revenge: *Hamlet, Macbeth* and *The Tempest*." In *Jonson and Shakespeare*, edited by Ian Donaldson. London: Macmillan, pp. 35–56.

Newmeyer, Frederick J. 1983. *Grammatical Theory: Its Limits and Its Possibilities*. Chicago: The University of Chicago Press.

Nietzsche, Friedrich. 1980. *On the Advantage and Disadvantage of History for Life*, translated with an Introduction by Peter Preuss. Indianapolis: Hackett.

Oatley, Keith. 1978. *Perceptions and Representations: The Theoretical Bases of Brain Research and Psychology*. London: Methuen.

Ortony, Andrew. 1975. "Why Metaphors are Necessary and Not Just Nice," *Educational Theory*, 25:45–53.

———, ed. 1979. *Metaphor and Thought*. Cambridge: Cambridge University Press.

Ortony, Andrew, D. L. Schallert, R. E. Reynolds, S. J. Antos. 1978. "Interpreting Metaphors and Idioms: Some Effects of Context on Comprehension," *Journal of Verbal Learning and Verbal Behavior*, 17:465–77.

Pagels, Heinz R. 1988. *The Dreams of Reason: The Computer and the Rise of the Sciences of Complexity*. New York: Bantam.

Paivio, Allan. 1986. *Mental Representations: A Dual Coding Approach*. Oxford: Clarendon Press.

Patterson, Lee. 1987a. "'No man his reson herde': Peasant Consciousness, Chaucer's Miller, and the Structure of the *Canterbury Tales*," *South Atlantic Quarterly*, 86, 4:457–95.

———. 1987b. *Negotiating the Past: The Historical Understanding of Medieval Literature*. Madison: The University of Wisconsin Press.

Pechter, Edward. 1987. "The New Historicism and Its Discontents: Politicizing Renaissance Drama," *Publications of the Modern Language Association*, 102, 3:292–303.

Peckham, Morse. 1965. *Man's Rage for Chaos: Biology, Behavior, and the Arts.* New York: Schocken.

———. 1978. "Perceptual and Semiotic Discontinuity in Art," *Poetics,* 7:217–30.

Petrie, Hugh G. 1979. "Metaphor and Learning." In *Metaphor and Thought,* edited by Andrew Ortony. Cambridge: Cambridge University Press, pp. 438–461.

Piaget, Jean. 1952. *The Origins of Intelligence in Children,* translated by Margaret Cook. New York: International Universities.

———. 1970. *Structuralism,* translated and edited by Chaninah Maschler. New York: Harper Row.

Piaget, Jean and Barbel Inhelder. 1969. *The Psychology of the Child,* translated by Helen Weaver. New York: Basic Books.

Piattelli-Palmarini, M. ed., 1980. *Language and Learning: The Debate between Jean Piaget and Noam Chomsky.* Cambridge, MA: Harvard University Press.

Poizner, Howard, Edward Klima, Ursula Bellugi. 1987. *What the Hands Reveal about the Brain.* Cambridge, MA: MIT Press.

Popper, Karl. 1963. *Conjectures and Refutations.* London: Routledge and Kegan Paul.

———. 1976. "The Myth of the Framework." In *The Abdication of Philosophy: Philosophy and the Public Good Essays in Honor of Paul Arthur Schilpp,* edited by Eugene Freeman. La Salle, IL: Open Court, pp. 23–48.

Popper, Karl and John C. Eccles. 1977. *The Self and Its Brain: An Argument for Interactionism.* London: Routledge and Kegan Paul.

Pratt, Mary Louise. 1981. "The Short Story: The Long and the Short of It," *Poetics,* 10:175–94.

Price, J. T. 1974. "Linguistic Competence and Metaphorical Use," *Foundations of Language,* 11:253–56.

Pylyshyn, Zenon W. 1979. "Metaphorical Imprecision and the 'Top-Down' Research Strategy." In *Metaphor and Thought,* edited by Andrew Ortony. Cambridge: Cambridge University Press, pp. 420–36.

Quine, Willard Van Orman. 1960. *Word and Object.* Cambridge MA: MIT Press.

———. 1969. "Natural Kinds," in *Ontological Relativity and other Essays.* New York: Columbia University Press, pp. 114–38.

Ricoeur, Paul. 1977. *The Rule of Metaphor*, translated by Robert Czerny with Kathleen McLaughlin and John Costello, SJ. London: Routledge and Kegan Paul.

Robertson, D. W., Jr. 1951. "Historical Criticism." In *English Institute Essays 1951*, edited by Alan S. Downer. New York: Columbia University Press, pp. 3–31.

———. 1962. *A Preface to Chaucer.* Princeton: Princeton University Press.

———, ed. 1970. *The Literature of Medieval England.* New York: McGraw-Hill.

Robertson, D. W., Jr. and B. F. Huppé. 1951. *Piers Plowman and the Scriptural Tradition.* Princeton, NJ: Princeton University Press.

Robinson, Lillian S. 1983. "Treason Our Text: Feminist Challenges to the Literary Canon," *Tulsa Studies in Women's Literature,* 2, 1: 83–98.

Root, Robert K. 1906. *The Poetry of Chaucer: A Guide to Its Study and Appreciation.* New York: Houghton, Mifflin.

Rorty, Richard. 1984. "Deconstruction and Circumvention," *Critical Inquiry*, 11, 1:1–23.

Rosch, Eleanor. 1978. "Principles of Categorization." In *Cognition and Categorization*, edited by Barbara B. Lloyd and Eleanor Rosch. Hillsdale, NJ: Erlbaum.

Rose, Jacqueline. 1986. "Hamlet—the *Mona Lisa* of Literature," *Critical Quarterly*, 28, 1–2:35–49.

Sacks, Oliver. 1984. *A Leg to Stand On.* New York: Harper Row.

———. 1985. *The Man Who Mistook His Wife for a Hat.* London: Picador.

Saintsbury, George. 1898. *A Short History of English Literature.* London: Macmillan.

Scarry, Elaine, ed. 1988. "Introduction," *Literature and the Body:*

Essays on Populations and Persons. Baltimore: The Johns Hopkins University Press.

Schauber, Ellen and Ellen Spolsky. 1977. "The Consolation of Alison: The Speech Acts of the Wife of Bath," *Centrum*, 5, 1:20–34.

———. 1979. "How to Know a Hypocrite When You Meet One." In *Rhetoric 78: Proceedings of Theory in Rhetoric: An Interdisciplinary Conference*, edited by Robert L. Brown, Jr., and Martin Steinmann, Jr. Minneapolis: The Minnesota Center for Advanced Study in Language, Style, and Literary Theory.

———. 1986. *The Bounds of Interpretation: Linguistic Theory and Literary Text.* Stanford, CA: Stanford University Press.

Schlissel, Lillian. 1982. *Women's Diaries of the Westward Journey.* New York: Schocken.

Scholes, Robert. 1974. *Structuralism in Literature: An Introduction.* New Haven, CT: Yale University Press.

Schultz, Elizabeth. 1981. "To Be Black and Blue: The Blues Genre in Black American Autobiography." In *The American Autobiography*, edited by Albert E. Stone. Englewood Cliffs, NJ: Prentice Hall, pp. 109–32.

Seamon, Roger. 1989. "Poetics against Itself: On the Self-Destruction of Modern Scientific Criticism," *Publications of the Modern Language Association*, 104:294–305.

Searle, John. 1969. *Speech Acts: An Essay in the Philosophy of Language.* Cambridge: Cambridge University Press.

———. 1976. "A Classification of Illocutionary Acts," *Language in Society*, 5, 1:1–23.

———. 1979. "What is an Intentional State?" *Mind*, 88:74–92.

———. 1982. "Chomsky's Revolution in Linguistics." In *On Noam Chomsky: Critical Essays*, 2nd Edition, edited by Gilbert Harman. Amherst, MA: The University of Massachusetts Press, pp. 2–33. Reprint of 1972 article in *The New York Review of Books.*

Shakespeare, William. 1985. *Hamlet Prince of Denmark*, edited by Philip Edwards. Cambridge: Cambridge University Press.

———. 1982. *Hamlet*, edited by Harold Jenkins. London: Methuen.

Shepard, R. N. and L. A. Cooper, eds., 1982. *Mental Images and Their Transformations.* Cambridge, MA: MIT Press.

Showalter, Elaine. 1979. "Towards a Feminist Poetics." In *Women Writing and Writing About Women*, edited by Mary Jacobus. London: Croom Helm.

———. 1981. "Feminist Criticism in the Wilderness," *Critical Inquiry*, 8, 2:179–205.

———, ed. 1985. *The New Feminist Criticism: Essays on Women, Literature, and Theory.* New York: Pantheon.

Slezak, Peter and W. R. Albury, eds. 1988. *Computers, Brains and Minds.* Dordrecht: Kluwer.

Smith, Barbara Herrnstein. 1978. *On the Margins of Discourse: The Relation of Literature to Language.* Chicago: The University of Chicago Press.

Spearing, A. C. 1972. *Criticism and Medieval Poetry*, 2nd Edition. New York: Barnes and Noble.

———. 1986. *Medieval to Renaissance in English Poetry.* Cambridge: Cambridge University Press.

Spence, Donald P. 1990. "Theories of the Mind: Science or Literature?," *Poetics Today*, 11, 2:329–47.

Spengemann, William C. 1980. *The Forms of Autobiography: Episodes in the History of a Literary Genre.* New Haven, CT: Yale University Press.

Sperber, Dan. 1975. *Rethinking Symbolism*, translated by Alice L. Morton. Cambridge: Cambridge University Press.

———. 1986b. "Inference and Implicature in Utterance Interpretation." In *Reasoning and Discourse Processes*, edited by Terry Myers, Keith Brown, and Brendan McGonigle. London: Academic Press.

Sperber, Dan and Diedre Wilson. 1986a. *Relevance: Communication and Cognition.* Oxford: Blackwell.

Spolsky, Bernard. 1989. *Conditions for Second Language Learning: Introduction to a General Theory.* Oxford: Oxford University Press.

Spolsky, Ellen. 1985. "Toward a Cognitively Responsible Theory of Inference: or, What Can Synapses Tell Us About Ambiguity?" *Theoretical Linguistics*, 12, 2–3:197–203.

———. 1988. "The Limits of Literal Meaning," *New Literary History*, 19, 2:419–40.

———. n.d. "Varieties of Visual Ambiguity: Reading Kinesis in Pictures." Paper read at Word and Image Conference, Zurich, 1990.

———. 1991. "The Uses of Adversity." In *The Uses of Adversity: Failure and Accomodation in Reader Response,* edited by Ellen Spolsky. Lewisburg, PA: Bucknell University Press, pp. 17–35.

Steiner, George. 1961. *The Death of Tragedy.* London: Faber and Faber.

———. 1988. "Tragic and counter-tragic," *TLS*, February 12–18 1988.

Steiner, Wendy. 1982. *The Colors of Rhetoric.* Chicago: The University of Chicago Press.

Stern, Josef. 1985. "Metaphor as Demonstrative," *Journal of Philosophy*, 82, 12:677–710.

Stillings, Neil. 1987. "Modularity and Naturalism in Theories of Vision," in *Modularity in Knowledge Representation and Natural-Language Understanding*, edited by Jay L. Garfield. Cambridge, MA: MIT Press, pp. 383–401.

Tanenhous, Michael K., Gary S. Dell, and Greg Carlson. 1987. "Context Effects in Lexical Processing: A Connectionist Approach to Modularity." In *Modularity in Knowledge Representation and Natural-Language Understanding*, edited by Jay L. Garfield. Cambridge, MA: MIT Press.

Taylor, Gordon O. 1983. *Studies in Modern American Autobiography.* London: Macmillan.

Todorov, Tzvetan. 1976. "The Origin of Genres," *New Literary History*, 8:159–70.

Tourangeau, Roger and Robert J. Sternberg. 1982. "Understanding and Appreciating Metaphors." *Cognition*, 11, 3:203–44.

Turner, Mark. 1987. *Death is the Mother of Beauty: Mind, Metaphor, Criticism.* Chicago: The University of Chicago Press.

Tverski, Amos and Itamar Gati. 1978. "Studies of Similarity." In *Cognition and Categorization*, edited by Eleanor Rosch and Barbara B. Lloyd. Hillsdale, NJ: Erlbaum.

Walzer, Michael. 1987. *Interpretation and Social Criticism*. Cambridge, MA: Harvard University Press.

Wellek, René and Austin Warren. 1956. *Theory of Literature*. Third Edition. New York: Harcourt, Brace & World.

Wertheimer, Max. 1923. "Laws of Organization in Perceptual Forms." In *A Source Book of Gestalt Psychology*, edited by Willis D. Ellis. London: Routledge and Kegan Paul. 1938.

White, Hayden. 1973. *Metahistory: The Historical Imagination in Nineteenth–Century Europe*. Baltimore: The Johns Hopkins University Press.

———. 1975. "The Problem of Change in Literary History," *New Literary History*, 7, 1:97–111.

———. 1978a. "Ethnological 'Lie' and Mythical 'Truth,'" *Diacritics*, 8, 1:2–9.

———. 1978b. *The Tropics of Discourse*. Baltimore: The Johns Hopkins University Press.

Williams, Raymond. 1977. *Marxism and Literature*. Oxford: Oxford University Press.

Wilson, John Dover. 1935. *What Happens in Hamlet?* Cambridge: Cambridge University Press.

Wimsatt, W. K., Jr., and Monroe Beardsley. 1946. "The Intentional Fallacy," *Sewanee Review*, 54. Reprinted in W. K. Wimsatt, Jr. 1954. *The Verbal Icon: Studies in the Meaning of Poetry*. Lexington, KY: University of Kentucky Press, pp. 3–18.

Winnicott, D. W. 1968. "Communication Between Infant and Mother, Mother and Infant, Compared and Contrasted." In *What is Psychoanalysis?* London: Balliere, Tindall and Cassell.

Witemeyer, Hugh. 1969. *The Poetry of Ezra Pound: Forms and Renewal, 1908–1920*. Berkeley, CA: University of California Press.

Wittgenstein, Ludwig. 1958. *Philosophical Investigations*. Second Edition, translated by G. E. M. Anscombe. Oxford: Blackwell.

Yeats, William Butler. 1961. *The Collected Poems*. London: Macmillan.

Index